CW01010957

# Romanism and the Reformation

*From the Standpoint of Prophecy*

By Henry Grattan Guinness

Published by Pantianos Classics

ISBN-13: 978-1545432211

First published in 1881

**Harry Grattan Guinness**

# Contents

# Preface

THE following lectures were delivered, by request, under the auspices of the Protestant Educational Institute, at Exeter Hall, in the spring of this year [1887]. That Institute exists to do a much needed work to keep alive, especially in the hearts of the rising generation, some measure of intelligent sympathy with the Protestant traditions of our country. England's Protestantism has long been England's glory, and the direct cause of her unrivaled prosperity and peculiar preeminence among the nations of Europe. That Protestantism is now sustaining a double attack, from without and from within. Yet few seem fully alive to the danger. The late Lord Beaconsfield saw it clearly enough however. "Your empire and your liberties are more in danger at this moment," he said, "than when Napoleon's army of observation was encamped at Boulogne." What would he have said had he lived to see the present position of affairs!

The Reformation of the sixteenth century, which gave birth to Protestantism, was based on Scripture. It gave back to the world the Bible. It taught the Scriptures; it exposed the errors and corruptions of Rome by the use of the sword of the Spirit. It applied THE PROPHECIES, and accepted their practical guidance. Such Reformation work requires to be done afresh. We have suffered prophetic anti-papal truth to be too much forgotten. This generation is dangerously latitudinarian indifferent to truth and error on points on which Scripture is tremendously decided and absolutely clear.

These lectures, simple and popular as they are, will, it is hoped, open many minds to perceive that the Bible gives no uncertain sound as to Romanism, and that those who will be guided by its teachings must shun an apostasy against which the sorest judgments are denounced.

The lectures are given as delivered, with the exception of the first and last, which have been extended and modified. In recasting and enlarging the opening lecture on the Daniel foreview, and the closing one on the Reformation, I have availed myself of the valuable help of my beloved wife, who has for so many years been my fellow laborer both in literary and evangelistic work.

I shall rejoice if these lectures obtain a wide circulation, for they contain, I am sure, truth for the times, ù truth deeply and increasingly needed, not only for the preservation of the civil and religious liberties of our country and empire, but for the practical guidance of the people of God in these last days.

*H. Grattan Guinness*
*Harley House, Bow, E., June 1st, 1887.*

# Preface to the Second Edition

From the first appearance of these lectures in the form in which they were originally published, I have been urged to produce a cheap popular edition suited for wide-spread distribution. I do so now the more willingly because the need of testimony to Protestant Truth is increasing instead of diminishing. Romanism and Ritualism are making extensive progress year by year, and seriously imperil "The Protestant Religion and Liberties of England." The duty of diffusing information on the true character and history of "Romanism and the Reformation" is one which presses on God's faithful people in these days. The apathy of many as to the present crisis only increases the danger, and intensifies the call for clear and cogent teaching suited to counteract the Romeward tendencies of these times. The testimony of Scripture, especially of the "sure word of Prophecy," should be set forth afresh, as in the days of the Reformation, that those in danger of departing from the faith once delivered to the saints may be warned, and those who have so departed may be delivered. The weapons of our warfare are not carnal, but spiritual, and mighty through God to the pulling down of strongholds. Our combat is with error, therefore let us diffuse the Truth. Books and pamphlets bearing on the questions at issue, and taking the side of Truth, should be circulated by the million. Let our readers do what they can in this direction, without delay, committing the result to Him who has promised that His word shall not return to Him void, but shall accomplish the ends for which He has sent it.

*H. GRATTAN GUINNESS.*
*HARLEY HOUSE, BOW, LONDON, E.*
*MAY 1ST, 1891.*

# Lecture One - The Daniel Foreview of Romanism

Fifty years ago the eminent statesman, Sir Robert Peel said, with remarkably clear foresight: "The day is not distant, and it may be very near, when we shall all have to fight the battle of the Reformation over again."

That day has come. It has been upon us for some time. It has found us unprepared, and as a result the battle is to some extent going against us. More than three centuries of emancipation from the yoke of Rome three hundred years of Bible light and liberty ù had made us overconfident, and led us to underestimate the power and influence of the deadliest foe, not only of the gospel of God, but also of Protestant England. Britain's honorable distinction of being the leading witness among the nations for the truth of the gospel and against the errors of Romanism had come to be lightly esteemed among us. Our fathers won this distinction through years of sore struggle and strife; they purchased it with their best blood, and prized it as men prize that which costs them dear. It had cost us nothing, we were born to it; we knew not its value by contrast as they did. In the early part of this century the power of Rome was in these lands a thing of the past, and it seemed to be fast decaying even in other lands. The notion grew up among us that there was no need to fear any revival of that deadly upas tree, which is the blight of all that is great and good, pure and prosperous. The light of true knowledge had for ever dispelled the dark fogs of superstition, so it was supposed; mediaeval tyrannies and cruelties cloaked under a pretense of religion could never again obtain a footing in these lands of light and liberty. We might despise and deride the corruptions and follies of Rome, but as to dreading her influence ù no. She was too far gone and too feeble to inspire fear, or even watchfulness.

This was all a delusion, and we have been roughly undeceived. The difficult and dangerous crisis through which England is now passing is the direct result of the course of action taken under this delusion, and God only knows what the ultimate consequences may be. A serpent may be scotched, yet not killed; it may retain life enough to turn and inflict on its foe a fatal wound. The ground may be purged from a destructive weed, but the little remnants left behind may sprout and spread so as speedily to pervade the plot anew. It has been thus with Romish influence in Protestant England.

Let facts speak. Fifty years ago there were not five hundred Roman priests in Great Britain; now there are two thousand six hundred. Fifty years ago there were not five hundred chapels; now there are fifteen hundred and seventy-five.

Fifty years ago there were no monasteries at all in Britain; now there are two hundred and twenty-five. There were even then sixteen convents, but now there are over four hundred of these barred and bolted and impenetrable prisons, in which fifteen thousand Englishwomen are kept prisoners at the mercy of a celibate clergy, who have power, unless their behests are obeyed, to inflict on these hapless and helpless victims torture under the name of penance. Fifty years ago there were but two colleges in our land for the training of Roman Catholic priests ù i.e., of men bound by oath to act in England as the agents of a foreign power, the one great object of which is avowed to be the dismemberment of our empire and the ruin of our influence in the world; now there are twenty-nine such schools. And, strangest of all, England, who once abolished monasteries and appropriated to national uses the ill-gotten gains of Rome, is now actually endowing Romanism in her empire to the extent of over a million of money per annum. The exact amount is 1,052,657 pounds.

Results even more serious have arisen from the dropping on the part of evangelical Christianity of its distinctive testimony against Romish doctrine and practice. An apostasy has taken place in the Reformed Church of England itself, and multitudes of its members, uninstructed in the true nature and history of the Church of Rome, and ignorant of the prophetic teachings of Scripture about it, have rejoiced in a return to many of the corruptions of doctrine and practice which their forefathers died to abolish. Our reformed faith is thus endangered both from without and from within, and it can be defended only by a resolute return to the true witness home by saints and martyrs of other days. We must learn afresh from Divine prophecy God's estimate of the character of the Church of Rome if we would be moved afresh to be witnesses for Christ against this great apostasy.

As Protestants, as Christians, as free men, as philanthropists, as those who are acquainted with the teachings of history, we deplore the existing state of things; we regard all these changes as a retrograde movement of the most dangerous character, and we feel constrained to renew the grand old PROTEST to which the world owes its modern acquisitions of liberty, knowledge, peace, and prosperity. We recognize it as a patent and undeniable fact, that the future of our race lies not with Papists, but with Protestants. Its leading nations this day are not Papal Italy, Spain, and Portugal, but Protestant Germany, England, and America. What has made the difference? The nations that embraced the Reformation movement of the sixteenth century have never since ceased to advance in political power, social prosperity, philanthropic enterprise, and general enlightenment; while the nations that refused it and held fast to the corruptions of Rome have as steadily retrograded in all these respects.

*"By their fruits ye shall know them."*

The present course of lectures is intended to arouse fresh attention to the great controversy between the Church of Rome and evangelical Churches. In this war the Roman army stands on one side, and Protestantism in one unbroken phalanx on the other. The regiments of Rome wear but one scarlet uniform, fly but one Papal flag, and use in their religious ceremonies but one dead language ù Latin; the Protestant army, on the other hand, consists of many divisions, clad in differing uniforms, flying different flags, and speaking different tongues. But, like the composite hosts of Germany in the struggle with France, they are all the stronger for their voluntary union; they can cordially join in the great struggle. The secondary denominational differences existing between Episcopalians, Presbyterians, and Nonconformists are all lost sight of in their common conflict with Rome; and the sole issue is between those who hold to the old gospel of Christ, and those who teach another gospel ù which is not another.

Our subject in these lectures is Romanism and the Reformation from the standpoint of prophecy: that is, we propose to give you, not any merely human view of the subject, but the Divine view; not the opinions of the lecturer about it, but the teachings of prophets and apostles, the judgment of the only wise God as expressed in His sacred word, in this blessed Divine revelation which sheds its beams on every subject of interest to the people of God. It is a fact, that though the canon of Scripture was closed ages before Romanism began to exist, and fifteen centuries before the Reformation, yet it presents the Divine judgment as to both. The Bible records the past in its histories and the future in its prophecies, which are simply history written beforehand. It expresses moreover moral judgments as to the individuals it describes and the acts which it records, and it similarly expresses moral judgments respecting the individuals and actions which it predicts. It warned the Church against the wiles of Rome Papal, even from the days of Rome Pagan. John, the victim of Nero and Domitian, painted for posterity pictures of the martyrs of the Inquisition, and of the cruelties of tyrants more merciless than the Caesars.

In viewing this question from the standpoint of prophecy, consequently, our object is, not merely to trace the fulfillment of sacred prediction in the broad facts of history, as a proof of the inspiration of Scripture ù though our lectures must of course do that ù but it is even more to present the Divine view of the Roman Papal system, to show what infinite reprobation and abhorrence Scripture pours upon it, and what an awful doom it denounces against it. If we know what God thinks of any system, we know what we ought to think of it and how we ought to act towards it. Forewarned is forearmed. Had the youth of the last two or three generations of England been carefully instructed in the Scriptures bearing on this subject, we should not have lived to see our country troubled and in peril of dismemberment through Jesuit intrigues, nor our national Church divided against itself, to its own imminent danger, and one section of it relapsing into the apostasy from which the Reformation had delivered it.

Let me first define distinctly the three terms in our title ù Romanism, the Reformation, and Prophecy. Let me answer the questions: What is Romanism? What was the Reformation? What is Prophecy?

**I.** ROMANISM IS APOSTATE LATIN CHRISTIANITY not apostate Christianity merely, but apostate LATIN Christianity. The Greek Church, the Armenian Church, the Coptic Church are all apostate in greater or less degrees, and the Protestant Church itself has no small measure of apostasy in it; but it is of Romanism, or Latin Christianity, alone that we now speak, because it is the great and terrible power of evil so largely predicted by the prophet Daniel and by the Apostle John; it is the special apostasy which bulks most largely in prophecy, and it is the culmination of Christian apostasy. It includes all whose public worship is conducted in Latin and who own allegiance to the Pope of Rome.

Dean Milman's history of the Church of Rome is called "The History of Latin Christianity." Archbishop Trench speaks of Gregory the Great as "the last of the Latin Fathers, and the first in the modern sense of the popes," and says he "did more than any other to set the Church forward on the new lines on which it must travel, to constitute a Latin Christianity with distinctive features of its own, such as broadly separate it from the Greek."1 Romanism is this Latin Christianity become apostate.

**II.** The Reformation was A RETURN TO PRIMITIVE OR NON-APOSTATE CHRISTIANITY accomplished between three and four centuries ago in this country, in Germany, and some other countries of Europe. One feature of this great movement was the abandonment of the use of Latin in public worship, and the translation of the Scriptures into living language, so that all nations might read the word of God in their own tongue, and understand for themselves its sacred messages. The names of Luther, Zwingle, Erasmus, Tyndale, Knox, Calvin, Latimer, Ridley, Cranmer, Hooper, and others, are associated with this "Reformation."

**III.** And, in the third place, Prophecy is THE DIVINELY GIVEN MIRROR OF THE FUTURE. "Things not seen as yet" are reflected on its surface with more or less distinctness. They may be partially discerned beforehand, and clearly identified when the time of fulfillment comes. Thus the first advent of Christ was shown, though but as in a glass darkly, thousands of years before it took place; and so the tragic episodes of the siege of Jerusalem were presented to the mind of Moses ages before the city was even built. Romanism and the Reformation both lay afar in the distant future when Daniel and John foresaw their history; but their prophetic visions and writings reflect both one and the other with a distinctness and clearness which is the exact equivalent of their magnitude and importance in the history of the Church and of the world.

Bear in mind these three brief definitions:

1. Romanism is apostate Latin Christianity.
2. The Reformation was a return to primitive non-apostate Christianity accomplished three centuries ago.
3. Prophecy is the mirror of the future.

Let us next inquire, What is this Romanism, or Latin Christianity, as distinguished from Greek, or Protestant, or any other form of the faith of Christ? As to its doctrines and practices, we will answer this question later on in our course of lectures, quoting from its own acknowledged standards. For the present we must confine ourselves to a consideration of its history. But before I give you a brief outline of this, I may state that there are three distinct sets of prophecies of the rise, character, deeds, and doom of Romanism. The first is found in the book of Daniel, the second in the epistles of Paul, and the third in the letters and Apocalypse of John; and no one of these three is complete in itself. It is only by combining their separate features that we obtain the perfect portrait. Just as we cannot derive from one gospel a complete life of Christ, but in order to obtain this must take into account the records in the other three: so we cannot from one prophecy gather a correct account of antichrist; we must add to the particulars given in one those supplied by the other two. Some features are given in all three prophecies, just as the death and resurrection of Christ are given in all four gospels. Others are given in only two, and others are peculiar to one. As might be expected from the position and training of the prophet who was a statesman and a governor in Babylon, Daniel's foreview presents the POLITICAL character and relations of Romanism. The Apostle Paul's foreview, on the other hand, gives ECCLESIASTICAL character and relations of this power; and John's prophecies, both in Revelation thirteen and seventeen, present the COMBINATION OF BOTH, the mutual relations of the Latin Church and the Roman State. He uses composite figures, one part of which represents the political aspect of Romanism as a temporal government, and the other its religious aspect as an ecclesiastical system.

In this lecture we deal with Daniel's political foreview, with his predictions of the great power of evil which was revealed to him as destined to arise in the fourth empire, and which he describes in chapter 7 of his book. Before we consider this prophecy you must allow me briefly to recall a few well-known historical facts, that none can deny or question.

The last twenty-five centuries of human history ù that is, the story of the leading nations of the earth since the days of Nebuchadnezzar ù has been divided into two chronologically equal parts, each lasting for about twelve and a half centuries. During the first half of this period four great heathen empires succeeded each other in the rule of the then known earth the Babylonian, Medo-Persian, Grecian, and Roman empires. They lasted from the eighth century before Christ to the fifth century of our era, and ended with the fall of the last emperor of Rome, Romulus Augustulus, A.D. 476. During the second half of this period no one great empire has ever ruled over the whole sphere dominated by these old pagan governments. Power has been more divided, and modern kingdoms have replaced ancient empires. A commonwealth of nations has for the last twelve hundred years existed in the territory once governed by old Rome, and no monarch has ever succeeded in subjecting them all to himself. This makes a broad distinction between ancient and modern times, and the dividing line is the fall of the old Roman empire, the break up of the last form of ancient civilization, the one which preceded our modern Christian civilization.

Rome itself that great and ancient city ù was founded about the beginning of the long period I have named, and has therefore been in existence for nearly two thousand six hundred years, though for many centuries it had but a local reputation. Gradually it rose to importance, and in the second century before Christ it attained supremacy in the earth. After that it was for about five hundred years the magnificent metropolis of the last and mightiest of the four great empires of antiquity, the seat of its government ù the very heart and center of the then known world. Nineveh and Babylon had each in its day been great metropolitan cities of wonderful size, wealth, and influence; but the realms they ruled were small compared to those over which Rome in its zenith of power exercised her imperial sway. She was for long ages, in the esteem of all civilized nations as well as in her own, "mistress of the world." Her proud pre-eminence of position was based on an unequaled degree of military strength and power. It was a rule, not of right, but of might, and it subjected the world to itself. Remains still extant, not only in all parts of Europe, but in Africa and Asia, and above all in Rome itself, sufficiently attest the wide extent of the sway of Rome, the luxury of her princes and people, and the refinements of her civilization. Roman roads, Roman camps, Roman baths, Roman coins, statues, and remains of every kind abound even in our own little isle, some of which have been examined with interest by most of us. Roman laws, Roman literature, and the fundamental relation of the Latin language to the languages of modern Europe afford clearer evidences still of the universal, mighty, and long-enduring influence of the ancient masters of he world.

Up to the beginning of the fourth century of our era Rome was a pagan city, and the emperor was the high priest of its religion. The ruins of its old heathen shrines still adorn the city. The Pantheon, which is now a church dedicated to the Virgin Mary and all the martyrs, was formerly a heathen temple dedicated to Cybele and all the gods of the ancient mythology. But in the fourth century of our era heathenism fell prostrate before that faith of Christ which for three centuries Rome had persecuted and sought to exterminate; the religion of Jesus of Nazareth overthrew the religion of Jupiter Olympius, and the Emperor Constantine established Christianity as the creed of the world. Rome had become the seat of a Christian bishop before that date, and in the division and decay of the Roman empire which soon followed, this bishop, owing to his metropolitan position, became a person of great importance and the head of Latin Christianity. As other rulers passed away, and as the power of Rome waned before the hordes of Gothic and Vandal invaders, the Christian bishopric, sole survival of the old institutions in Rome, raised its head like a rocky reef in the midst of a wild expanse of roaring billows. It remained when all else failed around it. At first it had itself been a small, weak, new thing under the shadow of a great, mighty, and ancient power. But time brought changes, and gradually it became the stable, strong, and only ancient thing in the midst of the turbulent young Gothic nations into which the fragments of the old Roman dominions slowly crystallized. To these rude and recently evangelized people the Church of Rome was naturally the mother Church, and the Bishop of Rome the chief of Christian bishops. The tendency of the Latin episcopate thus enthroned in the old metropolis of the world, in the midst of ignorant, superstitious, and childlike Gothic nations, was to become first a monarchical, and then an imperial power. This tendency was deep and enduring; it worked for centuries, till at last it produced that singular blasphemous usurpation and tyrannical government which we call the Papacy. The rise of this power was, like all great growths, gradual and slow. From the middle of the fifth century to the end of the thirteenth ù i, e. for between eight and nine hundred years it was steadily waxing greater and greater, rising higher and higher, reaching forth its branches more widely, and making more extravagant claims and pretensions. Time would of course fail me to trace the rise of ecclesiastical power in the Middle Ages to the monstrous proportions it assumed in the thirteenth century. After the conversion of Constantine, when Christianity became the established religion of the Roman world, the Church passed rapidly from a state of persecution, poverty, and distress to one of honor, wealth, and ease; and it degenerated as rapidly from its early purity. Covetousness and avarice came in like a flood, and ecclesiastical power became an object of eager ambition, even to ungodly men. The bishop was a wealthy, influential, worldly dignitary, instead of a humble Christian pastor. Opulence poured in upon the priesthood, alike from the fears and the affections of their converts; and their intellectual superiority over the barbarian nations had the effect of increasing still more their ascendancy. The time came when they alone retained any semblance of learning, or could prepare a treaty or write a document, or teach princes to read. By a variety of sordid frauds they contrived to secure to the Church immense wealth and an enormous share of the land. But they recognized their own subjection to the secular power, and respected mutually each other's independence. Claims to supremacy over other bishops began however before long to be advanced by the bishops of Rome, sometimes on one ground and sometimes on another, but it was long before they were admitted.

13

Papal authority indeed made no great progress beyond the bounds of Italy until the end of the sixth century. At this period the celebrated Gregory I, a talented, active, and ambitious man, was Bishop of Rome. He stands at the meeting place of ancient and mediaeval history, and his influence had a marked effect on the growth of Latin Christianity. He exalted his own position very highly in his correspondence and intercourse with other bishops and with the sovereigns of western Europe, with whom he was in constant communication. Claims that had previously been only occasionally suggested were now systematically pressed and urged. He dwelt much on the power conferred on the bishops of Rome in the possession of the keys of the kingdom of heaven, which were committed to Peter and his successors. The Gothic nations were too ignorant to unravel the sophistries of this clever and determined priest, and they permitted him to assume a kind of oversight of their ecclesiastical matters.

His successor, Boniface III, carried these pretensions still higher. He was the last of the bishops of Rome and the first of the popes. In his days the claim to supremacy over all other bishops was, not only definitely made, but it was acknowledged by the secular power and confirmed by an imperial edict. The wicked usurper Phocas, to serve his own selfish purposes, conceded to Boniface III in A.D. 607 the headship over all the Churches of Christendom. A pillar is still standing in Rome which was erected in memory of this important concession. This was a tremendous elevation, the first upward step on the ladder that led the bishops of Rome from the humble pastorate of a local Church to the mightiest throne in Europe. But still all that was claimed or granted was simple episcopacy, though of a universal kind; no thought of secular government existed at this period. The matter however did not stop here. This supreme episcopal jurisdiction led to constant interferences of the Roman bishop in the affairs of the various nations of Christendom, and to ever-increasing pretensions to authority in matters secular as well as ecclesiastical, until five hundred years later, in A.D. 1073, Pope Gregory VII took a great stride in advance and established

## *A THEOCRACY ON EARTH*

He was the first who claimed, as the representative of Deity, to be above all the kings of the world. This proud and self-exalting man strove, and strove successfully, not only to emancipate the spiritual power from all control by the State, not only to secure for it absolute independence, but, further, to subject the secular power of princes to the spiritual power of priests, and thus to establish at Rome in his own person and in the succession of the Roman pontiffs an absolute and supreme ruler of the world. Nor did he propound this new and startling doctrine as a theory only. With daring and audacity he excommunicated the German emperor Henry IV, released his subjects from allegiance to him, and forbade them to obey him as sovereign.2 He actually succeeded in exacting

14

humiliating concessions from the emperor, and yet he subsequently bestowed his kingdom on another. This pope turned the bishopric of Rome into a universal and unlimited monarchy, and the sovereigns of Europe were unable to oppose his unprecedented usurpations. He established also an undisguised and irresistible despotism over the national Churches in other lands, by enacting that no bishop in the Catholic Church should enter on the exercise of his functions until the pope had continued his election, ar law of far-reaching and vast importance, by which perhaps more than by any other means Rome sustained for centuries her temporal power as well as her ecclesiastical influence.

Many of the constant quarrels between our own early English kings and the popes of Rome, as well as many similar feuds on the Continent, arose out of this flagrant usurpation of national rights and invasion of national liberties. It virtually took from the Churches the power to appoint their own bishops, and placed them under a foreign despotism. The clergy of all nations were by this time enslaved to the Papacy, and by obeying its bulls of excommunication and giving effect to its interdicts they placed in the pope's hand a lever to move the world. During the interdict the churches in a country were all closed, bells silent, the dead unburied; no masses could be performed, no rites except those of baptism and extreme unction celebrated. This state of things was so dreadful to a superstitious age, that monarchs were obliged to yield lest their people should revolt. The result of every such interdict was an increase to the power of the Papacy, and they soon brought all refractory rulers in Europe to terms.

When the maxims of Gregory VII had been acted out for a century, and the power to trample on the necks of kings had come to be regarded by churchmen as an inherent right of the Papacy, the proud spirit of Papal aggression reached its climax. The period of climax may be dated from the pontificate of Innocent III, A.D. 1198. The leading objects which the Roman pontiffs had steadily pursued for centuries seemed at last attained: independent sovereignty, absolute supremacy over the Christian Church, and full control over the princes of Europe.

The historian Hallam says of this man: "He was formidable beyond all his predecessors, perhaps beyond all his successors. On every side the thunder of Rome broke over the heads of princes."3 He excommunicated Sweno, king of Norway; threatened the king of Hungary to alter the succession; put the kingdom of Castile under an interdict; and when Philip Augustus of France refused at his bidding to take back his repudiated wife, Innocent did not hesitate to punish the whole nation by putting France also under the same dreaded penalty, until her king humbly submitted to the pope's behest. King John of England and Philip II of Aragon were both constrained to resign their kingdoms and receive them back as spiritual fiefs from the Roman pontiff, who claimed also the right to decide the election of the emperors of Germany by his confirmation or veto. "The noonday of Papal dominion extends from the pontificate of Innocent III inclusively to that of Boniface VIII., or, in other words, throughout the thirteenth century. Rome inspired during this age all the terror of her ancient name; she was once more the mistress of the world, and kings were her vassals." 4

Innocent III claimed also the right to dispense with both civil and canon law when he pleased, and to decide cases by the plenitude of his own inherent power. He dispensed also with the obligation of promises made on oaths, undermining thus the force of contracts and treaties. The military power of the Papacy dates also from this man, as the crusades had left him in possession of an army. Systematic persecution of so-called heretics began also in this pontificate. The corruptions, cruelties, and assumptions of the Papacy had become so intolerable, that protests were making themselves heard in many quarters. It was felt these must be silenced at any cost, and a wholesale slaughter of heretics was commenced with a view to their extermination. The Inquisition was founded, the Albigenses and Waldenses were murderously persecuted, and superstition and tyranny were at their height. From this century Papal persecution of the witnesses for the truth never ceased until the final establishment of Protestantism at the end of the seventeenth century.

In A.D. 1294 Boniface VIII became pope, and by his superior audacity he threw into the shade even Innocent III. He deserves to be designated the most usurping of mankind, as witness his celebrated bull Unam Sanctam In this document the full claims of the Papacy come out. We have noted several ever-increasing stages of Papal assumption already, but now wereach the climax ù the claim which, if it were a true one, would abundantly justify all the rest; we reach the towering pinnacle and topmost peak of human self-exaltation. What was the claim of Boniface VIII? It was that

## *THE POPE REPRESENTS GOD ON EARTH*

As this claim is the most extraordinary and audacious ever made by mortal man, I will state it, not in my own words, but in the words of the highest Papal authority. In the summary of things concerning the dignity, authority, and infallibility of the pope, set forth by Boniface VIII, are these words: "The pope is of so great dignity and excellence, that he is not merely man, but as if God, and the vicar of God (non simplex homo, sed\par quasi Deus, et Dei vicarius). The pope alone is called most holy...Divine monarch, and supreme emperor, and king of kings..The pope is of so great dignity and power, that he constitutes one and the same tribunal with Christ (faciat unum et idem tribunal cum Christo), so that whatsoever the pope does seems to proceed from the mouth of God (ab ore Deo)..The pope is as God on earth (papa est QUASI DIAS IN TERRA)."

That which was claimed by Boniface VIII in the thirteenth century has been claimed ever since by a succession of popes down to Pius IX and Leo XIII in the nineteenth century. The pope speaks today as the vicar of Christ, as God's vice-regent. The great ecumenical council of 1870 proclaimed him such, and declared him to be INFALLIBLE! A professor of history in the Roman university, writing on the council of 1870, uses the following language, which strikingly expresses the Papal ideal: "The pope is not a power among men to be venerated like another. But he is a power altogether Divine. He is the propounder and teacher of the law of the Lord in the whole universe; he is the supreme leader of the nations, to guide them in the way of eternal salvation; he is the common father and universal guardian of the whole human species in the name of God. The human species has been perfected in its natural qualities by Divine revelation and by the incarnation of the Word, and has been lifted up into a supernatural order, in which alone it can find its temporal and eternal felicity. The treasures of revelation, the treasures of truth, the treasures of righteousness, the treasures of supernatural graces upon earth, have been deposited by God in the hands of one man, who is the sole dispenser and keeper of them. The life-giving work of the Divine incarnation, work of wisdom, of love, of mercy, is ceaselessly continued in the ceaseless action of one man, thereto ordained by Providence. This man is the pope. This is evidently implied in his designation itself, the vicar of Christ. For if he holds the place of Christ upon earth, that means that he continues the work of Christ in the world, and is in respect of us what Christ would be if He were here below, Himself visibly governing the Church." 5

Do you hear these words? Do you take them in? Do you grasp the thought which they express? Do you perceive the main idea and central principle of the Papacy? The pope is not simply man, but "as if God" and "the vicar of God," as God on earth. No wonder the sentence is addressed to every pope on his coronation, "Know thou art the father of princes and kings, and the governor of the world"; no wonder that he is worshipped by cardinals and archbishops and bishops, by priests and monks and nuns innumerable, by all the millions of Catholics throughout the world; no wonder that he has dethroned monarchs and given away kingdoms, dispensed pardons and bestowed indulgences, canonized saints, remitted purgatorial pains, promulgated dogmas, and issued bulls and laws and extravagants, laid empires under interdicts, bestowed benedictions, and uttered anathemas!

Who is like unto him on earth? What are great men, philosophers, statesmen, conquerors, princes, kings, and even emperors, of the earth compared to H IM? Their glory is of the earth, earthy; his is from above, it is Divine! He is the representative of Christ, the Creator and Redeemer, the Lord of all. He is as Christ; he takes the place of Christ. He is as God, as God on earth. This blasphemous notion is the keystone of the entire Papal arch; it is the stupendous axis on which the whole Papal world has rotated for ages, and is rotating at this hour.

But to complete this very brief sketch of the history of Romanism, I may just remind you that the long and checkered decline of Papal dominion may be dated from the pontificate of Boniface VIII, from the end of the thirteenth century. Early in the next century Clement V took the strange and fatal step of removing the seat of Papal government from Rome to Avignon, where it remained for seventy years, greatly to the detriment of its authority and power. There it was to some extent dependent on the court of France, and it also lost the affections of Italy and the prestige of Rome. Then came the great schism which seriously weakened and discredited the Papacy. Rival popes ruled at Rome and Avignon. Corruption and rapacity, demoralization and disaffection rapidly increased, and there supervened that darkest hour of the night which precedes the dawn.

Ere long Wycliffe, the morning star of the Reformation, arose, and at last came the blessed movement itself, with Martin Luther and the rest of the reformers, which delivered Germany, England, and other lands from the Papal yoke, dividing Christendom into two camps, Romanist and Protestant. Vainly did Rome seek with frantic efforts to arrest or reverse this movement! Hecatombs of martyrs, oceans of blood, centuries of war could not stop it. At the beginning of the sixteenth century Rome boasted that not a single heretic could be found; now Christendom contains a hundred and fifty millions of those whom the Papacy calls heretics, and whom it would exterminate by fire and sword if it could. It did succeed in crushing out the Reformation movement in France, Spain and Italy by awful Inquisition tortures, by bloody massacres, by cruel wars, by the revocation of the Edict of Nantes, by the deeds of such men as Philip of Spain with his armada, and the Duke of Alva with his cruelties in the Netherlands. Rome recovered some of the ground she lost in the Reformation, and she still exercises spiritual power over a hundred and eighty millions of mankind. Though her temporal power was overthrown for a time in the French Revolution, and to the joy of Italy brought to an end in 1870, her claim to it is in no wise abated, nor her pretension that she has a right to rule the world. The religion of Rome has so disgusted the continental nations, that, knowing nothing better, they have drifted into practical infidelity, and with one consent they have to a large extent despoiled the Church of her revenues, secularized her property and her religious houses, and repudiated her interference in their respective governments.

For the last five hundred years the authority of the Papacy has been declining. "Slowly and silently receding from their claims to temporal power, the pontiffs hardly protect their dilapidated citadel from the revolutionary concussions of modern times, the rapacity of governments, and the growing aversion to ecclesiastical influence..Those who know what Rome has once been are best able to appreciate what she is. Those who have seen the thunderbolt in the hands of the Gregories and the Innocents will hardly be intimidated at the sallies of decrepitude, the impotent dart of Priam amid the crackling ruins of Troy." So wrote Henry Hallam in the early part of this century; and while the fall of the temporal power has since taken place, and carried to low-water mark that steady ebb tide of Papal influence which he alleges, yet there has been during the last half century a revival of Romish influence in Protestant nations, which Hallam probably did not expect. I must not pause to estimate the causes or the importance of this revival here, but shall have occasion to allude to it again later on.

Let me now propose to you a puzzle. It is to condense into some brief, simple sentences, which could be read in a few minutes, an accurate, comprehensive, graphic summary of the thirteen hundred years of Papal history. Milman's "History of Latin Christianity" is here on the table. It occupies nine octavo volumes, and would take weeks to read. Ranke's "History of the Popes" is in three volumes, and does not cover the whole subject. D'Aubigne's "History of the Reformation" is in five volumes, and takes up only one episode of the long story. The Papacy has existed for thirteen centuries, has had to do with forty or fifty generations of mankind in all the countries of Christendom. Its history is consequently extremely complicated and various. It embraces both secular and ecclesiastical matters, and has more or less to do with all that has happened in Europe since the fall of the old Roman empire. The time is long, the sphere is vast, the story exceedingly complex. I want you to tell it all, in outline at least, in a narrative that you could read in less than five minutes or write in ten. You must bring in every point of importance: the time and circumstances of the origin of the Papacy, its moral character, its political relations, its geographical seat, its self-exalting utterances and acts, its temporal sovereignty, and a comparison of the extent of its dominions with those of the other kingdoms of Europe; its blasphemous pretensions, its cruel and long-continued persecutions of God's people, the duration of its dominion, its present decay, and the judgments that have overtaken it; and you must moreover add what you think its end is likely to be, and explain the relation of the whole history to the revealed plan of Divine providence.

You must get all this in not in the dry style of an annual Times summary of the events of the year ù but in an interesting, vivid, picturesque style, that will impress the facts on the memory, so that to forget them shall be impossible. Can you do it? I might safely offer a prize of any amount to the person who can solve this puzzle and write this story as I have described. But hard, even impossible as it would be for you to do this, even if you perfectly knew the history of the last thirteen centuries, how infinitely impossible would it be if that history lay in the unknown and inscrutable future, instead of in the past and present! If no eye had seen, nor ear heard it; if it was an untraversed continent, an unseen world, a matter for the evolution of the ages yet to come ù who then could tell the story at all, much less in brief?.

Now this is precisely what the prophet Daniel, by inspiration of the omniscient and eternal God, has done. He told the whole story of the Papacy twenty-five centuries ago. He omitted none of the points I have enumerated, and yet the prophecy only occupies seventeen verses of a chapter which can be read slowly and impressively in less than five minutes. This is because it was written in the only language in which it is possible thus to compress multum in parvo, the ancient language of hieroglyphics. God revealed the future to Daniel by a vision in which he saw, not the events, but the living, moving, speaking hieroglyphics of the events. These Daniel simply describes, and his description of them constitutes the prophecy written in the seventh chapter of his book. Our consideration of this remarkable prediction we must however postpone for the present, as we have already claimed your attention long enough for one lecture.

## Notes

1. "Mediaeval Church History," p. 14.
2. "Wherefore, trusting in the justice and mercy of God, and of his blessed mother, the ever- blessed Virgin Mary, on your authority (that of St. Peter and St. Paul), the above-named Henry and all his adherents I excommunicate and bind in the fetters of anathema; on the part of God Almighty, and on yours, I interdict him of all royal power and dignity. I prohibit every Christian from rendering him obedience as king. I absolve all who have sworn or shall swear allegiance to his sovereignty from their oaths." - Milman: "History of Latin Christianity," vol. 4., p. 121.
3. "The three great sovereigns of western Europe, the kings of Germany, of France, and of England, had seen their realms under Papal interdict, themselves under sentence of excommunication. But the Papal power under Innocent not only aspired to humble the loftiest. Hardly one of the smaller kingdoms had not already been taught, or was not soon taught, to feel the awful majesty of the Papacy. From the Northem Ocean to Hungary, from Hungary to the Spanish shore of the Atlantic, Innocent is exercising what takes the language of protective or parental authority, but which in most cases is asserted by the terrible interdict." - Milman: "History of Latin Christianity," vol. 5., p. 805.
4. Hallam: "History of the Middle Ages," p. 368, 4th ed.
5. Cited in "The Pope, the Kings, and the People." by Revelation William Arthur, M.A., vol. 1., p. 211.

# Lecture Two - The Daniel Foreview of Romanism, Second Part

Allow me to commence this lecture by reading to you Daniel's description of the divinely designed hieroglyph by which the history of Rome was prefigured. He has previously described the hieroglyphics of the Babylonian, Persian, and Grecian empires, and then he says:

After this I saw in the night visions, and behold a fourth beast, dreadful and terrible, and strong exceedingly; and it had great iron teeth: it devoured and brake in pieces, and stamped the residue with the feet of it: and it was diverse from all the beasts that were before it; and it had ten horns. I considered the horns, and, behold, there came up among them another little horn, before whom there were three of the first horns plucked up by the roots: and, behold, in this horn were eyes like the eyes of man, and a mouth speaking great things. I beheld till the thrones were cast down, and the Ancient of days did sit, whose garment was white as snow, and the hair of his head like the pure wool: his throne was like the fiery flame, and his wheels as burning fire. A fiery stream issued and came forth from before him: thousand thousands ministered unto him, and ten thousand times ten thousand stood before him: the judgment was set, and the books were opened. I beheld then because of the voice of the great words which the horn spake: I beheld even till the beast was slain, and his body destroyed, and given to the burning flame. As concerning the rest of the beasts, they had their dominion taken away: yet their lives were prolonged for a season and time. I saw in the night visions, and, behold, one like the Son of man came with the clouds of heaven, and came to the Ancient of days, and they brought him near before him. And there was given him dominion, and glory, and a kingdom, that all people, nations, and languages, should serve him: his dominion is an everlasting dominion, which shall not pass away, and his kingdom that which shall not be destroyed. I Daniel was grieved in my spirit in the midst of my body, and the visions of my head troubled me. I came near unto one of them that stood by, and asked him the truth of all this. So he told me, and made me know the interpretation of the things. These great beasts, which are four, are four kings, which shall arise out of the earth. But the saints of the most High shall take the kingdom, and possess the kingdom for ever, even for ever and ever. Then I would know the truth of the fourth beast, which was diverse from all the others, exceeding dreadful, whose teeth were of iron, and his nails of brass; which devoured, brake in pieces, and stamped the residue with his feet; And of the ten horns that were in his head, and of the other which came up, and before whom

21

three fell; even of that horn that had eyes, and a mouth that spake very great things, whose look was more stout than his fellows. I beheld, and the same horn made war with the saints, and prevailed against them; Until the Ancient of days came, and judgment was given to the saints of the most High; and the time came that the saints possessed the kingdom. Thus he said, The fourth beast shall be the fourth kingdom upon earth, which shall be diverse from all kingdoms, and shall devour the whole earth, and shall tread it down, and break it in pieces. And the ten horns out of this kingdom are ten kings that shall arise: and another shall rise after them; and he shall be diverse from the first, and he shall subdue three kings. And he shall speak great words against the most High, and shall wear out the saints of the most High, and think to change times and laws: and they shall be given into his hand until a time and times and the dividing of time. But the judgment shall sit, and they shall take away his dominion, to consume and to destroy it unto the end. And the kingdom and dominion, and the greatness of the kingdom under the whole heaven, shall be given to the people of the saints of the most High, whose kingdom is an everlasting kingdom, and all dominions shall serve and obey him.

In these verses you have the entire story of the Papacy, and what is more, you have its future as well as its past, the judgment of God as to its moral character and deserts.

And how vivid the coloring, how graphic the picture! I wish I could paint, or, better still, display in action before your eyes, such a dreadful and terrible and exceedingly strong wild beast, with its brazen claws and iron teeth, and ravening, ferocious nature, with its ten horns and its strange, head-like "little horn," able to see and speak and blaspheme the Almighty, so as at last to bring down destruction on the beast itself! I wish I could let you watch it ù rending and tearing its enemies, breaking their bones in pieces, devouring their flesh, and in wanton, fierce ferocity stamping on and trampling with its brazen-clawed feet what it cannot consume! If you had learned the ABC of the language of hieroglyphics you would at once recognize that such creatures as this are figures of godless empires, kingdoms which are brutal in their ignorance of God, in their absence of self-control, in their bestial instincts; which love bloodshed and are reckless of human agony, selfish, terrible, cruel, mighty. They represent and recall proud military heroes, like Julius Caesar, who trample down all that oppose them; cruel despots, who oppress their fellows; reckless conquerors like Tamerlane and Napoleon, to whom the slaughter of millions of mankind was a matter of no moment. This is the generic signification of all such hieroglyphs. But we are not left to guess the meaning and application of this particular monster. The symbol has a Divine interpretation. "The fourth beast," we read, "shall be the fourth kingdom upon the earth." That, beyond all question, was Rome, as all historians agree ù the fourth and last of the great universal empires of antiquity. The monster represents Rome, her whole existence as a supreme or

22

ruling power, after the fall of the Greek or Macedonian beast before her attacks (197 B.C.). It represents therefore the history of Rome for over 2,000 years in the past, and on into a time still future; for, be it well noted, this beast ravages and rules, and his characteristic little horn blasphemes and boasts, right up to the point when empires like to wild beasts come to an end, and "the Son of man and the saints of the Most High take the kingdom and possess it for ever."

It is important that we should clearly grasp one great historical fact; i.e. the rule of Rome has never, since it first commenced, ceased to exist, save once, for a very brief period during the Gothic invasions. It has changed in character, as we have seen, but it has continued. Rome ruled the known world at the first advent of Christ, and still rules hundreds of millions of mankind, and will continue so to do right up till the second advent of Christ. So this prophecy teaches; for not until the Son of man takes the dominion of the earth, and establishes a kingdom that shall never pass away, is the monster representing Roman rule destroyed. The rule of Rome, we repeat, has never ceased. It was a secular pagan power for five or six centuries; it has been an ecclesiastical and apostate Christian power ever since, that is to say, for twelve or thirteen centuries. There lay a brief period between these two main stages, during which professing Christian emperors ruled from Rome, followed by an interval when, for a time, it seemed as if the great city had received a fatal blow from her Gothic captors. It seemed so; but it was not so, for the word of God cannot be broken. The rule of Rome revived in a new form, and was as real under the popes of the thirteenth century as it had been under the Caesars of the first. It was as oppressive, cruel, and bloody under Innocent III. as it had been under Nero and Domitian. The reality was the same, though the forms had changed. The Caesars did not persecute the witnesses of Jesus more severely and bitterly than did the popes; Diocletian did not destroy the saints or oppose the gospel more than did the Inquisition of Papal days. Rome is one and the same all through, both locally and morally. One dreadful wild beast represents her, though the symbol, like the history it prefigures, has two parts. There was the undivided stage, and there has been the tenfold stage. The one is Rome pagan, the other Rome Papal; the one is the old empire, the other the modern pontificate; the one is the empire of the Caesars, the other is the Roman Papacy.

I speak broadly, omitting all detail for the present. We shall find more of that when we come by- and-by to John's later foreview. Daniel's was a distant view in the days of Belshazzar, too distant altogether for detail. No artist paints the sheep on the hillside if the hill be fifty miles off; he may sketch its bold outline, but he omits minor detail. So Daniel's distant foreview, dating from 2,500 years ago, shows the two great sections of Roman history ù the undivided military empire, followed by the commonwealth of Papal Christendom, the latter as truly Latin in character as the former; and he shows the end of Rome at the second advent of Christ. But he refrains from encumbering his striking sketch with confusing political details. He does not fail however to delineate fully the moral and religious features of the power ruling from Rome during the second half of the story, the power symbolized by the proud, intelligent, blasphemous, head-like "little horn" of the Roman beast. To this he devotes, on the contrary, the greater part of the prophecy; and I must ask you now carefully to note the various points that prove this horn to be a marvelous prophetic symbol or hieroglyph of the Roman Papacy, fitting it as one of Chubb's keys fits the lock for which it is made, perfectly and in every part, while it refuses absolutely to adapt itself to any other. The main points in the nature, character, and actings of this "little horn," which we must note in order to discover the power intended, are these:

1. Its place: within the body of the fourth empire.
2. The period of its origin: soon after the division of the Roman territory into ten kingdoms.
3. Its nature: different from the other kingdoms, though in some respects like them. It was a horn, but with eyes and mouth. It would be a kingdom like the rest, a monarchy; but its kings would be overseers or bishops and prophets.
4. Its moral character: boastful and blasphemous; great words spoken against the Most High.
5. Its lawlessness: it would claim authority over times and laws.
6. Its opposition to the saints: it would be a persecuting power, and that for so long a period that it would wear out the saints of the Most High, who would be given into its hand for a time.
7. Its duration: "time, times and a half," or 1260 years.
8. Its doom: it would suffer the loss of its dominion before it was itself destroyed. "They shall take away its dominion, to consume and destroy it to the end."

Here are eight different and perfectly tangible features. If they all meet in one great reality, if we find them all characterizing one and the same power, can we question that is the power intended? They do all meet in the Roman Papacy, whose history I have just briefly recalled, and we are therefore bold to say it is the great and evil reality predicted. A few words on each of these points, to convince you that this is the case.

**1. Its place.** No one can question that the Papacy is a Roman, as distinguished from a Greek or an oriental, power. Its seat is the seven-hilled city; its tongue is the Latin language of Caesar and of Pliny and of Tacitus; its Church is the Church of Rome, and is the only Church that is or ever has been named from a city. Others have been named from countries or from men; the Papal Church alone bears the name of a city, and that city is Rome. The Papacy fulfills the first condition therefore.

**2. Its time.** We have shown that the last Bishop of Rome and the first pope was Boniface III., A.D. 607. Now the western empire of Rome came to an end with the fall of Romulus Augustulus, A.D. 476; that is, 130 years earlier. During that time the ten kingdoms were forming in the body of the old empire, and during that time the simple pastor of the Church was transformed into a pope. The little horn grew up among the ten. The Papacy developed synchronously with the Gothic kingdoms.

**3. Its nature.** The power symbolized by the little horn is of course a kingdom, like all the other ten; but it is not merely this. It is "diverse," or different from all the other ruling dynasties with which it is associated. It is a horn of the wild beast, but it has human eyes and a human voice, denoting its pretensions to be a seer, or prophet, and a teacher. It takes the oversight of all the ten, it is an overseer or bishop, and it has "a mouth speaking great things." Its paramount influence depends, not on its mere material power, for it is small as a kingdom, a "little horn," but on its religious pretensions. Does not this exactly portray the Papacy? Was it not diverse or different from all the Gothic kingdoms amid which it existed? Was it a mere kingdom? Nay, but a spiritual reign over the hearts and minds as well as the bodies of men a reign established by means, not of material weapons, but of spiritual pretensions. It was founded not on force, but on falsehood and fraud, and the superstitious fears of the half-civilized and ignorant Gothic kingdoms.

The popedom has always been eager to proclaim its own diversity from all other kingdoms. It claims "a princedom more perfect than every human princedom," surpassing them "as far as the light of the sun exceeds that of the moon." It arrogates to itself a character as superior to secular kingdoms as man to the irrational beasts. Its laws are made not with the best human wisdom; but auctoritate, scientia, ac plenitudine, with fullness of Divine knowledge and the fullness of apostolic power. Is not the Papacy sufficiently diverse from all the rest of the kingdoms of western Europe to identify it as the little horn? What other ruling monarch of Christendom ever pretended to apostolic authority, or ruled men in the name of God? Does the pope dress in royal robes? Nay, but in priestly garments. Does he wear a crown? Nay, but a triple tiara, to show that he reigns in heaven, earth, and hell? Does he wield a scepter? Nay, but a crosier or crook, to show that he is the good shepherd of the Church. Do his subjects kiss his hand? Nay, but his toe! Verily this power is "diverse" from the rest, both in great things and little. It is small in size, gigantic in its pretensions. It is, or was for centuries, one among many temporal kingdoms in Europe. It is the only one which claims a spiritual authority and universal dominion.

**4. Its moral character.** The salient feature here is the "mouth speaking very great things." Great words spoken against the Most High, and "a look more stout than his fellows." Audacious pride and bold blasphemy must characterize the power that fulfills this point of the symbol.

25

We ask then, Has the Papacy exhibited this mark also? Time would fail me to quote to you verbatim its great words, its boastful self-glorifications, and its outrageous blasphemies against God! You will find pages of them quoted in my work on "The Approaching End of the Age," and volumes filled with them exist, for Papal documents consist of little else. The Papal claims are so grotesque in their pride and self-exaltation, that they almost produce a sense of the comic, and that feeling of pitying contempt with which one would watch a frog trying to swell itself to the size of an ox! I must however mention some of the claims contained in these "great words," which will show you the nature of Papal blasphemies. It is claimed, for instance, that "no laws made contrary to the canons and decrees of Roman prelates have any force," that "the tribunals of all kings are subject to the priests," that "no man may act against the discipline of the Roman Church," that "the Papal decrees or decretal epistles are to be numbered among the canonical Scriptures," and not only so, but that the Scriptures themselves are to be received only "because a judgment of holy Pope Innocent was published for receiving them." It is claimed that "emperors ought to obey, and not rule over pontiffs"; that even an awfully wicked pope, who is a "slave of hell," may not be rebuked by mortal man, because "he is himself to judge all men and to be judged by none," and "since he was styled God by the pious prince Constantine, it is manifest that God cannot be judged by man"! They claim that no law, not even their own canon laws, can bind the popes; but that just as Christ, being maker of all laws and ordinances, could violate the law of the Sabbath, because He was Lord also of the Sabbath, so popes can dispense with any law, to show they are above all law!

It is claimed that the chair of St. Peter, the see of Rome, is "made the head of the world"; that it is not to be subject to any man, "since by the Divine mouth it is exalted above all." In the canon laws the Roman pontiff is described as "our Lord God the pope," and said to be "neither God nor man, but both." But the climax of assumption, the keystone of the arch of Papal pretension, is probably to be found in the "extravagant" of Boniface VIII., the Unam Sanctam, which runs thus: "All the faithful of Christ by necessity of salvation are subject to the Roman pontiff, who judges all men, but is judged by no one." "This authority is not human, but rather Divine..Therefore we declare, assert, define, and pronounce, that to be subject to the Roman pontiff is to every human creature altogether necessary for salvation."

All these claims were incessantly and universally urged all down the centuries by the popes of Rome, and are still advanced, as boldly as ever, in official decretals, bulls, extravagants, decisions of canonists, sentences of judges, books, catechisms, sermons, and treatises of all kinds. There is no mistaking what they amount to. The pope claims Divine inspiration, his words are to be received as the words of God; no laws can bind him, he is supreme over all; the very Scriptures derive their authority from him; implicit obedience to him is the only way of salvation. He is exalted above all, supreme over all nations, kings, emperors, princes, bishops, archbishops, Churches, over all the world; he is as God on earth, and as such to be worshipped and obeyed. Let me quote you from his own lips some of the great words of the little horn. The following language affords a mere sample of thousands of such Papal blasphemies.

The greatness of priesthood began in Melchisedek, was solemnized in Aaron, continued in the children of Aaron, perfected in Christ, represented in Peter, exalted in the universal jurisdiction, and manifested in the pope. So that through this pre-eminence of my priesthood, having all things subject to me, it may seem well verified in me, that was spoken of Christ, "Thou has subdued all things under His feet, sheep and oxen, and all cattle of the field, the birds of heaven, and fish of the sea," etc.: where it is to be noted that by oxen, Jews and heretics, by cattle of the field, pagans be signified..by sheep and all cattle are meant all Christian men, both great and less, whether they be emperors, princes, prelates, or others; by birds of the air you may understand angels and potentates of heaven, who be all subject to me, in that I am greater than the angels, and that in four things, as afore declared, and have power to bind and loose in heaven, and to give heaven to them that fight in my wars; lastly, by the fishes of the sea, are signified the souls departed, in pain or in purgatory.

All the earth is my diocese, and I am the ordinary of all men, having the authority of the King of all kings upon subjects. I am all in all and above all, so that God Himself and I, the vicar of God, have but one consistory, and I am able to do almost all that God can do. In all things that I list, my will is to stand for reason; for I am able by the law to dispense above the law, and of wrong to make justice in correcting laws and changing them..Wherefore if those things that I do be said not to be done of man, but of God, what can you make me but God? Again, if prelates of the Church be called and counted of Constantine for gods, I then, being above all prelates, seem by this reason to be above all gods. Wherefore no marvel if it be in my power to change time and times, to alter and abrogate laws, to dispense with all things, yea, with the precepts of Christ; for where Christ biddeth Peter put up his sword, and admonishes His disciples not to use any outward force in revenging themselves, do not I, Pope Nicholas, writing to the bishops of France, exhort them to draw out their material swords? And whereas Christ was present Himself at the marriage in Cana of Galilee, do not I, Pope Martin, in my distinction, inhibit the spiritual clergy to be present at marriage feasts, and also to marry? Moreover where Christ biddeth us lend without hope of gain, do not I, Pope Martin, give dispensation for the same? What should I speak of murder, making it to be no murder or homicide to slay them that be excommunicated? Likewise against the law of nature, item against the apostles, also against the canons of the apostles, I can and do dispense; for where they in their canon command a priest for fornication to be deposed, I, through the authority of Sylvester, do alter the rigor of that constitution, considering the minds and bodies also of men to be weaker than they were then.

After that I have now sufficiently declared my power in earth, in heaven, in purgatory, how great it is, and what is the fullness thereof in binding, loosing, commanding, permitting, electing, confirming, disposing, dispensing, doing, and undoing, etc., I will speak now a little of my riches and of my great possessions, that every man may see by my wealth, and abundance of all things, rents, tithes, tributes, my silks, my purple miters, crowns, gold, silver, pearls and gems, lands and lordships. For to me pertaineth first the imperial city of Rome, the palace of Lateran; the kingdom of Sicily is proper to me; Apulia and Capua be mine. Also the kingdom of England and Ireland, be they not, or ought they not to be, tributaries to me? To these I adjoin also, besides other provinces and countries, both in the occident and orient, from the north to the south, these dominions by name. [Here follows a long list.] What should I speak here of my daily revenues, of my firstfruits, annats, palls, indulgences, bulls, confessionals, indults and rescripts, testaments, dispensations, privileges, elections, prebends, religious houses, and such like, which come to no small mass of money?..Whereby what vantage cometh to my coffers it may partly be conjectured..But what should I speak of Germany, which the whole world is my diocese, as my canonists do say, and all men are bound to believe; except they will imagine (as the Manichees do) two beginnings, which is false and heretical? For Moses saith, In the beginning God made heaven and earth; and not, In the beginnings. Wherefore, as I began, so I conclude, commanding, declaring, and pronouncing, to stand upon necessity of salvation, for every human creature to be subject to me (Foxe: "Acts and Monuments," vol. 4., p. 145).

It is futile to allege that the Papacy does not make these claims and speak these great words against God, but in His name and as His representative. The answer is patent. This prophecy foretells what the power predicted would do, not what it would profess to do. Does the Papacy give God the glory, or does it glorify itself? Facts cannot be set aside by false pretensions. Satan disguises himself as an angel of light. The head of a Christian Church would not overtly array himself against Christ; if he does so, it will be under semblance of serving Him.1

The Papacy has abundantly branded on her own brow this particular of the prophecy ù the boastful, blasphemous claim to Divine authority and absolute dominion. It has assumed Divine attributes, and even the very name of God, and on the strength of that name claimed to be above all human judgment.

**5. Lawlessness** was the next feature we noted in the little horn. We have given above some specimens of the Papal claim to set aside all laws Divine and human. The pope has also annulled the only surviving law of paradise, confirmed by the words of Christ. The Lord ordained, "What God hath joined together, let no man put asunder." The pope ordains, "We decide also that, according to the sacred canons, the marriages contracted by priests and deacons be dissolved, and the parties brought to do penance." The Papacy has further annulled the second commandment, given on the mount by the lips of God ù in theory, by the childish and false distinction between heathen idols and Christian images; and in practice, by hiding it from the people, and blotting it out from the catechisms of general instruction. The pope has further annulled the main laws of the gospel. He forbids the cup to the laity, although the Lord Himself has commanded, "Drink ye all of it." He forbids the people of Christ, in general, to use the word of God in their own tongue; though Christ Himself has charged them, "Search the Scriptures." He forbids the laity to reason or converse on the doctrines of the gospel; though St. Peter has commanded them, "Be ye ready to give a reason of the hope that is in you." The pope, finally, sanctions the invocation of saints and angels: though St. Paul has warned us, "Let no man beguile you of your reward in a voluntary humility and worshipping of angels"; though St. John has renewed the charge to the disciples of Christ, "Little children, keep yourselves from idols"; and an angel from heaven renews the caution, in his words to the same holy apostle, "See thou do it not, for I am thy fellow servant; worship God" (Birks, "First Two Visions of Daniel," pp. 258, 259).

**6. Systematic and long continued persecution of the saints** is one of the most marked features of the little horn of the prophecy. It is predicted that he should "wear out the saints of the Most High." His first great characteristic is blasphemous opposition to GOD; his next salient feature is oppressive cruelty towards men: and just as Christ allowed His people to suffer ten persecutions under the pagan emperors of Rome, so he allowed His faithful witnesses to be worn out by the cruelties of Papal Rome. "They shall be given into his hand." The Church has to tread in the footsteps of Christ Himself, who resisted unto blood striving against sin, and was put to death by the power of Rome. She is called to the fellowship of His sufferings; and while they secured the salvation of our race, hers have not been unfruitful, for the blood of the martyrs is the seed of the Church.

But we must compare the facts of history with the prediction of prophecy on this point, to see how deeply this mark is engraved on the Papacy as upon no other power that has ever existed in the earth. That the Church of Rome and her Papal head have persecuted largely and long, none can pretend to deny; in fact, so far from denying it, Rome glories in it, and regards it as one of her greatest merits. Other nations have now abandoned as unsound "the bloody tenet of persecution." Rome retains it still, approves it theoretically, and would carry it out as vigorously as ever practically, if she could. Other powers have persecuted to a small extent and occasionally, in the past, but never systematically and by law throughout ages. All but Rome now hold religious liberty to be an inherent right of man. Rome has, on the other hand, persecuted on principle, and steadily from the seventh century right on to the French Revolution and to some extent almost to the present time. She does so still in the secret recesses of her nunneries and monasteries, under the name of penance. Why else does she require shops for the sale of instruments of bodily torture, such as exist this day in London?

Rome's contention is, not that she does not persecute, but only that she does not persecute saints. She punishes heretics ù a very different thing. The first would be wicked, the last she esteems laudable. In the Rhemish New Testament there is a note on the words "drunken with the blood of saints," which runs as follows: "Protestants foolishly expound this of Rome, because heretics are there put to death. But their blood is not called the blood of saints, any more than the blood of thieves or man-killers, or other malefactors; and for the shedding of it no commonwealth shall give account." This is clear. Rome approves the murder of "heretics," and fully admits that she practices her principles.

The question therefore becomes this, Are those whom Rome calls "heretics" the same as those whom Daniel calls "saints"? If so, the identification of the Papacy is as complete in this respect as in all the previous points. In order to arrive at an answer to this question, let us take Rome's own definition of a heretic. The following statements are from authorized documents, laws, and decrees of the Papacy, dating from the time of Pope Pelagius in the sixth century, twelve hundred years ago. "Schism is an evil. Whoever is separated from the apostolic see is doubtless in schism. Do then what we often exhort. Take pains that they who presume to commit this sin be brought into custody..Do not hesitate to compress men of this kind, and if he despise this, let him be crushed by the public powers." This, it will be observed, makes a want of perfect submission to the pope, even though no false doctrine or evil practice be alleged, a ground for persecution. Pope Damasus, whose election to the pontificate was secured by a hundred and thirty-seven murders, authorizes persecution of those who speak against any of the holy canons, and adds, "It is permitted neither to think nor to speak differently from the Roman Church." This is one of the canons which it is blasphemy to violate; and he who ventures to differ, even in thought, on any point whatever from the Roman Church is therefore a heretic. Hundreds of decisions on detailed examples of heresy are all summed up in this one. The Roman decrees everywhere supply similar definitions. Whatever is short of absolute, unconditional surrender of all freedom of act or word, or even of thought and conscience, is heresy. Every evangelical Christian in the world is therefore, according to Romanist canons, a heretic, and as such liable to "punishment." And moreover Rome frankly admits that it is only where she cannot in the nature of things carry out her ecclesiastical discipline that she is justified in refraining from persecution. The Papacy teaches all her adherents that it is a sacred duty to exterminate heresy. From age to age it has sought to crush out all opposition to its own dogmas and corruptions, and Papal edicts for persecution are innumerable. The fourth Lateran Council issued a canon on the subject, which subsequently became an awful instrument of cruelty.

For long ages it was held and taught universally that whoever fell fighting against heretics had merited heaven. Urban II. issued a decree, acted on, alas! to this day in Ireland, that the murder of heretics was excusable. "We do not count them murderers who, burning with the zeal of their Catholic mother against the excommunicate, may happen to have slain some of them." If not absolutely murdered, heretics might be ill treated ad libitum, according to an ordinance of Gregory IX., who writes to the Archbishop of Milan: "Let those understand themselves to be absolved the debt of fidelity, homage, and all manner of service, who were bound by any compact, however firmly ratified, to those who have fallen into heresy." Systematic persecution and extermination of heretics among their subjects was constantly enjoined on kings and emperors; such were required solemnly to swear on their coronation that they would, according to their power, faithfully render their service to the pope. If they neglected to do it, the sovereign pontiff would declare the vassals free and give their realms to rigid Papists who would more effectually persecute. If monarchs became heretics themselves, they were to be deposed and anathematized. Thus Pius V. "issued a bull for the damnation and excommunication of Queen Elizabeth and her adherents," cutting her off from "the unity of the body of Christ," depriving her of her crown and kingdom, and pronouncing a curse on her and on all who continued to obey her.

The laws of the Papacy on this subject increase in malignity from the beginning down to modern times. Bellarmine argues for the necessity of burning heretics, a practice which Luther had asserted to be contrary to the Spirit of God. He says: "Experience teaches that there is no other remedy; for the Church has proceeded by slow steps, and tried all remedies. First, she only excommunicated. Then she added a fine of money, and afterwards exile. Lastly, she was compelled to come to the punishment of death. For heretics despise excommunication, and say that those lightnings are cold. If you threaten a fine of money, they neither fear God nor regard men, knowing that fools will not be wanting to believe in them, and by whom they may be sustained. If you shut them in prison, or send them into exile, they corrupt those near to them with their words, and those at a distance with their books. Therefore the only remedy is, to send them betimes into their own place."

Under these bloody maxims those persecutions were carried on, from the eleventh and twelfth centuries almost to the present day, which stand out on the page of history. After a signal of open martyrdom had been given in the canons of Orleans, there followed the extirpation of the Albigenses under the form of a crusade, the establishment of the Inquisition, the cruel attempts to extinguish the Waldenses, the martyrdom of the Lollards, the cruel wars to exterminate the Bohemians, the burning of Huss and Jerome, and multitudes of other confessors, before the Reformation; and afterwards the ferocious cruelties practiced in the Netherlands, the martyrdom of Queen Mary's reign, the extinction, by fire and sword, of the Reformation in Spain and Italy, by fraud and open persecution in Poland, the massacre of Bartholemew, the persecutions of the Huguenots by the League, the extirpation of the Vaudois, and all the cruelties and perjuries connected with the revocation of the Edict of Nantes. These are the more open and conspicuous facts which explain the prophecy, besides the slow and secret murders of the holy tribunal of the Inquisition" (Birks: "First Two Visions of Daniel," pp. 248,249).

A Romanist writer, who deplored the persecuting policy of his Church ù Professor Rossetti ù writes: It makes the heart of a true Christian bleed to think of this fatal error of the Latin Church, which by persecuting others laid the foundation of her own irreparable ruin. That the opinions held by these so-called heretics were most injurious to the Church of Rome cannot be denied, but the means taken to destroy them were, of all others, the most likely to strengthen them, and render them more deeply rooted. Daniel and St. John foretold that Satan's delegate would use horrid cruelties, and inundate Babylon with the blood of Christ's martyrs; and the pope, to prove that he was not that delegate, did use horrid cruelties, and cause Rome to overflow with the purest of Christian blood! So Sismondi, the historian writes: To maintain unity of belief the Church had recourse to the expedient of burning all those who separated themselves from her; but although for two hundred years the fires were never quenched, still every day saw Romanists abjuring the faith of their fathers and embracing the religion which often guided them to the stake. In vain Gregory IX., in A.D. 1231, put to death every heretic whom he found concealed in Rome. His own letters show that the heretics only increased in numbers.

It must never be forgotten that all Rome's ordinances against heresy, all its statutes of persecution, remain in its canon law unabrogated, unchanged, and as the Papacy is infallible in its own esteem ù unchangeable, "irreformable." Its present disuse of persecution practically is the result of the heavy judgments which have, since the Reformation, and especially since the French Revolution, overtaken it. It has now no army and no Inquisition of its own, nor is any single kingdom in Europe willing any longer to act as its executioner. It lacks the power ù it utterly lacks the power ù to persecute directly or indirectly. It can only stir up sedition and revolt in Protestant countries, and thus endeavor to injure and weaken Protestant powers, as it is doing today in Ireland and in the United States. It is too weak politically to defy modern society by reintroducing mediaeval tortures, massacres, religious crusades, and the auto da fe. But it is as willing as ever, and awaits the opportunity only. As a drunkard may retain his vicious appetite when he has no longer the means of gratifying it, so Rome long drunken with the blood of saints ù is restrained from further maddening and debasing draughts of her dreadful beverage by nothing but inability to procure them. The Papacy, by justifying as righteous all the horrible persecutions of the past, attests her readiness to renew them whenever the opportunity may serve.

As I shall have to recur to this subject when treating of St. John's foreview of Romanism, I will add nothing further on this point. I have said enough to show, that this sixth mark of the little horn attaches most distinctly to the Papacy, and indicates it alone among all the powers that have ever held sway on the Roman earth. It has martyred by millions the saints of God, the best and holiest of men. Its persecuting edicts range over the entire period of its existence; the present pope has endorsed them by his approval of the syllabus of Pius IX., and he threw over them the mantle of infallibility.

**7. Its duration.** A certain definite period is assigned to the rule of the little horn. That period is expressed in symbolic language, harmonious with the symbolic or hieroglyphic character of the whole prophecy. It is "time, times and a half," or "1,260 days." This is a miniature symbol of the empire, and the little horn of the Papacy of Rome. Scripture elsewhere gives us the scale on which it is to be enlarged, "a year for a day." It means therefore 1,260 years. The political supremacy and the persecuting power of the see of Rome were to last for this period and no longer. We have shown you that the popedom dates from the beginning of the seventh century. Twelve and a half centuries added brings us to the end of the nineteenth century ù in other words, to the days we live in, and in which Rome has ceased to be governed by its popes and has become the capital of the kings of Italy. I have no time to expound this chronological point fully to you this evening. If you wish to study it, you will find it carefully and exactly treated in my recent work, "Light for the Last Days." But it leads me to the final point in this identification.

**8. The doom of the predicted power.** What is the end of this symbolic horn? "They shall take away his dominion, to consume and to destroy it to the end." "The beast was slain, and his body destroyed and given to the burning flame." This last clause of prophecy is of course not yet fully accomplished, as it is the coming of the Son of man in the clouds of heaven that brings about the final consummation (v. 13). Speculations about the future we leave to futurists, and therefore it might at first sight seem as if we ought to say nothing on this point of the prophecy. But it is not so.

This doom consists clearly of two parts: first, the consuming and destroying to the end; and then the end itself, symbolized by the slaughter of the beast, the committal of his body to the burning flame. Now the first part of this doom is fulfilling, and has been fulfilling ever since the Reformation, and especially ever since the French revolution; though the second part is still future. We ask, Has there not been going on for the last few centuries a process by which the once mighty power of the Papacy has been sensibly consumed ù a weakening process, analogous to consumption in the human frame ù a wasting decay tending to extinction?

It must be borne in mind that this prophecy of Daniel takes up the political aspect of the great antichrist, not his religious character. It views him as a monarch of the Roman world, not as a bishop of the Christian Church. We come to that aspect of his career presently, when we take up Paul's foreview. Here it is one horn among ten, one kingdom among ten Latin kingdoms, though in some senses ruling over them all. The question is, Has there not been such a decay and diminution of Papal sovereignty, such a wasting and weakening of Papal power, such a loss of revenue, influence, and territory, as may be fairly said to fulfill this prediction?

Now I mentioned some facts at the beginning of this lecture which indicate a very considerable growth of Papal influence in England during the last fifty years. Many so fix their gaze on these facts as to get an impression that Romanism is gaining ground in the world generally. This is far from being the case, as a glance at the comparative positions of the Papacy in the thirteenth century and the two following ones, with its position now in the nineteenth, will show. Then Rome actually exercised the "dominion" which she can now only claim. Then, with the consent of his barons, the king of England agreed to hold his kingdom as the pope's feudatory, and to pay him annually one hundred thousand marks as an acknowledgment. Can you imagine Queen Victoria and the lords and commons of England agreeing to that sort of thing now? Then the great and valiant emperor of Germany stood for three winter days and nights barefoot in the courtyard of "His Holiness," waiting for the honor of an audience, in which he might beg the pope's pardon for having acted as an independent monarch! Can you imagine the Kaiser Wilhelm, of Berlin, doing that now? Then wherever he pleased the pope could suspend all the observances of religion, even to the burial of the dead and the marriage of the living, in any country with which he was offended. In what kingdom could he do so now? Long after his absolute dominion was gone, the pope had what were called concordats with different nations, in which it was agreed that, in return for the pope's spiritual support, they would uphold him when the last vestige of his temporal dominion was violently taken away.

Direct political power he now has none, though his position as head of the apostate Roman Church gives him still immense indirect influence. The ten kings as such have entirely shaken off his yoke, and he himself has no longer any sovereign jurisdiction. His territories are taken away, as well as his dominion. The wealth, which was once enormous, is equally gone; the immense landed estates belonging to the convents are, for the most part, confiscated to secular uses. But the greatest fact of all in this connection is the number of those who have rejected his religious pretension. At the Lateran Council, in 1513, after all the so-called heretics had been silenced by fire and sword, an orator, addressing the pope, said, "The whole body of Christendom is now subject to one head, even to thee; no one now opposes, no one now objects." Today there are about a hundred and fifty million Protestants in the world! Has not the dominion of the Papacy been consumed? Can a few thousand perverts in England weigh much against this stupendous fact, that 150,000,000 of mankind are no more subject to the Pope of Rome than to the Lama of Tibet? When we take into account all the twelve centuries of Papal history, and remember that this emancipation belongs to the last three only, we must admit that the predicted consumption has made considerable progress. The political dominion and the temporal possessions are gone; the Papacy is no longer a kingdom, but only an ecclesiastical power, and, counting the Greek Church, there are far more so- called Christians outside than inside the pale of the apostate Latin Church, of which it is the head.

This feature of the prediction is then as clearly applicable to Romanism as all the rest. Let me inquire, can any one suggest any other power in which all these marks, or the majority of them, meet? They are eight in number, and definite in character. The prophecy lays its finger on the place where we are to find the great enemy ROME; on the point of time in the course of history at which we may expect to see him arise the division of the Roman territory into a commonwealth of kingdoms; it specifies the nature of the power politico-ecclesiastical; its character blasphemously self-exalting, lawless, and persecuting; it measures its duration l,260 years; and specifies its doom ù to have its dominion gradually consumed and taken away, and then to be suddenly destroyed for ever, because of its blasphemous assumptions, by the epiphany in glory of the Son of man, introducing the kingdom of God on earth.

The proof that the Papacy is the power intended is strictly cumulative. If it answered to one of these indications there would be a slight presumption against it; if to several, a strong one; if to the majority, an overwhelming one; while if it answer to all, then the proof that it is the power intended becomes to candid minds irresistible. There is not a single clause in the prophecy that cannot be proved to fit the Roman Papacy exactly, except the last, which is not yet fulfilled. Rome, which in her pagan phase defiled and destroyed the literal temple of God at Jerusalem, in her Papal days defiled and destroyed the anti-typical spiritual temple of God ù the Christian Church. Was it not worthy of God to warn that Church beforehand of the coming of this dreadful antichristian power, and to cheer her in all the sufferings she would have to endure from its tyranny by a knowledge of the issue of the great and terrible drama? Was it not right that the Roman power, pagan and Papal, should occupy as paramount a place on the page of Scripture as it has actually done on the page of history? The eighteen Christian centuries lay open before the eye of the omniscient God, and no figure stood out so prominently in all their long course as that of the great antichrist. The pen of inspiration sketched him in a few bold, masterly strokes; and there is no mistaking the portrait. In subsequent lectures I shall have much to say to you of the antichristian doctrines and practices of the Papacy. Tonight we have but studied the broad outline drawn in the days of Belshazzar, which forms a broad foundation for what must follow.

Notice, in conclusion, the evidence of inspiration afforded by this wonderful prophecy. Could Daniel foresee the things that were coming on the earth? How should he happen to light on the notion that there would be four universal empires, and four only, and that after the fourth there would arise ù what the world had never seen before a commonwealth often kingdoms? How could he depict so strange and peculiar a power as the Papacy? How could he conceive it? A little, weak kingdom, yet controlling all kingdoms! a human dynasty like any other, yet exalting itself against God, and slaughtering His saints! a power so wicked that heaven itself is moved for its destruction, and the whole Roman earth ruined on its account! Supposing for a moment this was a sketch from imagination: how comes it that history has so wonderfully realized it? The prediction did not produce its own fulfillment, for they who fulfilled it denied its application to themselves. It was not concocted to fit the events, for the events did not begin for a thousand years after it was published. The events were not arranged by men to fit the prophecy, for they extend over forty successive generations. There is no solution of the problem save the true one: "Holy men of old spake as they were moved by the Holy Ghost"; "He revealeth the deep and secret things: He knoweth what is in the darkness, and the light dwelleth with Him."

Let me then solemnly charge you, reverence this holy volume, heed its warnings, dread the judgments it denounces, believe its promises, obey its precepts, study its sacred predictions; for be ye very sure it is the inspired word of the only living and true God, who is, as Nebuchadnezzar declared of old, "a God of gods, a Lord of kings, and a revealer of secrets."

## Note

**1** *"Let us suppose a rebel in some distant province to forge the royal seal and handwriting, and pretend to act in the name of the sovereign. He then claims to himself entire and unreserved allegiance. He abrogates whatever laws he pleases, and enacts contrary ones in their room. He enforces his own statutes by the severest punishments against those who still adhere to the old laws of the kingdom. He clothes himself with the robes of state, applies to himself the royal titles, claims immunity from the laws, even of his own enacting; and pretends that all the statutes derive their sole force from his sanction, and must borrow their meaning from his interpretations. Last of all, he banishes, strips of their goods, imprisons, and puts to death all those subjects who abide by the laws of the king and reject his usurpation. Surely, in this case, the pretence of governing in the monarch's name does not excuse, but aggravates the rebellion. It lessens greatly, it is true, the guilt of the deceived subjects, but increases, in the same proportion, the crime of their deceiver"* (Birks: "The First Two Visions of Daniel," p. 221).

# Lecture Three - Paul's Foreview of Romanism

You will remember that in my last lecture I stated that the three foreviews of Romanism presented in prophecy by Daniel, Paul, and John respectively, have three distinctive characters. Daniel gives mainly its political relations and its broad moral features; Paul presents its ecclesiastical relations and its religious features; and John, by the two compound hieroglyphs which he employs and which we will consider in the next lecture, exhibits the combination of the two aspects ù a politico-ecclesiastical power. He shows also the changing relations between its contrasted yet united elements during their long joint career, and foretells the distinctive doom of each.

It must never be forgotten that the Roman Papacy was for long ages an absolute, unlimited, tyrannical monarchy, a worldly, secular government. It had its territorial dominions, its provinces, cities, and towns; it had its court, its nobles, its ambassadors, its army, its police, its legislature, its jurisprudence, its laws, its advocates, its prisons, its revenues, its taxes, its exchequer, its mint, its arsenals, its forts, its foreign treaties, and its ambitious, selfish plans and policy, just as much as any mere secular kingdom. But it was also something very different ù it was the head of the Latin Church; it was a great ecclesiastical power; it was a religion as well as a government. As such it had its dioceses and parishes, its spiritual hierarchy of archbishops, bishops, priests, and deacons, its theological schools and colleges and professors, its abbots and deans, its councils and synods and chapters, its monasteries and convents, its orders of mendicant and other friars, its services and sacraments, its creeds and confessions, its doctrines and discipline, and its penances and punishments. Romanism is a comprehensive term, including both these widely different organizations. Both had their center in the seven-hilled city, and both regarded the Roman pontiff as head. Just as in the old pagan times the Caesars themselves had been both emperors and high priests of the national religion, so the popes in mediaeval times were fountainheads of authority both in the kingdom and in the Church. The ecclesiastical position of the emperors was however rather a name than a reality; while that of the popes was most real. They were practically and effectively head in both realms.

From his remote point of view, in the Babylonian era, the statesman-prophet Daniel saw mainly the political status of the Papacy. From his five-hundred-years-later standpoint, under the empire of Rome, the Christian Apostle Paul saw and foretold most clearly the ecclesiastical character of the coming antichrist; and this evening we are to consider this latter foreview of Romanism ù we are to study it as a Church system. I must ask you at your leisure to study very carefully three or four passages in the writings of the Apostle Paul, especially the third and fourth chapters of his first letter to Timothy, and the second chapter of his second epistle to the Thessalonians. You will see that Paul's foreview consists of two parts: the first gives a general view of a great apostasy, which would in due time arise in the Church; and the second a carefully drawn portrait of the power in which that apostasy would be headed up. He had even previously predicted the apostasy in his parting address to the elders of the Church at Ephesus, recorded in #Acts 20.

He had told them that there would arise ù not from the outside world, but from among themselves, the pastors or bishops of the Church ù "grievous wolves, not sparing the flock." "Of your own selves shall men arise, speaking perverse things, to draw away disciples alter them; therefore watch, and remember how I ceased not to warn you." This was but a brief and passing glance into the dark future; but the momentary glimpse suffices to show the outline of the evils which time was to develop, and which Paul so fully predicted later on. Ten pagan persecutions lay before the Church; but Paul does not predict them. Myriads of Christians were to do literally what he did figuratively, to fight with wild beasts in Roman amphitheaters; but the Apostle's prophetic gaze rests not on any such spectacle. No! a worse evil by far was to befall the Church: an enemy was to arise in her midst, an apostasy was to originate in her bosom, and eat like a cancer into her vitals. Her own leaders were to mislead her; her very pastors, instead of feeding the flock, would feed on it, and devour it like ravening wolves. Perverse pastors, selfish, mercenary bishops, would draw away disciples after themselves, instead of drawing them to Christ as Paul had done. He had coveted no man's silver or gold, as he reminds them: but these apostate bishops who should arise would be of a wholly different character, robbing and oppressing the Church as wolves the flock; they would be the direct opposites of the Good Shepherd who gave His life for the sheep, and of the apostolic ministry which follows in His steps.

This first warning prediction of the Apostle Paul was addressed, it is true, especially to the elders or bishops of Ephesus; but in view of all that has happened since, it is easy to see that the Ephesian branch of bishops were at any rate representative, for the words are a prediction of the ecclesiastical corruption that culminated in the Papacy. It strikes the keynote as to the nature of the evil from which the Church was destined to suffer so long and so widely. The pagan persecutions, which threatened to exterminate the early generations of Christians, were harmless to the Church compared to the internal corruption and cruel tyranny introduced by her own bishops later on. Paul's foreview, from the first, was of an ecclesiastical evil, one arising not from the throne of the emperors but from the bench of bishops, not outside but inside the Church. You will feel the importance of this fact later on in our course more than you can do now; I urge you to take special note of it.

In the picture of the coming apostasy which Paul draws in 1 Timothy he adds many an additional and dark detail. After giving practical precepts for the organization and government of the infant Church, and specifying the qualifications essential in its bishops and deacons (one of which was that they should be married men), and after summing up the faith of Christ in a brief epitome of "the mystery of godliness," he writes ù and we may well believe he did so with a heavy heart:

Now the Spirit speaketh expressly, that in the latter times some shall depart from the faith, giving heed to seducing spirits, and doctrines of devils; speaking lies in hypocrisy; having their conscience seared with a hot iron; forbidding to marry, and commanding to abstain from meats, which God hath created to be received with thanksgiving of them which believe and know the truth. For every creature of God is good, and nothing to be refused, if it be received with thanksgiving, for it is sanctified by the word of God and prayer.

Here we have, not only a prediction that there would be an "apostasy," or falling away from the faith in the Christian Church, but a description of its origin and character. Its origin was to be satanic; its doctrines were to be doctrines of devils, or demons. It was to assume authority, and to lay down laws and prohibitions. Prominent among these was to be the prohibition of marriage; that is, of the very relationship which the inspired apostle had just previously enjoined on bishops and deacons in the words, "A bishop must be blameless, the husband of one wife;..one that ruleth well his own house, having his children in subjection with all gravity"; and in the word, "Let the deacons be the husbands of one wife, ruling their children and their own houses well." Marriage, although thus divinely ordained, would be prohibited, and meats, though created to be received with thanksgiving, would be forbidden. Thus the apostasy would be marked by a departure from primitive faith and pure religion, and by the authoritative inculcation in its place of asceticism ù the substitution of an external religiousness, and self-imposed sacrifices, for true holiness, but a cover for the reverse. Its professors would be hypocrites and liars, men so sinful as to have lost their conscience against sin; "speaking lies in hypocrisy; having their consciences seared with a hot iron."

This feature of false profession reappears in the corresponding prophecy in 2 Timothy concerning the "last days," in which the abettors and adherents of the apostasy are described as men "having a form of godliness, but denying the power thereof." These men were not then to be open opponents of godliness, but, on the contrary, they would be great professors. They were to have a form of godliness: but only a form- ù a form covering no reality; a hollow form, a hypocritical form. Thus the two great Pauline prophecies of the apostasy in "the latter times" and "last days" warn the Church, not against professed irreligionists, but against professed religionists, against covert enemies of the Gospel: men cloaked in the garment of self-denial and superior sanctity; clever imitators of the apostles, like the magicians of Egypt, who withstood Moses, not by denying his miracles, but by counterfeiting them; cunning men, who should "creep into houses, and lead captive silly women laden with sins, led away with divers lusts"; and withal educated men, men of letters, "ever learning, and never able to come to the knowledge of the truth." Mark this well: the men whom Paul described as leaders of the apostasy which he foresaw were not low, ignorant infidels, but learned hypocrites, lying professors of religion, and self-deceived ascetics.

It is in this same strain that he writes also to the Thessalonians. The coming of Christ, he tells them, would not take place before the occurrence of an "apostasy," or falling away from the faith. This apostasy was to result from the working of what he calls "the mystery of iniquity" a remarkable expression, in direct contrast to the "mystery of godliness," from which the apostasy is a departure. (Compare 1 Timothy 3:16.) The iniquity in question was hidden. It was a "mystery." People did not recognize it as iniquity; they were deceived by it. From this "mystery of iniquity" was to spring in due time "the man of sin," whose coming was to be "after the working of Satan." The outcome and issue of this Satan-inspired apostasy would be "all deceivableness of unrighteousness," "lying wonders," and the belief of lies under the influence of "strong delusion" on the part of those who had "pleasure in unrighteousness."

All of this is consistent. These Pauline prophecies teach the same thing. They warn the Church against the same danger. They predict the same sort of apostasy; an apostasy marked, not by open hostility to the gospel, not by the denunciation of godliness and the unblushing profession of infidelity or atheism, but by "hypocrisy," "deceit," a "form of godliness," external religiousness, the practice of asceticism, cloaking corruption ù by a beautiful garment of light covering the form of the very prince of darkness.

But this apostasy was to have a head, and the coming and character of that head are the great subject of Paul's Thessalonian prophecy. A mistaken apprehension of his first letter to them had led the Thessalonians to expect an immediate advent of Christ, and in his second epistle Paul sets himself to correct this error by further instruction as to the future. He tells them of something that was destined to precede the return of Christ, a great apostasy, which would reach its climax in the manifestation of a certain mighty power of evil; to which he attaches three names, and of which he gives many particulars similar to those which Daniel gave of his "little horn," such as the place and time of its origin, its nature, sphere, character, conduct, and doom.

The names which the apostle gives to this head of the apostasy in this prophecy are "that man of sin,...the son of perdition," and "that wicked" or "lawless" one. These expressions might convey to the mind of superficial readers the idea that the predicted head of the apostasy would be an individual. Careful study however shows this to be a false impression ù an impression for which there is no solid foundation in the passage. The expressions themselves, when analyzed grammatically, are seen to bear another signification quite as well, if not better, and the context demands that they be understood in a dynastic sense. "The man of sin," like "the man of God," has a broad, extended meaning. When we read "that the man of God may be perfect, thoroughly furnished unto all good works," we do not suppose it means any one individual man, although it has the definite article. It indicates a whole class of men of a certain character, a succession of similar individuals. The use of the indefinite article (analogous to the omission of the article in Greek) does indeed limit an expression of the kind. A man of sin could be only one, just as a king of England could mean only an individual. The king, on the other hand, may include a whole dynasty. A king has but the life of an individual, the king never dies. When, in speaking of the Jewish tabernacle in Hebrews, Paul says that into the holiest of all "went the high priest alone once every year," he includes the entire succession of the high priests of Israel. That a singular expression in a prophecy may find its fulfillment in a plurality of individuals is perfectly clear from John's words, "As ye have heard that antichrist shall come, even so now there are many antichrists." 1

Any doubt or ambiguity as to the true force of the expression "the man of sin" is however removed by a consideration of the context of this passage. Grammatically it may mean either an individual or a succession of similar individuals. The context determines that it actually does mean the latter. "The mystery of iniquity," in which this man of sin was latent, was already working in Paul's day. The apostasy out of which he was to grow was already in existence. "The mystery of iniquity doth already work." The man of sin, on the other hand, was to continue till the second advent of Christ, which is still future; for he is destroyed, as it is distinctly stated, only by the brightness of the epiphany. The interval between Paul's days and those of the still future advent was then to be filled by the great apostasy in either its incipient working as a mystery of iniquity or its open manifestation and great embodiment in the career of "the man of sin and son of perdition." That career must consequently extend over more than a thousand years, for the process of gestation is certainly briefer than the duration of life. In this case of the man of sin the two together occupy at least eighteen centuries. What proportion of the period can we assign to the hidden, mysterious growth of this power, and what to its wonderfully active and influential life? The life must of course occupy the larger half, to say the least of it, and therefore, as no individual lives on through ages, we may be sure that it is a succession of men, a dynasty of rulers, that is intended by the ambiguous expression. We, students of the nineteenth century, may be sure of this, though the students of early centuries could not.

Paul himself probably supposed that the antichrist he foretold would be an individual, for it is not always given to prophets to understand the messages they are inspired to deliver. "Not unto themselves, but unto us" they minister, as Peter tells us. At any rate, the early Church thought so, as their writings prove. They expected an individual antichrist, who should be followed by an immediate advent of Christ. But it must be remembered that the apostles and the early Church knew nothing of the eighteen centuries of delay which have actually taken place. They could not have guessed or even conceived that well-nigh two thousand years would pass before the second advent. They expected it in their own day. Paul wrote as if he himself would see it: "We who are alive and remain unto the coming of the Lord"; and no revelation was given the effect of which would have been to rob the early Church of that sweet and sanctifying hope. On the contrary, the prediction of the apostasy and the antichrist who should head it up are purposely so worded as not to extinguish that hope. Even in Daniel, where chronological limits are assigned to the Roman "little horn," the expression which conveys them is symbolic, and could be interpreted with certainty only by the fulfillment.

No duration at all is mentioned in this prophecy by Paul, only the two limits. "Already" the apostasy was developing, and it would not be destroyed till the advent. That much was clearly revealed, but not the length of the interval between the starting point in apostolic days in the first century, and the advent, which has not yet ù in the nineteenth ù taken place. There was a good reason for the form of the prophecy ù for the ambiguous use of the singular number. It neither asserted nor excluded a dynastic meaning. Time alone could decide, and time has decided.

Bearing this in mind, let us now look at Paul's prophetic portrait of the great antichristian power he foresaw and foretold.

It is a strange one, with marked and most peculiar features. He is represented as seated in the temple or house of God; i.e. the Church, "the habitation of God through the Spirit," God's dwelling-place ù a sacred sphere, the most sacred on earth. There in the midst, exalted and enthroned, sits a sinful mortal, an enemy of God, a "man of sin," engaged in receiving from a multitude of deluded apostate Christians worshipful submission and adoration. Beneath him, like a dark cloud or vapor, out of which he has arisen, is a "mystery of iniquity." There is a chronological date upon the cloud. Close examination shows inscribed on it the words, "doth already work," indicating its existence in Paul's day, eighteen centuries ago. On one side lies a broken arch, covered with Roman sculpture. This arch had at one period blocked the way from the dark under the cloud to the exalted seat occupied by the "man of sin." In Paul's day it stood firm, a massive hindrance; but he foresaw that it would be "taken out of the way." By some mighty stroke it has been rent, and lies in fragments. The barrier has been "taken out of the way." Through the ruinous gap the mystery of iniquity has come up into the holy place in the form of "all deceivableness of unrighteousness." Mingled with a vast mass of deceit there are certain leading lies, which are firmly believed, and many "lying wonders."

The countenance of the "man of sin" is marked by pretended sanctity. There is in it a look of elevation, marred by pride. The features are full of power and intelligence. His head is circled with a crown of a peculiar form, unlike that worn by ordinary kings, and upon it is the title "King of kings and Lord of lords," ù implying that he is ruler both of the Church and of the world, because he claims to be as God on earth. His hand is lifted in the attitude of one bestowing divine favors. His semblance is that of benignity and blessing, while the spirit of the man is that of the great adversary. Behind him, half concealed, is a dark figure difficult to make out, with a face full of malignity. There is a gleam of defiance in his eye, and a deadly purpose in his aspect. He too wears a crown, and the name written on it in yellow, sulfurous letters is, "god of this world." He stands close to the "man of sin," ù too close to be seen by the worshipping multitude ù directing and inspiring all his utterances and all his movements. With extraordinary skill he wields a worldwide power through this chosen agent, a power which has been exercised in various ways for six thousand years, deluding men to their destruction, but which reaches its climax in this combination of satanic craft with ecclesiastical exaltation. By the mouth of the "man of sin" he speaks to the multitude thronging the holy temple, or house of God, in a tone of authority, commanding them to submit to his teachings and guidance, and to abase themselves in his presence. His words are, "Fall down and worship me." The deluded multitude blindly obeys him, as though his voice was the voice of God! Under the feet of the "man of sin" are two venerable volumes, bearing the titles "Laws Human and Divine." He is trampling on them both, treading them underfoot! Some in the crowd are pointing to this fact, and stand in a protesting attitude. In the distance there are prophets and apostles looking on. Far above ù a perfect contrast in every respect to the self-exalting "man of sin" ù is seen the self-humbling and self-sacrificing Son of God. He too is seated, seated on a radiant throne, from which celestial glory is streaming. His attitude is that of one coming in judgment for the destruction of the "man of sin" and his sinful worshipers. Many of the protesters are looking at him in anticipation of His advent, and seem to have something of His likeness. The face of the man of sin is the face of a false apostle, the dark face of a Judas. Written upon the wall of the temple, in letters of light, just above the proud, false, central figure, is the name "son of perdition." The man of sin is a Judas ù a secret enemy while a seeming friend ù a "familiar friend," yet a fatal foe who betrays with a kiss and a "hail, master!"

There are several features in this portrait which I must ask you to specially notice. Observe the place occupied by the man of sin ù the "temple" or house of God. This is not, and cannot be, any Jewish temple. Paul, who uses this expression in his prophetic portrait of Romanism, employs it both in Corinthians and Ephesians with reference to the Christian Church. In the second Epistle to the Corinthians, writing to Gentile Christians, he says, "Ye are the temple of the living

God; as God hath said, I will dwell in them, and walk in them." In Ephesians he calls the Church "a holy temple," a "habitation of God through the Spirit"; and he would never have applied it to the Jewish temple, which, with all other Jewish things, he regarded as mere shadows of Christian realities. To Paul emphatically the temple of God was the Church of Christ. This is the temple in which his prophetic eye saw the man of sin seated. It is no question of his bodily location in any structure of wood and stone, but of something far higher. The temple of God is that "spiritual house" in which He dwells. It is built of "living stones," of true believers. It is here that the man of sin was to usurp the place of God. This is the "mystery," the dread danger, the deadly evil, predicted by the Apostle. It is no person in a temple of stone, but a power in the Christian Church.

Observe next the character of the man of sin. He is at once an imitation of Christ, and a contrast to Him. He occupies His position, but is totally unlike Him, and opposed to Him. He has usurped His place and His prerogatives; but, so far from truly representing Him, he represents His great enemy. As Christ acts for God, so the man of sin acts for Satan, who indeed produces him for this very purpose. His coming is "after the working of Satan." Christ and he are antagonistic powers: the power of light, and the power of darkness; the Majesty of heaven, and the might of hell. And as the Son of God humbled Himself, so the "man of sin" exalts himself. There is infinite self- abasement in the one, the Divine nature stooping to humanity; and infinite self-exaltation in the other, the human and satanic assuming to be Divine. Observe here that it is not asserted that the man of sin will say that he is God, but that he will show himself as such. The words are, "He as God sitteth in the temple of God, showing himself that he is God" or is Divine, or a Divine being. (apodelknuJnta eanton oti esti Qeov) There is no article here before the name God. The expression indicates that the man of sin would show himself by acts and professions to be possessed of superhuman and Divine dignity, authority, and power.

Observe the position of the man of sin. Notice the word kaqisai, "sitteth," and connect with it kaqedra, a seat, a word which occurs three times in the New Testament. It is used twice with reference to the seats in the temple of those who sold doves, who turned the house of God into a house of merchandise and den of thieves; and once in the sentence, "the Pharisees sit in Moses' seat." From kaqedra comes "cathedral," "the bishop's seat," and also the expression ex cathedra, or from his seat, officially. There, in that exalted cathedral position, and claiming to represent God, the man of sin was to act and abide as the pretended vicar, but real antagonist, of Christ, undermining His authority, abolishing His laws, and oppressing His people. Observe the words, "who opposeth." It is possible effectually to oppose another without being his avowed antagonist; so the professions of the predicted power might be friendly, while his actions would be those of an opponent of the gospel of Christ.

We have said that the principles which were ultimately to produce the man of sin had already begun to operate in Paul's own day. His words are, "The mystery of iniquity doth already work"; and these principles would continue to work until the full development of the apostasy, and its final destruction at the Second Advent: that is, throughout the eighteen Christian centuries.

The sphere of their operation therefore cannot be the Jewish temple, which was destroyed in the first century, but must needs be the professing Christian Church. An important point in the prophecy is the existence in apostolic times of a certain restraining power, withholding while it lasted the manifestation of the man of sin. Paul, for good reasons, speaks of it in guarded language, as "he who letteth," or "that which hinders." What it was Paul knew, and the Thessalonians knew from him: "Remember ye not, that, when I was yet with you, I told you?" The early Church - from whom alone we can learn what Paul told them by word of mouth, but refrained from committing to writing has left it on record that the Apostle had told them that this hindering power was the dominion of the Roman Caesars; that while they continued to reign at Rome, the development of the predicted power of evil was impossible. Hence it would seem that ROME would be the seat of the man of sin. During the continuance of the Roman empire there was no opportunity for him to rise; he would only be manifested on its fall. While the Caesars reigned he could not appear, but when they passed away he would succeed them.

Notice particularly that, just as the expression, "he that letteth," comprehends the line of succession of the Caesars, so the expression, "he that sitteth," may well comprehend an analogous line or succession of rulers. Both expressions refer to dynasties, and not to individuals.

The distinctive names given by Paul to the great head of the apostasy are expressive of his character. They are the "man of sin," the "son of perdition," and "that wicked" (o anomov, the lawless one). First, it was to be to an extraordinary extent sinful itself, and the occasion of sin in others; secondly, it would be like Judas, and share his doom; and, thirdly, it would set at defiance all laws, whether human or Divine. It would be inspired by Satan, and, on account of its evil character and actions, it would be doomed to destruction; it would eventually "go to its own place" ù the bottomless pit, from whence it emanated. Its doom was to fall in two stages: the Lord Himself would consume it by the spirit of His mouth, and destroy it by the brightness of His epiphany, or advent in power and glory. There would be first a consumption, then a destruction. It would continue until the second coming of Christ a statement which, as you will observe, involves the Lord's return before the millennium, since there can be no millennium under the reign of the man of sin, nor prior to his utter destruction.

Let us now compare this portrait of the man of sin drawn by the Apostle Paul with the portrait of the self-exalting power foretold by Daniel, which we studied last week. The comparison will demonstrate their identity.

1. Both are Roman. The self-exalting horn or head represented by Daniel is Roman; it belongs to the fourth or Roman empire. So also does Paul 's man of sin, for the imperial government seated at Rome needed to be removed in order to make way for its rise and dominion. It was to be the successor of the Caesars at Rome. They have the same geographical seat.
2. They have the same chronological point of origin: both arise on the fall of the old undivided empire of Rome. And they have he same chronological termination: Daniel's little horn perishes at the coming of the Son of man in glory, and Paul's man of sin is destroyed at the epiphany.
3. Both exalt themselves against God. Daniel mentions the proud words of the blasphemous little horn, and Paul the audacious deeds of the man of sin, showing himself as Divine.
4. Both begin as small, inconspicuous powers, and develop gradually to very great and influential ones.
5. Both claim to be teachers of men. Daniel's little horn was to have eyes, as a bishop, or overseer (the meaning of the word bishop, episkopov, is overseer); and that he was to have a mouth, that is, he was to be a teacher; while Paul assigns to the man of sin ecclesiastical eminence, a proud position in the temple of God, or Christian Church.
6. Both are persecutors. Daniel describes the little horn as a persecutor wearing out the saints, and Paul speaks of the man of sin as "opposing," and calls him the "lawless one."

To sum up. The two have the same place Rome; the same period ù from the sixth century to the second coming of the Lord in glory; the same wicked character, the same lawlessness, the same self-exalting defiance of God, the same gradual growth from weakness to dominion, the same episcopal pretensions, the same persecuting character, the same twofold doom.

These resemblances are so important, so numerous, so comprehensive, and exact, as to prove beyond all question that the self-exalting, persecuting power predicted by Daniel and this man of sin foretold by Paul are one and the same power. Even Romanists admit this to be the case, and call the power thus doubly predicted the antichrist.

In the Douay Bible, with notes, issued under Romish authority, and bearing the signatures of Cardinals Wiseman and Manning, the "man of sin" is interpreted as follows: "'He sitteth in the temple of God,' etc. By all these words is described to us the great antichrist,...according to the unquestionable authority and consent of the ancient Fathers." Rome allows thus that the "little horn" of Daniel and the "man of sin" of Paul foreshow one and the same power, and admits that power to be the antichrist.

So far then for our examination of the prophecies of the Roman antichrist, given, some of them a thousand, and others five hundred years before the actual appearance of the predicted power. Strange and incomprehensible must these prophecies have appeared, both to those who gave them and to those who received them. Little could they imagine the tremendous scale,both geographical and chronological, on which they were to be fulfilled! They understood clearly that an awful apostasy was to intervene between the early Church and the advent; but how far it would extend and how long it would last they knew not, and could not know. A terrible enemy to God and to His Church was to arise, strange as it might seem, in that Church itself; and yet it was to have its seat in Rome, which was in their day the throne of the pagan persecutors of Christianity. How could these things be? Much was revealed, but much was left still utterly mysterious, and which time only could interpret.

Turn now from prophecy to the history, and let the latter interpret the former. We see what was predicted, let us ask what has happened. What are the historical facts? The history of the Christian Church does not record a steady progress in the pathway of truth and holiness, an uninterrupted spread of the kingdom of God on earth. On the contrary, it tells the story of a TREMENDOUS APOSTASY. Even in the first century, as we learn from the New Testament, there set in a departure from the gospel, and a return to certain forms of ritualism, as among the Galatians. In the second and third centuries, antichristian doctrine and antichristian practices, sacramentarianism and sacerdotalism, invaded the Church, and gradually climbed to a commanding position, which they never afterwards abandoned. In the fourth century, with the fall of paganism, began a worldly, imperial Christianity, wholly unlike primitive apostolic Christianity, a sort of Christianized heathenism; and in the fifth and sixth centuries sprang up the Papacy, in whose career the apostasy culminated later on.

The mighty Caesars had fallen; Augustus, Domitian, Hadrian, Diocletian, were gone; even the Constantines and Julians had passed away. The seat of sovereignty had been removed from Rome to Constantinople. Goths and Vandals had overthrown the western empire; the once mighty political structure lay shivered into broken fragments. The imperial government was slain by the Gothic sword. The Caesars were no more, and Rome was an actual desolation. Then slowly on the ruins of old imperial Rome rose another power and another monarchy ù a monarchy of loftier aspirations and more resistless might, claiming dominion, not alone over the bodies, but over the consciences and souls of men: dominion, not only within the limits of the fallen empire, but throughout the entire world. Higher and higher rose the Papacy, till in the dark ages all Christendom was subject to its sway.

"Under the sacerdotal monarchy of St. Peter," says Gibbon, "the nations began to resume the practice of seeking on the banks of the Tiber their kings, their laws, and the oracles of their fate." And this was a voluntary submission. As a kingdom, the Papacy was not at that time in any position to enforce it. Not by military power, but by spiritual and religious pretensions, did the Bishop of Rome attain supremacy in the Church and in the world; it was by his lofty claim to be the vice-regent of Christ, by his assumption that he was as God on earth ù it was by means of his episcopal position that he attained by degrees supreme power, not in the Church only, but in the world.

The growth of this power to these gigantic proportions was a most singular phenomenon. Tyndale, the Reformer, speaking of it, says: To see how the holy father came up, mark the ensample of the ivy. First it springeth up out of the earth, and then awhile creepeth along by the ground, till it find a great tree. Then it joineth itself beneath, unto the body of the tree, and creepeth up a little and a little, fair and softly. At the beginning, while it is yet thin and small, the burden is not perceived; it seemeth glorious to garnish the tree in winter. But it holdeth fast withal, and ceaseth not to climb up till it be at the top, and even above all. And then it sendeth its branches along by the branches of the tree, and overgroweth all, and waxeth great, heavy, and thick; and it sucketh the moisture so sore out of the tree and his branches, that it choketh and stifleth them. And then the foul, stinking ivy waxeth mighty in the stump of the tree, and becometh a seat and a nest for all unclean birds, and for blind owls, which hawk in the dark, and dare not come to the light.

Even so the Bishop of Rome, now called pope, at the beginning crope along upon the earth, and every man trod on him. As soon as there came a Christian emperor, he joined himself to his feet and kissed them, and crope up a little, with begging now this privilege, now that..And thus, with flattering and feigning and vain superstition, under the name of St. Peter, he crept up, and fastened his roots in the heart of the emperor, and with his sword climbed above all his fellow bishops, and brought them under his feet. And as he subdued them by the emperor's sword, even so, after they were sworn faithful, he, by their means, climbed up above the emperor, and subdued him also, and made him stoop unto his feet and kiss them.. And thus the pope, the father of all hypocrites, hath with falsehood and guile perverted the order of the world, and turned things upside down.

"All the kings of the West reverence the pope as a God on earth," said Gregory II., and he spoke truly. Sismondi describes how Pepin and the Franks received him as a divinity. His dogmas were regarded as oracles; his bulls and sentences as the voice of God. "The people think of the pope as the one God that has power over all things in earth and in heaven." Marcellus, addressing the pope at the Lateran Council, said, "Thou art another God on earth"; and "our Lord God the pope" was an oft accepted title. These are facts, substantial facts of history, which can be proved by countless documents, and which indeed no Romanist will deny. The people rendered and the pope received worship ù worship due to God alone. At the coronation of Pope Innocent X., Cardinal Colonna, in his own name and that of the clergy of St. Peter's, addressed the following words to the pope, "kneeling on his knees": "Most holy and blessed father! head of the Church, ruler of the world, to whom the keys of the kingdom of heaven are committed, whom the angels in heaven revere, and the gates of hell fear, and all the world adores, we specially venerate, worship, and adore thee!" What blasphemous exaltation is here! Have not Paul's words been fulfilled? Has not this man of sin, sitting in the temple of God, shown himself that he is God, or allowed himself to be treated as Divine, nay, even claimed to be so treated? He allowed himself to be styled "the Lamb of God, which taketh away the sin of the world," because he gave and sold indulgences for sin. He was even more merciful than Christ; for He left souls in purgatory, and the pope took them out! He could command even the angels of heaven, and add saints to the celestial choir, raising dead men to form part of heaven's hierarchy as "saints," and causing them henceforth to be worshipped by the Church on earth.

IN ALL THIS THE POPE WAS AS GOD UPON EARTH. It was his to speak and govern as God; it was the world's to bow down, to believe, and to obey.

See him in his robes of more than kingly royalty, with his crown of more than terrestrial dominion ù not one, but three, three in one, a triple crown. The proud tiara of the Papacy symbolizes power on earth, in heaven, and in hell; in all three the pope claims to rule. He is far above all kings. He is the vice-regent of God, the regent of the universe! He never rises from his pontifical throne to any person whomsoever, nor uncovers himself before mortal man. He does not even condescend to honor any human being by the least inclination of his head. His nuncios and legates take precedence of the ambassadors of all crowned heads. Cardinals, the chief princes of the Church, adore his holiness upon their bended knees, kissing his right hand, and even his feet! At his coronation they set him on the high altar of St. Peter's, and adore him as the representative of Deity. He is carried in lofty state on men's shoulders, beneath a canopy hung with fringe of gold. People, prelates, princes, and cardinals exalt and worship him with the most solemn ceremonies. He is head of the universal Church, arbiter of its rights and privileges. He wears the keys, as the sign of his power to open the gates of heaven to all believers. He holds two swords, as judging in things temporal and spiritual. He is "the sole and supreme judge of men, and can himself be judged of no man." He is the husband of the Church, and as such wears a ring, indicating her perpetual betrothal to himself. Thousands upon thousands kneel before him; they struggle to get near his person; they stretch forth their hands to obtain his indulgences, and crave his quasi-Divine benediction, that "smoke of smoke," as Luther called it. The deluded multitude rend the air with acclamations at his approach. In his processions all is gorgeous magnificence. Swiss guards and other attendants form his cortege, in scarlet cloaks, embroidered with gold, with silver maces and rich caparisons, silk housings, red velvets, purples, satins laced with gold, long flowing robes sweeping the ground, some crimson, some black, some white, and caps adorned with precious stones, and helmets glittering in the sun. His litter is lined with scarlet velvet, fringed with gold, and he himself is clothed in a white satin cassock, with rochet, stole, and mozette, all of red velvet if it is winter, or of red satin if it is summer. At his adoration by the canons and clergy of St. Peter's, he is clothed in a white garment and seated on a throne, and thus attired he "presides in the temple of the Lord."

Mark these words: he "presides in the temple of the Lord." I took them from Picart's description of the Roman ceremonial, a Roman Catholic authority. It is the Romanists themselves who use this significant phrase of the Papal pontiff: he "presides in the temple of the Lord." Exalted to this position, he is incensed, and the cardinals, one at a time, in solemn, deliberate state and idolatrous submission, kiss his hand, his foot, and even his stomach. He is surrounded by cardinals, archbishops, bishops, abbots, priests, and princes. Enormous fans of peacock's feathers are carried on either side of his chair, as used to be done to the pagan monarchs of olden times. He directs the affairs of the greatest empire upon earth, governing by an almost infinite number of men, whom he keeps constantly in subjection to himself, and from whom he demands frequent periodical account. He distributes spiritual gifts, and exalts to the highest preferments, not only on earth, but also in heaven: for is it not his to make bishops and archbishops, to canonize whom he will, and to decree their perpetual memorial and worship in the world?

All power is delivered unto him. He forgives sins; he bestows grace; he cancels punishments, even in purgatory; he restores the lapsed; he excommunicates the rebellious; he can make that which is unlawful, lawful; he cannot err; his sentences are final, his utterances infallible, his decrees irreformable. O dread dominion! O dizzy height! O blasphemous assumption! O sublime, satanic tyranny! who is like unto thee, thou resuscitated Caesar, thou false Christ? Lord of the conscience, thou sittest there as a very deity, QUASI DEUS, as God. Thou sittest supreme, as thine own words are witness, "in the temple of the Lord."!

Look again at the confessional, where every priest sits as an image of the pope his master, with the sacred consciences of men and women beneath his feet, as though he were a god! For mark, he searches the heart, the very secrets of the soul; he demands the discovery and confession of all its sins; he makes himself master of all its thoughts and intents; he sits in that temple, the temple of the human conscience, which God claims solely for Himself. Oh, awful position! And there he presumes to reign, to decide, to absolve from sin; "Absolvo te," I absolve thee, is his word. The sinner regards him as holding the place of Jesus Christ. This Romish work is a witness that it is so. This is the Ursuline Manual. Here, in the chapter for the direction of those who go to confession, and every Papist does, are these words, "Confessors should not be viewed in any other light than..as holding the place of Jesus Christ" (p. 177). And again, on p. 182, "When you leave the confessional, do not disturb your mind by examining whether you have been confessed well, or have forgotten any of your sins; but rest assured that, if you have made your confession with sincerity, and the other requisite dispositions, you are, according to the express decisions of the Council of Trent, fully absolved from every sin." "Who can forgive sins, but God only?" See how the "man of sin" sits in God's temple, and robs Him of His place and His prerogative!

Look at this other book. It is the volume of the laws and constitution of the Jesuits. Here, on p. 10, the Jesuit is taught that his superior, whoever he may be, must be recognized, reverenced, and submitted to with perfect and complete subjection of act and thought, as occupying the place of Jesus Christ. Thus the priest in the confessional and the superior in the Jesuit order, and the bishop and archbishop and cardinal, all reflect the sacerdotal supremacy of the pope, who sits there in God's very temple, the temple of conscience and of the Christian Church, as a usurping god ù quasi Deus, as if God Himself.

But we must pass on from this point, the position assumed by the man of sin in the Church of God, and ask whether Romanism has fulfilled the other predictions of St. Paul as to "lying wonders" and "signs," or false miracles, and the deceits of unrighteousness. Has she employed these as a means of gaining "power," deluding her votaries that she might the more effectually enslave them? To exalt the priesthood, and especially its head, the Papal high priest, Rome has spared nothing. She has trampled alike on the intellect and conscience of mankind, and despised the eternal well-being of souls by inducing them to believe lies.

The man of sin was to come with all power and signs and lying wonders, in all deceivableness of unrighteousness. Just as the apostles wrought miracles to confirm the gospel they preached ù or rather, as the Lord wrought with them and confirmed the word with signs following ù so Satan would work with antichrist, endorsing his pretensions with false miracles designed to overthrow the gospel. Bishop John Jewell, of Salisbury, wrote in the sixteenth century: Of the first sort of false miracles, we have seen an infinite number in the days of our fathers in the kingdom of antichrist. Then was there an appearance of spirits and visions of angels: our lady came swimming down from heaven; poor souls came creeping and crying out of purgatory, and jetted abroad; and kept stations, casting flakes of fire, and beset highways, and bemoaned their cases, the pains and torments were so bitter.

They sought for help, and cried for good prayers; they cried for dirges, they cried for masses of requiem, for masses of scala coeli, for trentals of masses. Hereof grew portsale of pardons, and hereof grew the province of purgatory, the most gainful country that ever was under the cityof Rome.

But these miracles were no miracles at all; they were devised by subtle varlets and lazy lordanes for a purpose, to get money. Oftentimes the spirit has been taken and laid in the stocks; the angel has been stript; the good lady has been caught; the conveyance of the miracle has appeared; the engines, and sleights, and the cause, and the manner of the working have been confessed.

In those days idols could go on foot; roods could speak; bells could ring alone; images could come down, and light their own candles; dead stocks could sweat, and bestir themselves; they could turn their eyes; they could move their hands; they could open their mouths; they could set bones and knit sinews; they could heal the sick, and raise up the dead.

These miracles were conveyances and subtleties, and indeed no miracles; the trunks by which they spake, the strings and wires with which they moved their faces and hands, all the rest of their treachery, have been disclosed. These are the miracles of which Paul speaks ù miracles in sight, in appearance, but indeed no miracles.

..It was also arranged that the saints should not have power to work in all places. Some wrought at Canterbury, some at Walsingham, some at York, some at Buxton, some in one place, some in another, some in the towns, some in the fields. Even as Jeremiah said among the Jews, chapter 11, "According to the number of thy cities were thy gods." Hereof grew pilgrimages and worshipping of images, and kissing of reliques; hereof grew oblations, and enriching of abbeys; every man had his peculiar saint on whom he called; every country was full of chapels, every chapel full of miracles, and every miracle full of lies. These miracles are wrought by antichrist; they are his tools, wherewith he worketh; they are his weapons, wherewith he prevaileth; they are full of lying, full of deceitfulness, and full of wickedness: so shall antichrist prevail, and rule over the world. By these miracles he shall possess the ears, the eyes, and the hearts of many, and shall draw them after him." 2

It was alleged that miracles were not only wrought by the saints, but even by the relics of the saints. In Calvin's tractate on the subject of relics, he proves that the great majority of the relics in use among Romanists are spurious, having been brought forward by imposters, so that every apostle is made to have three or four bodies, and every saint two or three, and that the garments of Christ are almost infinite in number! As His body ascended to heaven, relics of it were not of course available; but spurious relics of everything He ever used or handled have been multiplied ad nauseam. Even the body of Christ has not escaped; the teeth, the hair, and the blood are exhibited in hundreds of places; the manger in which He was laid at His birth, the linen in which He was swaddled, His cradle, the first shirt His mother put on Him, the pillar against which He leant in the temple, the water-pots that were at the marriage in Cana of Galilee, and even the wine that was made in them, the shoes that He used when He was a boy, the table on which He observed the Last Supper, and hundreds of similar things are shown many of them in a number of places to this day. And as to the relics connected with our Lord's sufferings and death, they are just innumerable. The fragments of the true cross scattered over the globe would, if catalogued, fill a volume. "There is no town, however small, which has not some morsel of it; and this not only in the principal cathedral church of the district, but also in parish churches. There is scarcely an abbey so poor as not to have a specimen. In some places larger fragments exist, as at Paris, Poitiers, and Rome. If all the pieces which could be found were collected into a heap, they would form a good ship load; though the gospel testifies that a single individual was able to carry the real cross. What effrontery then thus to fill the whole world with fragments which it would take more than three hundred men to carry!...In regard to the crown of thorns, it would seem that its twigs had been planted that they might grow again; otherwise I know not how it could have attained such a size..I would never come to an end were I to go one by one over all the absurd articles they have drawn into this service. At Rome is shown the reed which was put into our Savior's hands has a scepter;..the sponge which was offered to Him containing vinegar mixed with gall. How, I ask, were those things recovered? They were in the hands of the wicked. Did they give them to the apostles that they might preserve them for relics, or did they themselves lock them up that they might preserve them for some future period? What blasphemy to abuse the name of Christ by employing it as a cloak for such driveling fables!"3

Among the images that Rome worships, a certain class are miraculous. The figure on the crucifix of Burgos, in Spain, is said to have a beard which grows perpetually, and there are similar ones in three or four other places. The stupid people believe the fable to be true. Other crucifixes are said to have spoken ù a whole number. Others shed tears, as for instance one at Treves; and another at Orleans. From others the warm blood flows periodically. Miraculous images of the virgin are even more numerous. As they hold that the body of the virgin ascended to heaven like that of her Son, they cannot pretend to have her bones like those of the saints. Had it been otherwise, they would have given her a body of such size as would fill a thousand coffins. But they have made up for this lack by her hair and her milk. There is no town however small, no monastery or nunnery however insignificant, which does not possess some of this ù some in small, others in large quantities. As Calvin says: "Had the breasts of the most holy virgin yielded a more copious supply than is given by a cow, and had she continued to nurse during her whole lifetime, she could scarcely have furnished the quantity which is exhibited. I would fain know," he asks, "how it was collected so as to be preserved until our time. Luke relates the prophecy which Simeon made to the virgin, but he does not say that Simeon asked her to give him some milk." The fabrication of these relics was a lucrative trade throughout the middle ages; especially were dead bodies invested with sacredness by attaching to them the names of saints and martyrs. Toulouse, for instance, thinks it possesses six bodies of the apostles: James, Andrew, James the Less, Philip, Simeon, and Jude; but duplicates of these bodies are also in St. Peter's and other churches in Rome. Matthias has also another at Treves; and there are heads and arms of him existing at different places sufficient to make up another body. What shall we say of the spirit that encourages the belief in lies and deceives men in this style? The degradation inflicted on the ignorant and unlearned by these fables is terrible, as any one who watches their effect in Ireland or on the Continent is aware. Whether the miracles of the man of sin be real or pretended, true or false, it matters little. The main point is, they are directed to establish falsehood. "He relies for his success on the effects to be wrought in human minds by wonders and deceits accomplished in the energy of Satan." He employs wonders and deceits, a pretense to miraculous powers. Romanism has availed herself of such fraudulent practices to an enormous extent, and has profited by them both financially and otherwise.

But lying wonders to impose on the ignorant and superstitious masses were not the only means by which the Papacy attained its power in the middle ages; spurious documents, impostures of another kind, were used to influence the royal, noble, and educated classes. Principal among these were the celebrated decretal epistles, a forgery which produced the most important consequences for the Papacy, though its spurious nature was ultimately detected. Gibbon writes: Before the end of the eighth century, some apostolical scribe, perhaps the notorious Isidore, composed the "decretals" and the "donation of Constantine" ù the two magic pillars of the spiritual and temporal monarchy of the popes. This memorable donation was introduced to the world by an epistle of Pope Adrian I, who exhorts Charlemagne to imitate the liberality and revive the name of the great Constantine" (Gibbon: "Decline and Fall of the Roman Empire," chapter 49). Their effect was enormous in advancing both the temporal power and the ecclesiastical supremacy of the popes. The donation of Constantine founded the one, and the false decretals the other. The latter pretended to be decrees of the early bishops of Rome limiting the independence of all archbishops and bishops by establishing a supreme jurisdiction of the Roman see in all cases, and by forbidding national councils to be held without its consent. "Upon these spurious decretals," says Mr. Hallam in his "History of the Middle Ages," "was built the great fabric of Papal supremacy over the different national Churches ù a fabric which has stood after its foundation crumbled beneath it, for no one has pretended to deny for the last two centuries that the imposture is too palpable for any but the most ignorant ages to credit."

It is evident then that Romanism has fulfilled this part of the prophecy of the "man of sin," even him whose coming was to be after the working of Satan with all power and signs and lying wonders and all deceivableness of unrighteousness. The power of the popes was built up on frauds and deceits of this character, and has been maintained over all the nations subject to it ever since by pretended miracles, spurious relics, lying wonders, and unrighteous deceits. And all these have been employed to oppose the gospel and establish falsehood.

In considering the ecclesiastical aspect of Romanism, we must never forget that it is the outcome and climax of the predicted apostasy, whose features Paul describes in Timothy. We must close this lecture with a few remarks on the departure from the faith which occupies so prominent a place in that description. Some should "depart from the faith, giving heed to seducing spirits and doctrines of devils, speaking lies in hypocrisy, forbidding to marry, and commanding to abstain from meats." The faith must of course here be taken in a broad sense, as including all the doctrines and commandments of the Christian religion. The apostasy was to be marked by a departure from this faith, by the teaching of false doctrines, and the inculcation of anti-scriptural practices. That Popery is completely at variance with the Bible on all the important points of the faith of Christ may be safely asserted, and can be abundantly proved. We can select but a few of the principal points.

**1.** The Apostle Paul teaches that the Holy Scriptures are able to make us "wise unto salvation," that they are capable of rendering the man of God "thoroughly furnished"; and James speaks of the engrafted word of God as "able to save the soul." The true doctrine therefore is that Scripture contains all that is necessary to salvation. What is the doctrine of Romanism on this point? One of the articles of the Council of Trent asserts that, not only should the Old and New Testaments be received with reverence as the word of God, but also "the unwritten traditions which have come down to us, pertaining both to faith and manners, and preserved in the Catholic Church by continual succession." In considering this decree, and its fatal effects in exalting mere human traditions to the level of Divine revelation, one is reminded of the solemn words which close the Apocalypse: "If any man shall add unto these things, God shall add unto him the plagues that are written in this book." Christ taught, on the contrary, that tradition was to be rejected whenever it was opposed to Scripture. "Why do ye also transgress the commandment of God by your tradition?" "In vain do they worship me, teaching for doctrines the commandments of men." "Laying aside the commandment of God, ye hold the tradition of men." "Making the word of God of none effect through your tradition."

**2.** Again. The Bible teaches us the duty of reading and searching the Scriptures. The Lord Jesus Himself said, "Search the Scriptures"; but Romanism forbids the general reading of Scripture, asserting that such a use of the word of God in the vulgar tongue causes more harm than good, and that it must never be practiced except by special permission in writing obtained from a priest. If any presume to read it without that, they are not to receive absolution. Booksellers who sell the Bible to any desiring to obtain it are to have penalties inflicted upon them, and no one is to purchase a Bible without special license from their superior. This is extended to receiving a gift of the Bible.

**3.** The true faith teaches us that every man is bound to judge for himself as to the meaning of Scripture. "Prove all things, hold fast that which is good." "To the law and to the testimony: if they speak not according to this word, it is because there is no light in them." But the Council of Trent decrees, that "no one confiding in his own judgment shall dare to wrest the sacred Scriptures to his own sense of them contrary to that which is held by holy mother Church, whose right it is to judge of the meaning." If any one disobeys this decree he is to be punished according to law.

**4.** Scripture teaches us most abundantly that Christ is the only head of the Church. God gave Him to be the head over all things to the Church, which is His body; but Romanism teaches that the pope is the head of the Church on earth. "The pope is the head of all heads, and the prince, moderator, and pastor of the whole Church of Christ, which is under him," says Benedict XIV; and the Douay catechism, taught in all Papal schools, says, "He who is not in due connection and subordination to the pope must needs be dead, and cannot be counted a member of the Church."

**5.** Scripture teaches us that the wages of sin is death, and "that whoever shall keep the law, and yet offend in one point, is guilty of all." "Cursed is every one that continueth not in all things which are written in the book of the law to do them." But Popery teaches that there are some sins which do not deserve the wrath and curse of God, and that venial sins do not bring spiritual death to the soul.

**6.** The Bible teaches us that a man is justified by faith without the deeds of the law, and that we are justified freely by His grace through the redemption that is in Christ Jesus. But Popery denounces this doctrine. The Council of Trent asserted that whosoever should affirm that we are justified by the grace and favor of God was to be accursed, and so all those who hold that salvation is not by works, but by grace.

**7.** Scripture teaches us to confess sin to God only. "Against thee, thee only, have I sinned, and done this evil in thy sight." "Every one of us shall give account of himself to God." "If we confess our sins, he is faithful and just to forgive us our sins." But Romanism denies this, and says that sacramental confession to a priest is necessary to salvation, and that any one who should denounce the practice of secret confessions as contrary to the institution and command of Christ, and a mere human invention, is to be accursed.

**8.** Scripture teaches us, again, that God only can forgive sins, and that the minister's duty is simply to announce His forgiveness. "Repentance and remission of sins" was to be preached in His name among all nations. "God was in Christ, reconciling the world unto himself, not imputing their trespasses unto them; and hath committed unto us the word of reconciliation." He commanded us to preach to the people, that "through his name whosoever believeth in him shall receive remission of sins." The Council of Trent asserts, on the contrary, whosoever shall affirm that the priest's absolution is not a judicial act, but only a ministry to declare that the sins of the penitent are forgiven, or that the confession of the penitent is not necessary in order to obtain absolution from the priest, let him be accursed.

**9.** Scripture teaches us that no man is perfectly righteous, and certainly that none can do more than his duty to God. "If we say we have no sin, we deceive ourselves." "In thy sight shall no man living be justified." "When ye shall have done all those things which are commanded you, say, We are unprofitable servants: we have done that which was our duty to do." The Council of Trent, on the contrary, asserts that the good works of the justified man, his fasts, alms, and penances, really deserve increase of grace and eternal life, and that God is willing, on account of His most pious servants, to forgive others. It teaches that a man may do more than is requisite, and may give the overplus of his good works to another.

**10.** Scripture teaches us that faith in Christ removes sin and its guilt, "that the Lamb of God taketh away the sin of the world," that by His death Christ put away our sins, that "the blood of Jesus Christ cleanseth us from all sin." But Romanism teaches that the venial sins of believers have to be expiated by a purgatory after death, and that the prayers of the faithful can help them. The Creed of Pope Pius IV contains the clause: "I constantly hold that there is a purgatory, and that the souls detained therein are helped by the suffrages of the faithful."

**11.** Scripture teaches us that "by one offering He hath perfected for ever them that are sanctified," that He was once offered to bear the sins of many. But Romanism asserts, on the contrary, that in each of the endlessly repeated masses in its innumerable churches all over the world there is offered to God "a true, proper, and propitiatory sacrifice for the living and the dead."

**12.** Scripture, as we have already shown, teaches us that the marriage of the ministers of Christ is a lawful and honorable thing. Peter was a married man; Paul asserts his liberty to marry, and says that a bishop must be the husband of one wife, having his children in subjection with all gravity, and that the deacons also must be the husbands of one wife, ruling their children and their own houses well. Romanism, on the other hand, teaches "that the clergy may not marry, and that marriage is to them a pollution."

**13.** Scripture says, "Thou shalt worship the Lord thy God, and Him only shalt thou serve." Barnabas and Paul with horror forbade the crowds to worship them, and the angel similarly forbade John, saying, "See thou do it not." Romanism enjoins the worship both of angels and saints and their relics. "The saints reigning together with Christ are for us, and their relics are to be venerated."

**14.** The Bible again teaches that images are not to be worshipped. "Thou shalt not bow down to them, nor serve them." "I am the Lord: My glory will I not give to another, neither My praise to graven images." But Romanism teaches her rotaries to say, "I most firmly assert, that the images of Christ, and of the mother of God ever virgin, and also of the of the other saints, are to be had and retained, and that due honor and veneration are to be given to them."

**15.** And above all, Scripture teaches us that there is one God, and one Mediator between God and man, the Man Christ Jesus, neither is there salvation in any other. But Romanism teaches that there are other mediators in abundance besides Jesus Christ, that the Virgin Mary and the saints are such. "The saints reigning together with Christ offer prayers to God for us."

I must not go further, and contrast Bible and Romish teachings on the subject of the Lord's supper, extreme unction, and a multitude of other points, but may say, in one word, that there is not a doctrine of the gospel which has not been contradicted or distorted by this system, and that it stands branded before the world beyond all question as fulfilling Paul's prophecy of the apostasy ù that it should be characterized by departure from the faith.

Perhaps I cannot give you a better idea of the distinctive teachings of Romanism as to controverted points of doctrine, than by reading to you the Creed of Pope Pius IV. This creed was adopted at the famous Council of Trent, held in the sixteenth century, when the doctrines of the Reformation were already widely diffused through Europe, and joyfully accepted and held by the young Protestant Churches of many lands. The Council of Trent was indeed Rome's reply to the Reformation. The newly recovered truths of the gospel were in its canons and decrees stigmatized as pestilent heresies, and all who held them accursed; and in opposition to them this creed was prepared and adopted. It commences with the Nicene Creed, which is common to Romanists and Protestants; but to this simple and ancient "form of sound words" it adds twelve new articles which are peculiar to Rome, and contain her definite rejection of the doctrines of Scriptures recovered at the Reformation.

**1.** I most firmly admit and embrace apostolical and ecclesiastical traditions, and all other constitutions and observances of the same Church.

**2.** I also admit the sacred Scriptures according to the sense which the holy mother Church has held, and does hold, to whom it belongs to judge of the true sense and interpretation of the Holy Scriptures; nor will I ever take or interpret them otherwise than according to the unanimous consent of the Fathers.

**3.** I profess also, that there are truly and properly seven sacraments of the new law, instituted by Jesus Christ our Lord, and for the salvation of mankind, though all are not necessary for every one; namely, baptism, confirmation, eucharist, penance, extreme unction, orders, and matrimony; and that they confer grace; and of these, baptism, confirmation, and orders cannot be reiterated without sacrilege.

**4.** I also receive and admit the ceremonies of the Catholic Church received and approved in the solemn administration of all the above said sacraments.

**5.** I receive and embrace all and every one of the things which have been defined and declared in the holy Council of Trent concerning original sin and justification.

**6.** I profess likewise that in the mass is offered to God a true, proper, and propitiatory sacrifice for the living and the dead; and that in the most holy sacrifice of the eucharist there is truly, really, and substantially the body and blood, together with the soul and divinity, of our Lord Jesus Christ; and that there is made a conversion of the whole substance of the bread into the body and of the whole substance of the wine into the blood, which conversion the Catholic Church calls transubstantiation.

**7.** I confess also, that under either kind alone, whole and entire Christ and a true sacrament are received.

**8.** I constantly hold that there is a purgatory, and that the souls detained therein are helped by the suffrages of the faithful.

**9.** Likewise that the saints reigning together with Christ are to be honored and invocated; that they offer prayers to God for us; and that their relics are to be venerated.

**10.** I most firmly assert that the images of Christ, and of the mother of God ever virgin, and also of the other saints, are to be had and retained, and that due honor and veneration are to be given them.

**11.** I also affirm that the power of indulgences was left by Christ in the Church, and that the use of them is most wholesome to Christian people.

**12.** I acknowledge the holy catholic and apostolic Roman Church, the mother and mistress of all Churches; and I promise and swear true obedience to the Roman bishop, the successor of St. Peter, the prince of the apostles and vicar of Jesus Christ.

**13.** I also profess and undoubtedly receive all other things delivered, defined, and declared by the sacred canons and general councils, and particularly by the holy Council of Trent; and likewise I also condemn, reject, and anathematize all things contrary thereto, and all heresies whatsoever, condemned, rejected, and anathematized by the Church. This true catholic faith, out of which none can be saved, which I now freely profess, and truly hold, I, N., promise, vow, and swear most constantly to hold and profess the same whole and entire, with God's assistance, to the end of my life; and to procure, as far as lies in my power, that the same shall be held, taught, and preached by all who are under me, or are entrusted to my care, by virtue of my office. So help me God, and these holy gospels of God.

This creed of Pope Plus IV is the authoritative Papal epitome of the canons and decrees of the Council of Trent. The importance of this council "depends upon the considerations, that its records embody the solemn, formal, and official decision of the Church of Rome ù which claims to be the one, holy, catholic Church of Christ ù upon all the leading doctrines taught by the reformers; that its decrees upon all doctrinal points are received by all Romanists as possessed of infallible authority; and that every Popish priest is sworn to receive, profess, and maintain everything defined and declared by it." 4

As an illustration of its reception and maintenance in the present day by the infallible head of the Romish Church, and by the whole conclave of Roman

Catholic bishops, I refer you to their action in the comparatively recent Council of the Vatican.

See the almost incredible spectacle of 1870! See those seven hundred bishops of the Church throughout the world gathered in Rome at the high altar of St. Peter's. See them and hear them! In this Romish book, entitled "The Chair of Peter," p. 497, is a description of the scene. áááááá "The pope recited in a loud voice the profession of faith, namely the Creed of Nice and Constantinople, together with the definitions of the Council of Trent, called the Creed of Pope Pius IV; alter which it was read aloud from the ambo by the Bishop of Fabriano; 'then for two whole hours,' to use the words of one of the prelates present, 'the cardinals, patriarchs, primates, archbishops, bishops, and other fathers of the council, made their adhesion to the same by tossing the Gospel at the throne of the head of the Church.' A truly sublime spectacle, those seven hundred bishops from all parts of the earth, the representatives of more than thirty nations, and of two hundred millions of Christians, thus openly making profession of one common faith, in communion with the one and supreme pastor and teacher of all!"

Yes; the Creed of Trent, the canons and decrees of Trent, the Creed of Pius IV, those twelve articles which Rome has added to the ancient Nicene Creed, the sacrifice of the mass, transubstantiation, communion in one kind, the seven sacraments, traditions, Romish interpretation, Popish ceremonies, justification by works, purgatory, invocation of saints, indulgences, the worship of images, the absolute supremacy of the pope as the vicar of Christ, and no salvation out of union and communion with him, and submission to him: they confessed and professed them all, and swore adhesion to them, and kissed the holy Gospels in solemn token thereof before heaven and earth.

O Creed of Pius ù or Impious as he deserves to be called; O doctrines of Trent, "solemn, formal, official" decision of the Church of Rome upon all the great doctrines taught by the Reformers, Rome's reply to the Reformation, her deliberate final rejection and anathema of its blessed teachings and confessions drawn from the holy word of God; O Creed of Trent and of the impious priest whose word supplants the word of God with fables and blasphemies and lies: thou art the awful decision of apostate Latin Christendom on the controversy of the ages, A DECISION TO WHICH ROME MUST NOW UNCHANGEABLY ADHERE, sealed as infallible, confessed to be irreformable! O momentous fact! O fatal Creed of Trent! thou art a millstone round the neck of the Roman pontiff, the cardinals, the archbishops, the bishops, the priests, the people of the whole Papal Church, a mighty millstone that must sink them in destruction and perdition! There is no shaking thee off. Alas! they have doomed themselves to wear thee; they have wedded and bound themselves to thy deadly lies; they have sealed, have sworn to thee as infallible and irreformable, and condemned themselves to abide by thee forever! It is done. Rome's last word is spoken. Her fate is fixed, fixed by her own action, her own utterance, her own oath. Individuals may escape, may flee the system; but as a Church it is past recovery, and utterly beyond the reach of reformation. Oh that thousands might escape from it while yet there is time! Oh that they would hear the earnest, the urgent call, "Come out of her, My people"! Oh that they would wake from their blind and abject submission to the tyranny of hypocrites while there is room for repentance! And now, in conclusion. We have shown briefly but clearly that Romanism is the offspring of a mystery of iniquity which began to work in apostolic times; that it is characterized by hypocrisy, by asceticism, by the prohibition of meats and marriage, by superstition and idolatry, by the worship of relics and images, of saints and angels, by the multiplication of mediators by false miracles, by lying signs and wonders, and by doctrines and decrees antagonistic to the teachings and command of Christ. We have shown that the Papal pontiffs have exalted themselves above all bishops, and above all kings, that they have fabricated new articles of faith and new rules of discipline; that they have altered the terms of salvation; that they have sold the pardon of sins for money, and bartered the priceless gifts of grace for selfish gain; that they have bound their deadly doctrines on the souls of countless millions by monstrous tyrannical threats and denunciations; that they have pertinaciously rejected the light of truth; that they have resolutely and wrathfully resisted those who have rebuked their impiety; that they have thundered against them their bulls and interdicts, their excommunications and anathemas; that they have made war with them, and with the faithful saints of many ages, and prevailed against them, and worn them out with long and cruel persecutions, with infamous and inhuman massacres; that they have waged against them no less than a war of extermination, wielding in this the whole strength and machinery of the resistless Roman empire, as well as the spiritual forces of the apostate Christian Church; that with the mighty working of Satan, with all power, signs, and miracles of falsehood they have OPPOSED CHRIST, have opposed His doctrines, His precepts, His people, and His cause, and in opposing Christ have OPPOSED GOD HIMSELF, and made war with Him who is the Lord of heaven and earth, and have uttered against Him their daring prohibitions and anathemas; that they have enthroned themselves in His holy temple, and trampled on His sacred laws, and trodden down His saints and servants, and arrogated to themselves His place, and power, and prerogatives; and while perpetrating acts of enormous and indescribable wickedness, have blasphemously claimed to be His sole representatives both in the church and in the world, to be inspired by His spirit, to be INFALLIBLE in their teachings and decrees, to be Vice-Christs, to be Vice- Gods ù in other words, to be AS CHRIST, AND AS GOD HIMSELF VISIBLY REVEALED UPON THE EARTH.

We have further shown that prophets and apostles foresaw and foretold the rise, reign, and doom of such a great apostate power, describing it as a "little horn" of the fourth or Roman empire, possessed of intelligence and oversight, having a mouth speaking great things and blasphemies; a power both political and ecclesiastical; a Roman ruler, yet an overseer in the Christian Church; a power arising on the break up of the old Roman empire, and coexisting with the kings of its divided Gothic state; a power inspired by Satan, and prevailing by means of false miracles and lying wonders; a power springing from a "mystery of iniquity" and characterized by all deceivableness of unrighteousness; a lawless, self-exalting power, claiming Divine prerogatives, and receiving from deluded millions the submission and homage which should be rendered to God alone; a power characterized by exceeding personal sinfulness, and by the widespread promotion of sin in others; above all, a persecuting power, a power making war with the saints, and wearing them out, and prevailing against them throughout its long career of proud usurpation and triumphant tyranny.

These inspired words of prophecy and those indisputable facts of history agree. The Roman Papacy is revealed by the far-reaching light of the divinely written word. Its portrait is painted; its mystery is penetrated; its character, its deeds are drawn; its thousand veils and subterfuges are torn away. The unsparing hand of inspiration has stripped it, and left it standing upon the stage of history deformed and naked, a dark emanation from the pit, bloodstained and blasphemous, blindly struggling in the concentrated rays of celestial recognition, amid the premonitory thunders and lightnings of its fast approaching doom.

## Notes

**1** *The following legal distinction should be borne in mind in weighing this point. It is given in "Blackstone's Commentary," book 1, chapter 1. "Persons are divided by the law into either natural persons or artificial. Natural persons are such as are formed by the God of nature; artificial are such as are created and devised by human laws for the purposes of society and government, which are called corporations or bodies politic." Thus there is a sort of perpetual person in whom a community subsists, as well as the person whose life is confined within the limits of one individual existence. Each is equally real, and either may be spoken of in the singular. "The parson of a parish" may mean either a man or a succession of men. So "the pope of Rome" may intimate one single bishop or the long succession ù a perpetual person. So "the man of sin." See on this subject a careful investigation in "The Apostasy Predicted by St Paul," by Dr. O. Sullivan (Curry, Dublin).]*

**2** *Jewell on 2 Thessalonians, p. 245.*

**3** *"Admonition Showing the Advantages which Christendom might Derive from and Inventory of Relics." ù Calvin: Tracts, vol. 1, p. 289.*

**4** *W. Cunninghame, D.D.: "Historical Theology," vol. 1., p. 483.*

# Lecture Four - John's Foreview of Romanism

In the three preceding lectures we considered first the POLITICAL character and relations of Romanism, as prefigured in the prophecies of Daniel; and next its ECCLESIASTICAL character and relations, as predicted in the epistles of Paul. We have now to consider the combination of these two aspects, or the POLITICO-ECCLESIASTICAL character of Romanism, as presented in the prophecies of John. The Apocalypse, or "Revelation of Jesus Christ," is an advance on all other prophecies. It gives the complete story of Christ's kingdom, exhibiting it both from an external and an internal point of view, and unveiling its political as well as its ecclesiastical history. In its faithful reflection of the future it gives central prominence to the Roman power and apostasy. On this subject it enters into detail, and exhibits the mutual relations of the Latin Church and Roman State, using composite figures for this purpose-figures one part of which represent the political aspect of Romanism as a temporal government, and the other its religious aspect as an ecclesiastical system.

Two great foreviews of Romanism are given in the Apocalypse: that concerning its rise and reign in Revevelation 13, and that relating to its decline and fall in chapters 17-19.

Both of these prophecies are double. The first is the prophecy of "the beast" and the "false prophet"; the second is that of "the beast" and "the harlot." The false prophet acts for "the beast," the harlot rides upon "the beast." In each case there are two powers, perfectly distinct yet closely connected. The "beast" and the "false prophet" can neither be confounded nor separated. Similarly, the "beast" and "harlot" are associated. The beast carries the harlot during all her long career of crime and cruelty, and they both come to their ruin in the same judgment era of the vials of God's righteous wrath which terminate the present dispensation.

Before considering the interpretation of these wonderful Apocalyptic visions, it will be necessary to devote a few moments to the relation which exists between the prophecies of DANIEL and those of JOHN. We are exhibiting the prophecies of Romanism as a whole, and in order to do this it is necessary to trace the simple yet profound connection between the foreview granted to the Jewish prophet in Babylon in the days of Nebuchadnezzar and Belshazzar, and that given to the Christian apostle in Patmos, in the days of Domitian.

The prophecies of Daniel and the book of Revelation may be considered as two parts of a single prophecy; their subject is the same, and their symbols are the same. They reveal the course of cruel, idolatrous Gentile empires, followed by the eternal kingdom of God; and in doing this they employ the same symbols. Daniel revealed the four empires; John the fourth only, for the first three had in his time passed away. Babylon, Persia, Greece had fallen; but Rome was still in the zenith of its greatness, destined to endure for many ages, and to rule, even to our own day, a large section of the human race. To John therefore was shown with considerable fullness, the future of the Roman power. The Apocalypse contains a marvelous foreview of the rise, reign, decline, and fall of the Roman Papacy, of the sufferings and triumphs of the saints of God during its continuance, and their enthronement at its close.

The Roman empire is presented to Daniel and to John under one and the same striking and special symbol, a ten-horned wild beast. Daniel saw the Medo-Persian empire as a two-horned ram, one horn being higher than the other (#Dan 8:3). He saw the Grecian empire as a four-horned goat (#Dan 8:8-20); and he saw the Roman empires as a ten-horned wild beast Thus these three great empires as seen by Daniel were two-horned, four-horned, ten-horned. This is remarkable and easy to be remembered. Now Daniel's ten-horned beast reappears in the Apocalypse. Here we have an important link between the Old Testament and the New, and a clue to the meaning of the last book of Scripture. Let us try to be clear on this point. The four wild beasts represent Babylon, Persia, Greece, Rome. The fourth is ten-horned. This ten-horned beast of Daniel reappears in the Apocalypse, the divinely given symbol of the fourth and final earthly empire. You see it in chapters 12,13, and 17 of the book of Revelation. Compare now the passages. First, #Dan 11:7: "I saw in the night visions, and behold a fourth beast, dreadful and terrible, and strong exceedingly; and it had ten horns."

Next, #Rev 12:3: "A great red dragon, having ten horns."

#Rev 13:1: "I saw a beast rise up out of the sea, having ten horns."

Lastly, #Rev 17:3: "A scarlet-colored beast, having ten horns."

It is universally admitted that this fourth, or ten-horned beast, represents the Roman empire. The angel himself so interprets it. I want you particularly to notice the fact that we are not left to speculate about the meaning of these symbols; that the all-wise God who selected them, and gave them to us, has condescended to give us their interpretation. All these principal visions are divinely interpreted.

First, as to the vision of the fourfold image there is an inspired interpretation of a most detailed character. You remember the words with which it begins, "This is the dream, and we will tell the interpretation thereof before the king."

Then in the vision of the four wild beasts, there is the interpretation beginning thus, "So he told me, and made me know the interpretation of the things." So with the vision of the second and third empires in Daniel 13, there is the interpretation. Daniel says: "I heard a man's voice..which called, and said, Gabriel, make this man to understand the vision," and so forth.

The same method is followed in the Apocalypse. The opening vision of the seven candlesticks is interpreted. You remember the words, "The seven candlesticks which thou sawest are the seven Churches." And similarly, the vision of the woman seated on the seven-headed, ten-horned beast, in chapter 17, is interpreted: every part of it is interpreted. Observe the angel's words: "I will tell thee the mystery of the woman, and of the beast that carrieth her, which hath the seven heads and ten horns." Mark in your Bibles, if you will, these four sentences in the angelic interpretation: "The beast which thou sawest." "The ten horns which thou sawest." "The waters which thou sawest." "The woman which thou sawest."

These four sentences are the key to the Apocalypse. The beast, the horns, the waters, the woman are all interpreted; and their interpretation involves, or carries in it, the interpretation of the Apocalypse. The seven heads of the beast are also interpreted, and so interpreted as to tie down the symbol to the ROMAN empire. For the angel mentions an important note of time; he says of the seven heads, "five are fallen, and ONE IS, and the other is not yet come." The heads of this beast then, when the vision was revealed, were past, present, and future; five were past, the sixth then existed, the seventh was not yet come. This demonstrates the power in question to be the Roman empire. The then reigning power in John's day was symbolized by the sixth head of a seven-headed beast. This is certain. And the then reigning power was that of the Caesars of pagan Rome. This is equally certain. Therefore the Roman Caesars were represented by the sixth head of the symbolic beast. Now, to make the assurance doubly sure, mark the closing sentence in the angelic interpretation: "The woman which thou sawest is that city which reigneth over the kings of the earth." Note the words, "which reigneth" (h ecousa basileian), or as it is in Latin, "quae habet regnum super reges terrae": "and the woman which thou sawest is the great city which has (or holds) the kingdom (or government) over the kings of the earth." The great city "which reigneth," not which did reign, nor which shall reign, but "which reigneth", or was actually reigning then. What great city was reigning then over the kings of the earth? Rome, and none other. Rome then is the power which is signified.

We have now got the KEY to the Apocalypse; we are no longer lost in a crowd of uninterpreted symbols. The beasts of Daniel and John are empires. The ten-horned beast is the Roman power. This beast appears three times in the Apocalypse; it is expounded by the angel. This expounded symbol is the key to the entire prophecy.

And I stood upon the sand of the sea, and saw a beast rise up out of the sea, having seven heads and ten horns, and upon his horns ten crowns, and upon the heads the name of blasphemy. And the beast which I saw was like unto a leopard, and his feet were as the feet of a bear, and his mouth as the mouth of a lion: and the dragon gave him his power, and his seat, and great authority. And I saw one of his heads as it were wounded to death; and his deadly wound was healed: and all the world wondered after the beast. And they worshipped the dragon that gave power unto the beast: and they worshipped the beast, saying, Who is like unto the beast? who is able to make war with him? And there was given unto him a mouth speaking great things and blasphemies; and power was given unto him to continue forty and two months. And he opened his mouth in blasphemy against God, to blaspheme His name, and His tabernacle, and them that dwell in heaven. And it was given unto him to make war with the saints, and to overcome them: and power was given him over all kindreds, and tongues, and nations. And all that dwell upon the earth shall worship him, whose names are not written in the book of life of the Lamb slain from the foundation of the world (#Rev 13:1-8). The head is the governing power in the body. The heads of this beast represent successive governments. Mark the "deadly wound" inflicted on the last of its seven heads, and the marvelous healing of that wound, or the revival of the slain head or government, then mark the tyrannical and dreadful doings of this revived or eighth head. It becomes a great and terrible enemy of God's people, a Roman enemy not an early Roman enemy, not a pagan Caesar, not a Nero or a Domitian, but one occupying a later place, a final place; for none succeeds him in that empire, since it is foretold that his destruction will be accomplished at the advent of Christ in His kingdom.

A comparison of this Roman enemy of God's people described by John with the "little horn" foreshown by Daniel, demonstrates the important fact of their identity. They are one and the same. Observe the following points:

**I.** The persecuting horn seen by Daniel is a horn of the Roman empire; it is a Roman horn. And the persecuting head seen by John is a head of the Roman beast. In this they are alike. Each is Roman.

**II.** The persecuting horn grows up in the later, or divided state of the Roman empire; it rises among the ten Gothic horns. The persecuting head seen by John also grows up in the same later state of the Roman empire, for it follows the seven heads, and is the last. The sixth was said by the angel to be in existence in John's time, and the seventh was to last only a short season, ù be wounded to death, and then revived in a new and final and peculiarly tyrannical and persecuting form. The "little horn" in Daniel belongs to the later ten-horned, or Gothic, period of the Roman empire; and the revived head of the empire seen by John belongs to the same period. You will note this point their period is the same. This is the second mark of their identity.

**III.** Each has a mouth. Now here is a very distinct and remarkable feature. The other horns and heads were dumb; but this speaks. Of the persecuting Roman horn we read in Darnel, it had "a mouth"; and of the persecuting Roman head we read in John, "there was given to him a mouth."

**IV.** In each case this mouth speaks the same things. Of the mouth of the Roman horn Darnel says, in chapter 7, "it spake great things" (#Dan 7:8), "the great words which the horn spake" (#Dan 7:11), "very great things" (#Dan 7:20), "great words against the Most High" (#Dan 7:25). While of the Roman head in the Apocalypse John says:

"There was given unto him a mouth speaking great things and blasphemies..And he opened his mouth in blasphemy against God, to blaspheme His name, and His tabernacle, and them that dwell in heaven" (#Rev 13:6).

The horn speaks; the head speaks: each speaks great things; each speaks blasphemies. This striking correspondence is a further indication of their identity. Each has (otoma laloun megala) (#Dan 7:8). (otoma laloun megala) (#Rev 13:5).

The expression is exactly the same in the Septuagint translation of Daniel and in the Apocalypse.

**V.** The horn has great dominion. It plucks up three horns; it has "a look more stout than his fellows" (v. 20); it makes war and prevails; its great "dominion" is eventually taken away and destroyed; "they shall take away his dominion" (v. 26). Similarly the head has great dominion; "power was given him over all kindreds and tongues and nations." The application of these words should not be pressed beyond the sphere to which they belong. In that sphere, for a certain period, the power of the horn or head was to be supreme and universal. In the fact of their dominion they are alike.

**VI.** Each makes war with the saints: each is terrible as a persecutor of God's people. Daniel says: "The same horn made war with the saints, and prevailed against them..He shall wear out the saints of the Most High.. They shall be given into his hand until a time, and times, and the dividing of time." John says: "It was given unto him to make war with the saints and to overcome them" (#Rev 13:7); "He shall make war against them, and shall overcome them, and kill them" (#Rev 11:7).

John describes the method of this warfare, in what way and for what reason the "saints" or "martyrs of Jesus" "should be killed" (#Rev 13:15); and it is of these martyrs the voice from heaven says, "Blessed are the dead which die in the Lord from henceforth: yea, saith the Spirit, that they may rest from their labors; and their works do follow them" (#Rev 14:13).

In their persecution of the saints Daniel's "horn" and John's revived "head" are alike.

**VII.** The duration of each is the same. This too is a noteworthy feature. The duration of the persecuting horn is mystically stated in Daniel as "time, times, and the dividing of time," or three and a half times (#Dan 7:25). And the duration of the persecuting head in the Apocalypse is stated to be forty-two months. "Power was given unto him to continue forty and two months" (#Rev 13:5). And these are the same period. This will appear from a comparison of the seven passages in which this period occurs in Daniel and the Apocalypse; in these it is called 1,260 days, forty-two months, and three and a half times. Now 1,260 days are forty-two months, and forty-two months are three and a half years. What these symbolic periods represent is another question; our point here is their identity. The persecuting horn and persecuting head are exactly the same in their duration. This is another proof of the sameness of the reality they represent.

**VIII.** They end in the same manner and at the same time. This completes the evidence of their identity. The persecuting horn is slain by the Ancient of days revealed in judgment, and the glory of His kingdom (#Dan 7: 9-11,22). The persecuting head is slain by the "King of kings and Lord of lords" revealed in that judgment in which He treads the winepress of the fierceness and wrath of Almighty God. The judgment is the same (#Rev 19:11,20). The "little horn" and revived "head" then, are alike in place, time, character, authority, persecuting action, duration, and doom. They arise at the same point, they last the same period; they do the same deeds; they come to their end at the same moment, and by the same revelation of Christ in the glory of His kingdom. They cannot prefigure two powers absolutely alike in all these respects; but one and the same. Even the Church of Rome admits their identity. It teaches that both are symbols of the same great persecuting power.

The way is now clear to consider the interpretation of this prophecy. It is indeed determined already by this very identification. The little horn of Daniel prefigures, as we have proved before, the Papacy of Rome. So then does this revived head. We will examine briefly the evidence which sustains this conclusion; but as we have already sketched the history, we need not dwell at any length on the different points. We will take the prophetic features in the order in which we have already presented them, considering first the facts relating to the rise, and then those concerning the reign, of the power in question.

First then as to its rise. The predicted head rises from the Roman empire. It is therefore Roman. So is the Papacy. We have called the system which owns the pope as head Romanism, because its seat is the seven-hilled city.

Secondly, the predicted persecuting power grows up in the second stage of Roman history. It is the seventh or last head of the old empire revived. Now this is the exact position of the Papacy. The Papacy belongs to the second or Christian stage of the Roman empire. It grew up among its Gothic horns or kingdoms. It was the revival of a power which had been slain. When the pagan empire was overthrown the Papal rose in its place. First the Caesars ruled in Rome, then the popes. The Goths overthrew the Roman empire in the fifth century; Romulus Augustulus abdicated the imperial dignity in A.D. 476. This was the "deadly wound" of the seventh head. From that date the Papacy grew with freedom, grew up among the Gothic horns or kingdoms. Note this feature ù the Papacy belongs to the second or Christian stage of the Roman empire. It was a horn among the Gothic horns. It was a revived head. The power of the Caesars lived again in the universal dominion of the popes.

The Papacy was small at its beginning, but grew to great dominion; it exercised as wide a sway as the Caesars it succeeded; all Europe submitted to its rule; it claimed, and still claims, a power without a rival or a limit. Hallam, as we have already remarked, says of the thirteenth century, the noonday of Papal power: "Rome inspired during this age all the terror of her ancient name. She was once more mistress of the world, and kings were her vassals."1 Remember the proud title taken by the popes, rector orbis ù ruler of the world. In this also the Papacy fulfills the prophecy.

Observe, secondly, that extraordinary feature both in Daniel and the Apocalypse, the mouth of this power. Both the horn, in Daniel, and the head, in John, has a mouth, otoma laloun megala - "a mouth speaking great things." This feature is marvelously fulfilled in the Papacy. What a mouth has that Latin ruler! What a talker! what a teacher! what a thunderer! How has he boasted himself and magnified himself, and excommunicated and anathematized all who have resisted him! Has the world ever seen his equal in this respect? All the Gothic kings were his humble servants. He was, by his own account, and is, the representative of Christ, of God, ruler of the world, armed with all the powers of Christ in heaven, earth, and hell. He is infallible; his decrees are irreformable. A mouth indeed is his, a mouth speaking great things!

Notice, in the third place, his warring with the saints. In the Apocalypse we read, "It was given to him to make war with the saints, and to overcome them." I will not do more here than remind you of the fact that, terribly as the saints suffered under the Caesars of pagan Rome, they suffered far more terribly and far longer under Papal Rome. Let the massacres of the Albigenses, the Waldenses, the Hussites, the Lollards, the massacres in Holland and the Netherlands, the massacre of St. Bartholomew, the massacre in Ireland in 1641, the tortures of the Inquisition, the fires of the stake kindled over and over in every country in Europe ù let these speak and testify to the fulfillment of prophecy. Yes; the Papacy has made war with the saints, and overcome them, and worn them out, and would have totally crushed and annihilated them, but for the sustaining hand and reviving power of God. In its prolonged, cruel, and universal persecution of the saints, the Papacy has fulfilled this solemn prophecy.

Notice, in the fourth place, the predicted duration of this persecuting power. Daniel mysteriously announces its duration as three and a half times; John as forty-two months. The symbolical nature of the prophecy, as well as the vastness of the subject, forbid us to take these times literally. As the beast is symbolic, and its various parts symbolic, so the period of its persecuting head is symbolic. You find this period mentioned seven times over in Daniel and Revelation, and called 1,260 days, forty-two months, and also three and a half "times." These are, as we have said, the same period. Calculate for yourself, and you will find it so. Now, both in the law and prophets, a day is used as the symbol of a year. Moses, Ezekiel, Daniel use it thus. The seventy weeks of Daniel, or 490 days to Messiah, were fulfilled as 490 years; that is, they were fulfilled on the year-day scale. On this scale the forty-two months, or 1,260 days, are 1,260 years. We ask then, Has the Papacy endured this period? An examination of the facts of history will show that it has. From the era of its rise in the sixth century, at the notable decree of the emperor Justinian, constituting the Bishop of Rome head of all the Churches in Christendom, A.D. 533, 1,260 years extended to 1793, the date of the tremendous Papal overthrow in the French Revolution. Here we have a fact of great importance. Note it well. To this we add the further fact, that from the analogous decree of the emperor Phocas, confirming the headship of the pope over Christendom, in the year 607, 1,260 years extended to 1866-7, the initial date of the recent remarkable overthrow of Papal governments which culminated in the loss of the pope's temporal power in 1870. In that year the Papacy assumed the highest exaltation to which it could aspire, that of infallibility, and lost the temporal sovereignty, which it had held for more than a thousand years. Thus the predicted period has been fulfilled. What an evidence is this! The Papacy has fulfilled the prophecy, not only in its geographical and historical position, its moral character, its political power, its blasphemous pretensions, its tyrannical career, but in its very chronology, ù in the point of its rise, the period of its duration, the era of its decline, the crisis of its overthrow. We have already directed your attention to the fact that the Papacy is a complex power, and requires complex symbols for its prefiguration. It is both a secular and an ecclesiastical power; and the ecclesiastical power has arrogated to itself the right to create the secular, or endow it with divine authority, and has also wielded the energies of the secular power in pursuance of its own unholy ends. Revelation 13 represents both these organizations as "beasts." The one is represented as a ten- horned, the other as a two-horned beast. The former rises, as does each of the beasts of Daniel, from the sea; the latter rises from the earth. The one springs up in storm, the other in stillness. Striving and warring winds attend the birth of the one; the other grows up quietly from a low, terrestrial origin, like an ivy plant or a noxious, earth-born weed. The ten horns of the one are strong iron kingdoms; the two horns of the other are gentle and lamb-like. The two beasts stand side by side; they act together in everything. The earth-born beast is the "prophet" of the sea-born beast, and he is a "false prophet." He compels subjection to the secular power, especially to its new head, that head which had been slain and healed. He establishes an idolatrous worship of that head, or a submission to it as Divine in authority. He "exercises" all the power of the ten-horned beast in his warfare against the saints and servants of God. He works false miracles, and accomplishes lying wonders, and even brings down fire upon the earth in imitation of the prophets of the Lord; that is, he causes judgments to descend on those who resist. He uses the instrument of excommunication, a weapon of celestial authority, and wields it with terrible effect. He lays kingdoms under interdicts, and nations under anathemas. He makes idolatry compulsory, delivering to the secular arm all who refuse to render it, that they may be put to death. He prohibits all dealings with so called "heretics," all traffic and communion with them. He allows none to buy from them, and none to sell to them. He institutes the system which is now called "boycotting," a system of persecution which was freely wielded by the Popish priesthood in the middle ages, and is still employed, as we know, in certain Papal lands.

How could the mutual relations of the political and ecclesiastical powers in the apostate Roman empire be better represented than by these wonderful symbols? Here are a monarchy and a priesthood in close, nefarious association; the priesthood anoints the monarchy, serves it, uses it. Together they rule, and together they persecute. No symbol can represent everything, no parable can correspond in all respects with the reality it depicts. It is surely enough if the principal features and primary relations are exhibited in the symbol, or reflected by the parable. This is just what is done in the apocalyptic prophecy. Look at the facts. The Papacy has been a political power for more than a thousand years. The popes of Rome have been secular monarchs. They have possessed territories, levied taxes, laid down laws, owned armies, made wars. The Papal monarchy has been for ages an integral part of the Roman empire. The Papacy has also been a sacerdotal power, and is so still. While its temporal government has fallen, its spiritual remains. Further, the Papacy is served by an extensive sacerdotal organization, embracing about a thousand bishops and half a million priests. This organization controls the convictions and actions of two hundred millions of persons, belonging to more than thirty nations. If the best symbol to represent the Roman empire with its rulers be a ten-horned beast, what better symbol to represent the Papal hierarchy than a two-horned beast, whose horns are like those of a lamb, while it has the voice of a dragon? And what better name for that hierarchy could be found than the "false prophet"? Does it not pretend to utter the messages of heaven? And as Moses and Elijah called down the fire of God's judgments on the enemies of Israel, has not this hierarchy brought down again and again, in the estimation of millions, the judgments of God on those who have resisted its will, whether individuals or nations? Has not this been one of its most tremendous and irresistible weapons? Read the history of the middle ages and of the sixteenth century. What nation in Europe has not been laid from time to time under Papal interdicts, and compelled by these means to submit to the decisions of the Roman pontiff? And has not the priesthood too been the author and instigator of a wholesale system of idolatry and persecution? Has it not employed the power of the State in enforcing idolatry, and cruelly persecuted to death millions of the faithful who would not bow the knee to the modern Baal? In all this, history only too faithfully corresponds to prophecy. Deep calls to deep, and the utterances of inspiration are caught up and echoed by the experience of generations. The voices of the prophets come back in thunder from the course of ages, and the proof that God has spoken reverberates throughout the world. Having briefly considered John's prophecy concerning the rise and reign of the Papal power, we have now to glance at his prediction of its fall and overthrow. This you will find in Revelation 17-19. We have not time to read these chapters now; you are doubtless familiar with them, and will do well to study them carefully and thoroughly. They contain the second complex or duplicate prophecy concerning Romanism ù the career and judgment of "Babylon the Great."

In this prophecy John beholds the ten-horned BEAST representing the Roman empire bearing a mystical WOMEN, dressed in purple and scarlet, decked with gold, precious stones, and pearls; a harlot, and the mother of harlots and abominations, the guilty paramour of kings, the creel persecutor of saints; intoxicated, but not with wine drunken with the blood of the saints and of the martyrs of Jesus. What a vision! what a prophecy!

You remember the angel's interpretation of this vision: "The woman which thou sawest is that great city which reigneth over the kings of the earth." We showed that that city was Rome, indisputably Rome. That Babylon the Great means Rome is admitted by Romanists themselves. Cardinal Bellarmine says that "Rome is signified in the Apocalypse by the name of Babylon." Cardinal Baronius admits that "all persons confess that Rome is denoted by the name of Babylon in the Apocalypse of John." Bossuet observes that "the features are so marked, that it is easy to decipher Rome under the figure of Babylon" (Rome sous la figure de Babylone). But, while admitting that Babylon the Great, seated on the seven hills, means Rome, Papal interpreters assert that it means heathen Rome, and not Christian Rome ù the Rome of the Caesars, and not that of the popes.

In reply to this, we answer, first, that the name upon the harlot's brow is "mystery," and that heathen Rome was no mystery. The true character of heathen Rome was never concealed. On the other hand, Christian Rome is a "mystery"; it is not what it seems. In profession, it is Divine; in character, satanic. We say, in the second place, that there is a marked and intentional contrast in the Apocalypse between the two cities Babylon and Jerusalem, which is overlooked by the Papal interpretation. Babylon, in the Apocalypse, is a city and a harlot. Jerusalem, in the same book, is a city and a bride. The former is the corrupt associate of earthly kings; the latter, the chaste bride of the heavenly King. But the latter is a Church; the former then is no mere heathen metropolis. The contrast is between Church and Church; the faithful Church and the apostate Church.

In the third place, we point to the fact that the judgment described in Revelation 18, falls upon Babylon when her sins had reached to heaven; that is, in the darkest part of her career. But when Alaric destroyed Rome in A.D. 410 that city had improved, it had become Christian; it was purified at that time from its pagan idolatries. Nor had it then sunk into the darkness of the Papacy. It was not in the fifth century that Rome reached the utmost height of her iniquity. The capture of the city by the soldiers of Alaric, when it was neither pagan nor Papal, could not have been the judgment here foretold.

In the fourth place, we point to the fact that the destruction of Babylon foretold in the Apocalypse is total and final; as a great "mill-stone" she is plunged into the deep; there is no recovery. This cannot refer to the mere burning of Rome in A.D. 410, for that event was speedily followed by the complete restoration of the city. When the Babylon of Revelation 18, falls, the smoke of its burning goes up for ever; it is found no more at all.

In the fifth place, we point to the fact that the foretold destruction of Babylon is accomplished by the horns or governments which were previously subject to her rule. We freely admit that the Goths destroyed ancient Rome, but the Goths were not previously subject to Rome. The Gothic nations did not first submit to Rome obediently, and then cast her off, and rend, and trample, and destroy her. All this however these nations did in the case of Papal Rome. For centuries they were subject to her sway; then they cast her off. Look at the French Revolution; see the deeds of France. Look at Italy in 1870. See the Continent today.

In the sixth place, we point to the fact that the foretold destruction of Babylon is immediately to be followed by "the marriage of the Lamb." This is clearly foretold in Revelation 19. But the capture of Rome by Alaric was not followed by that event. Alaric captured Rome fifteen centuries ago, while the marriage of the Lamb is still future. This utterly excludes the notion that the destruction of Rome by Alaric is the judgment intended, and that Babylon the Great represents pagan Rome. And as Babylon the Great does not represent Rome pagan, it must represent Rome papal; there is no other alternative.

Now, in conclusion, read this wonderful prophecy concerning "Babylon the Great" in the clear and all-revealing light of history. I ask those of you who have read the history of the last eighteen centuries, did not Rome Christian become a harlot? Did not Papal Rome ally itself with the kings of the earth? Did it not glorify itself to be as a queen, and call itself the Mistress of the World? Did it not ride upon the body of the beast, or fourth empire, and govern its actions for centuries? Did not Papal Rome array itself with gold and precious stones and pearls? Is not this its attire still? We appeal to facts. Go to the churches and see. Look at the priests; look at the cardinals; look at the popes; look at the purple robes they wear; look at their scarlet robes; see the encrusted jewels; look at the luxurious palaces in which they live; look at the eleven thousand halls and chambers in the Vatican, and the unbounded wealth and glory gathered there; look at the gorgeous spectacles in St. Peter's at Rome, casting even the magnificence of royalty into the shade. Go and see these things, or read the testimony of those who have seen them. Shamelessly Rome wears the very raiment, the very hues and colors, portrayed on the pages of inspired prophecy.

You may know the harlot by her attire, as certainly as by the name upon her brow.

But to come to the darkest feature. Has not the Church of Rome drunk most abundantly the precious blood of saints and martyrs? We appeal to facts. What of the Albigenses in the thirteenth century? What of the Waldenses from the thirteenth century on to the time of Cromwell and the commonwealth? You have not forgotten Milton's poem about them, those memorable lines. And what of the persecutions of Protestants in France, those dreadful persecutions mercilessly continued for more than three hundred years? What of the massacre of St. Bartholomew, and the revocation of the Edict of Nantes? What of the fires of Smithfield? What of the terrible Inquisition?

Stay, I will take you to the Inquisition. You shall enter its gloomy portals; you shall walk through its dark passages; you shall stand in its infernal torture chamber; you shall hear the cries of some of its victims; you shall listen to their very words. What agonies have been suffered in these somber vaults, unseen by any human eyes save those of fiendish inquisitors! What cries have been uttered in this dismal place which have never reached the open world in which we live. Locked doors shut them in; stone walls stifled them. No sound escaped, not even that of a faint and distant moan. But now and then a victim found release; one and another have come forth from the torture chamber pale and trembling, maimed and mutilated, to tell the things they experienced when in the hands of the holy inquisitors. We shall call in some of these as witnesses.

This book is Limborch's "History of the Inquisition." It tells the story of its origin seven hundred years ago, and of its establishment and progress in France, Spain, Italy, Portugal, Poland, Sicily, Sardinia, Germany, Holland, and other parts of the world; it describes its ministers and methods, its vicars, assistants, notaries, judges, and other officials; it describes the power of the inquisitors, and their manner of proceeding. It unveils their dread tribunal; opens their blood-stained records; describes their dungeons, the secret tortures they inflicted, the extreme, merciless, unmitigated tortures, and also the public so called "acts of faith," or burning of heretics. What a record! What a world of tyranny and intolerable anguish compressed into that one word<e>the Inquisition! Tyranny over the conscience! Men in the name of Jesus Christ stretching and straining, maiming and mangling their fellow men, to compel them to call light darkness, and darkness light; to call the Gospel of Christ a lie, and the lie of Satan truth; to confess that wrong is right, and acknowledge right is wrong; to bow down to man and worship him as God; to call the teachings of Christ heresy, and the teachings of antichrist Diviner Tremendous was the power of that dread tribunal. In Spain and Portugal it completely crashed the Reformation. No secrets could be withheld from the inquisitors; hundreds of persons were often apprehended in one day, and in consequence of information resulting from their examinations under torture, thousands more were apprehended. Prisons, convents, even private houses, were crowded with victims; the cells of the inquisition were filled and emptied again and again; its torture chamber was a hell. The most excruciating engines were employed to dislocate the limbs of even tender women. Thousands were burned at the stake. The gospel was gagged and crashed, and Christ Himself in the persons of His members subjected to the anguish of a second Golgotha.

Let us look into the chamber of horrors in the Spanish Inquisition. "The place of torture," says a Spanish historian, quoted by Limborch, p. 217, "the place of torture in the Spanish Inquisition is generally an underground and very dark room, to which one enters through several doors. There is a tribunal erected in it in which the inquisitor, inspector, and secretary sit. When the candles are lighted, and the person to be tortured brought in, the executioner, who is waiting for him, makes an astonishing and dreadful appearance. He is covered all over with a black linen garment down to his feet, and tied close to his body. His head and face are all concealed with a long black cowl, only two little holes being left in it for him to see through. All this is intended to strike the miserable wretch with greater terror in mind and body, when he sees himself going to be tortured by the hands of one who thus looks like the very devil."

The degrees of torture are described by Julius Clams and other writers quoted by Limborch. They were various, and included the following:

1. The being threatened to be tortured.
2. Being carried to the place of torture.
3. The stripping and binding.
4. The being hoisted up on the rack.
5. What they called "squassation."

This was the torture of the pulley. Besides this there was the torture of the fire, or chafing- dish full of burning charcoal applied to the soles of the feet. Then there was the torture of the rack, and of another instrument called by the Spaniards "escalero"; then that of pouring water into a bag of linen stuffed down the throat; and that of iron dice being forced into the feet by screws; and of canes placed crosswise between the fingers, and so compressed as to produce intolerable pain; then the torture of cords drawn tightly round various parts of the body, cutting through the flesh; and of the machine in which the sufferer was fixed head downwards; and, lastly, the torture of red-hot irons applied to the breasts and sides till they burned to the bone.

Here, on p. 219, is the account of the stripping of victims, men and women, preparatory to torture; the stripping from them of every vestige of clothing by these holy inquisitors, and how they put on them short linen drawers, leaving all the rest of the body naked for the free action of the tormentors. Here, on page 221, is the account by Isaac Orobio of what he suffered when in their hands. It was towards evening, he says, when he was brought to the place of torture in the Inquisition. It was a large, underground room, arched, and the walls covered with black hangings. The candlesticks were fastened to the wall, and the whole room enlightened with candles placed in them. At the end of it there was an enclosed place like a closet, where the inquisitor and notary sat at a table; so that the place seemed to him as the very mansion of death, everything appearing so terrible and awful. Then the inquisitor admonished him to confess the truth before his torments began. When he answered that he had told the truth, the inquisitor gravely protested that since he was so obstinate as to suffer the torture, the holy office would be innocent (what exquisite hypocrisy) if he should even expire in his torments. When he had said this, they put a linen garment over his body, and drew it so very close on each side as almost squeezed him to death.

When he was almost dying, they slackened all at once the sides of the garment, and, after he began to breathe again, the sudden alteration put him to the most grievous anguish and pain. When he had overcome this torture, the same admonition was repeated, that he would confess the truth in order to prevent further torment. As he persisted in his denial, they tied his thumbs so very tight with small cords as made the extremities of them greatly swell, and caused the blood to spurt out from under his nails. After this he was placed with his back against a wall and fixed upon a bench; into the wall were fastened iron pulleys, through which there were ropes drawn and tied round his arms and legs in several places. The executioner, drawing these ropes with great violence, fastened his body with them to the wall, his arms and legs, and especially his fingers and toes, being bound so tightly as to put him to the most exquisite pain, so that it seemed to him just as though he was dissolving in flames. After this a new kind of torture succeeded. There was an instrument like a small ladder, made of two upright pieces of wood and five cross ones sharpened in front. This the torturer placed over against him, and by a single motion struck it with great violence against both his shins, so that he received upon each of them at once five violent strokes, which put him to such intolerable anguish that he fainted away. After this he came to himself, and they inflicted on him a further torture. The torturer tied ropes about Orobio's wrists, and then put these ropes about his own back, which was covered with leather to prevent his hurting himself; then falling backwards he drew the ropes with all his might till they cut through Orobio's flesh, even to the very bones. And this torture was repeated twice, the ropes being tied about his arms at the distance of two fingers' breadth from the former wound, and drawn with the same violence. On this the physician and surgeon were sent for out of the neighboring apartment to ask whether the torture could be continued without danger of death. As there was a prospect of his living through it, the torture was then repeated, after which he was bound up in his own clothes and carried back to his prison. Here, opposite to this recital, is a picture representing these various tortures. After prolonged imprisonment, Orobio was released and banished from the kingdom of Seville.

Before we let fall the curtain upon this awful subject, let us listen for a moment to some of the words of William Lithgow, a Scotsman, who suffered the tortures of the Inquisition in the time of James I. After telling of the diabolical treatment he received, which was very similar to that I have just described, he says, "Now mine eyes did begin to startle, my mouth to foam and froth, and my teeth to chatter like the dobbling of drumsticks. Oh, strange, inhuman, monster man-manglers!

And notwithstanding of my shivering lips in this fiery passion, my vehement groaning, and blood springing from my arms, my broken sinews, yea, and my depending weight on flesh-cutting cords, yet they struck me on the face with cudgels to abate and cease the thundering noise of my wrestling voice. At last, being released from these pinnacles of pain, I was handfast set on the floor with this their ceaseless imploration: 'Confess, confess, confess in time, or thine inevitable torments ensue.' Where, finding nothing from me but still innocent, ù Oh! I am innocent. O Jesus, the Lamb of God, have mercy on me, and strengthen me with patience to undergo this barbarous murder ù '"

Enough! Here let the curtain drop. I should sicken you were I to pursue the subject further; it is too horrible, too damnable.

Here in this paper I have some of the ashes of the martyrs, some of their burned bones. I have bits of rusted iron and melted lead which I took myself with these hands from the Quemadero in Madrid, the place where they burned the martyrs, not far from the Inquisition. It was in the year 1870 that I visited it, just before the great ecumenical council was held at Rome, by which the pope was proclaimed infallible. I was in Spain that spring, and visited the newly opened Quemadero. I saw the ashes of the martyrs. I carried away with me some relics from that spot, which are now lying upon this table.

Hear me, though in truth I scarcely know how to speak upon this subject. I am almost dumb with horror when I think of it. I have visited the places in Spain, in France, in Italy most deeply stained and dyed with martyr-blood. I have visited the valleys of Piedmont. I have stood in the shadow of the great cathedral of Seville, on the spot where they burned the martyrs, or tore them limb from limb. I have stood breast-deep in the ashes of the martyrs of Madrid. I have read the story of Rome's deeds. I have waded through many volumes of history and of martyrology. I have visited, either in travel or in thought, scenes too numerous for me to name, where the saints of God have been slaughtered by Papal Rome, that great butcher of bodies and of souls. I cannot tell you what I have seen, what I have read, what I have thought. I cannot tell you what I feel. Oh, it is a bloody tale! I have stood in that valley of Lucerna where dwelt the faithful Waldenses, those ancient Protestants who held to the pure gospel all through the dark ages, that lovely valley with its pine-clad slopes which Rome converted into a slaughter-house. Oh, horrible massacres of gentle, unoffending, noble-minded men! Oh, horrible massacres of tender women and helpless children! Yes, ye hated them, ye hunted them, ye stuck them on spits, ye impaled them, ye hanged them, ye roasted them, ye flayed them, ye cut them in pieces, ye violated them, ye violated the women, ye violated the children, ye forced flints into them, and stakes, and stuffed them with gunpowder, and blew them up, and tore them asunder limb from limb, and tossed them over precipices, and dashed them against the rocks; ye cut them up alive, ye dismembered them; ye racked, mutilated, burned, tortured, mangled, massacred holy men, sainted women, mothers, daughters, tender children, harmless babes, hundreds, thousands, thousands upon thousands; ye sacrificed them in heaps, in hecatombs, turning all Spain, Italy, France, Europe, Christian Europe, into a slaughter-house, a charnel house, an Akeldama. Oh, horrible; too horrible to think of! The sight dims, the heart sickens, the soul is stunned in the presence of the awful spectacle. O harlot, gilded harlot, with brazen brow and brazen heart! red are thy garments, red thine hands. Thy name is written in this book. God has written it. The world has read it. Thou art a murderess, O Rome. Thou art the murderess Babylon ù "Babylon the Great," drunken, foully drunken; yea, drunken with the sacred blood which thou hast shed in streams and torrents, the blood of saints, the blood of the martyrs of Jesus. Were there naught else by which to recognize thee, O persecuting Church of Rome, this dreadful mark would identify thee. This is thy brand; by this we know thee. Thou art that foretold Babylon. We know thee by thy place. We know thee by thy proud assumptions, by the throne on which thou sittest, by those seven hills, by the beast thou ridest, by the garments thou wearest, by the cup thou bearest, by the name blazoned on thy forehead, by thy kingly paramours; by thy shameless looks, by thy polluted deeds; but oh, chiefly by this, by thy prolonged and dreadful persecution of the saints, by those massacres, by that Inquisition, by the fires of that burning stake. Mark how its ruddy flames ascend; see how its accusing smoke goes up to heaven!

In this sacred prophecy behold thy picture, read thy name; read, ay, read thy written doom. The French revolution broke upon thee; it was a stage in thy judgment, and no more. The beast who carried thee for centuries in abject submission turned against thee, cast thee off, stripped thy garments from thee, rent thee with its horns. It was foretold it would be so. It is fulfilled, but that fulfillment is not the end. It is but the beginning of the end. Tremble, for thy doom is written from of old. The hand upon the wall has written it; the finger of Almighty God has engraved it. Dreadful have been thy sins; dreadful shall be thy punishment. Thou hast burned alive myriads of the members of Christ, thou hast burned them to cinders and to ashes: thy doom is to be burned; thy doom is the appalling flame whose smoke ascends for ever.

I have done. Prophecy has spoken; history has fulfilled its utterance. Rome pagan ran its course; Rome Papal took its place. "Babylon the Great" has risen, has reigned, has fallen; her end is nigh. "Come out of her, My people," come out of her before the final judgment act in the great drama of the apostasy. "Come out of her," saith your God, "that ye be not partakers of her sins, and that ye receive not of her plagues."

FOR AS A MILLSTONE CAST BY A MIGHTY ANGEL INTO THE SOUNDING DEEP, SHE SHALL WITH VIOLENCE BE THROWN DOWN, AND SHALL BE FOUND NO MORE FOR EVER.

## Note

1.  *Hallam: History of the Middle Ages, Fourth Edit., p. 368.*

# Lecture Five - Interpretation and Use of These Prophecies in Pre-Reformation Times

ROMANISM foretold. Such has been our subject in the four previous lectures the Scripture prophecy, and the Papal history. That a deep and widespread apostasy has taken place in the Christian Church; that this apostasy has produced paganized forms of Christianity, the chief of which is that of the Romish Church; that the apostasy of the Romish Church has culminated in the Papacy; that the Papacy has lasted through long centuries, and lords it still over half Christendom; that it has persecuted the faithful unto blood, striving for the destruction of the gospel of God as if it were deadly heresy, and for the extermination of the saints of God as of accursed heretics; that it would have been completely triumphant still but for the glorious Reformation, which burst its bonds, emancipated the enslaved consciences of millions, and created a new departure in the convictions and actions of the world ù such are the facts with which history presents us. They are broad, unquestionable facts, which are so notorious as to be beyond all controversy, so long lasting as to fulfill the records of a thousand years.

And that this great apostasy was foretold; that it was foretold ages before its accomplishment by Old Testament prophets and New Testament apostles; that Daniel dwelling in Babylon foretold it, and John, the exile in Patmos, and Paul, the Apostle to the Gentiles; that these men, surrounded as they were by ancient heathenism, and knowing nothing by the evidence of their senses or by observation of the complete corruption of Christianity which has since darkened the world, as a long and awful eclipse of the Sun of righteousness ù that these men, prophets and apostles, living in antecedent times, should have predicted the extraordinary events which have come to pass, and should have painted them in vivid colors on the venerable pages of the writings they have left us; and that those predictions have for eighteen centuries confronted apostate Christendom with their accusations, and reflected as in a faithful mirror the entire history of its ways: this is the profound prophetic truth we have endeavored to elucidate.

We have now to study THE INTERPRETATION AND USE of these marvelous prophecies by the Christian Church. How has the Christian Church understood and employed them? Of what practical benefit have these prophecies been to her during the last eighteen centuries? It is evident that they were written for her guidance, protection, and sanctification. The prophecies of Paul and John are addressed to Christian Churches. The voice of inspiration expressly invites the whole Church to study them, and the Church has obeyed this command. She has read, marked, learned, and inwardly digested the "sure word of prophecy."

What moral effect has it had upon her? To what extent has it guided her footsteps and sustained her hopes? If these prophecies have proved to be a mighty power in her history; if they have preserved the faith of the Church in times of general apostasy; if they have given birth to great reformation movements; if they have inspired confessors, and supported martyrs at the stake; if they have broken the chains of priestcraft, superstition, and tyranny, and produced at last a return on the part of many millions of men to a pure, primitive Christianity ù they have answered their purpose, and justified their position in the sacred Scriptures of truth. Nor may we lightly esteem that interpretation which has produced such results. Had the prophecies been misinterpreted, applied otherwise than according to the mind of the spirit, we cannot believe that they would have been thus productive of blessed consequences. The fact that, understood and applied as they were by the reformers, they have produced spiritual and eternal good to myriads of mankind is a proof that they were rightly applied, for "by their fruits ye shall know them" is true, not only of teachers, but of their teachings. Protestantism, with all its untold blessings, is the fruit of the historic system of interpretation.

On the other hand, all that leads us to expect that the sufferers under antichristian tyranny would correctly interpret the prophetic word written for their guidance and support prompts also the expectation that their persecutors would as surely wrongly interpret it. As apostate Jews wrongly interpreted the prophecies of the Old Testament, so we should expect apostate Christians wrongly to interpret those of the New. In our study of the last eighteen centuries of interpretation we shall not expect to find the true interpretation therefore among the apostates, but among the faithful; not among the persecutors, but among the persecuted; not among those who have waged war against the gospel of Christ, but among those who have confessed its pure teachings, and sealed that confession with their blood.

We shall not be surprised to find antagonistic schools of prophetic interpretation, but, on the contrary, we shall expect such; and we shall expect the apostates and persecutors to belong to one school, and the faithful confessors and martyrs to another. If an officer of justice arrest a man because he perceives that he answers exactly to a description of a notorious criminal published by the Government as a help to his identification, is it likely that the man himself will admit that the description fits him? He will of course deny the correspondence, but his denial will carry no weight. On turning to the history of prophetic interpretation this is precisely what we find. With many varieties as to detail we find there have existed, and still exist, two great opposite schools of interpretation, the Papal and the Protestant, or the futurist and the historical. The latter regards the prophecies of Daniel, Paul, and John as fully and faithfully setting forth the entire course of Christian history; the former as dealing chiefly with a future fragment of time at its close.

The former, or futurist, system of interpreting the prophecies is now held, strange to say, by many Protestants, but it was first invented by the Jesuit Ribera, at the end of the sixteenth century, to relieve the Papacy from the terrible stigma cast upon it by the Protestant interpretation. This interpretation was so evidently the true and intended one, that the adherents of the Papacy felt its edge must, at any cost, be turned or blunted. If the Papacy were the predicted antichrist, as Protestants asserted, there was an end of the question, and separation from it became an imperative duty.

There were only two alternatives. If the antichrist were not a present power, he must be either a past or a future one. Some writers asserted that the predictions pointed back to Nero. This did not take into account the obvious fact that the antichristian power predicted was to succeed the fall of the Caesars, and develop among the Gothic nations. The other alternative became therefore the popular one with Papists. Antichrist was future, so Ribera and Bossuet and others taught. An individual man was intended, not a dynasty, the duration of his power would not be for twelve and a half centuries, but only three and a half years; he would be an open foe to Christ, not a false friend; he would be a Jew, and sit in the Jewish temple.

Speculation about the future took the place of study of the past and present, and careful comparison of the facts of history with the predictions of prophecy. This related, so it was asserted, not to the main course of the history of the Church, but only to the few closing years of her history. The Papal head of the Church of Rome was not the power delineated by Daniel and St. John. Accurately as it answered to the description, it was not the criminal indicated. It must be allowed to go free, and the detective must look out for another man, who was sure to turn up by and by. The historic interpretation was of course rejected with intense and bitter scorn by the Church it denounced as Babylon and the power it branded as antichrist, and it is still opposed by all who in any way uphold them.

It is held by many that the historic school of interpretation is represented only by a small modern section of the Church. We shall show that it has existed from the beginning, and includes the larger part of the greatest and best teachers of the Church for 1800 years. We shall show that the Fathers of the Church belonged to it, that the confessors, reformers, and martyrs belonged to it. and that it has included a vast multitude of erudite expositors of later times. We shall show that all these have held to the central truth that prophecy faithfully mirrors the Church's history as a whole, and not merely a commencing or closing fragment of that history.

It is held by many that the futurist school of interpretation is represented chiefly by certain Protestant commentators and teachers, who deny that the prophecy of the "man of sin" relates to the Pope of Rome.

We shall show that the futurist school of interpretation, on the contrary, is chiefly represented by teachers belonging to the Church of Rome; that the popes, cardinals, bishops, and priests of that apostate Church are all futurists, and that the futurist interpretation is one of the chief pillars of Romanism.

Two interpretations of prophecy are before us, the historic and the futurist.

The historical school of interpretation regards these prophecies as reflecting the history of the fourth or Roman empire, in all its most important aspects, from first to last, including especially the dark apostasy which has long prevailed in Christendom, the testimony and sufferings of God's faithful people amid this apostasy, and the ultimate triumph of their cause.

On the other hand, the futurist school of interpretation regards these prophecies as dealing almost exclusively with the distant future of the consummation; regards them as dealing chiefly, not with what has been for the last eighteen hundred years, but with what will be in some final spasm at the close. The war against the saints waged by the Roman "little horn" of the prophecies of Daniel, the proud usurpations of the "man of sin," and his antagonism to the cause of true religion, foretold by Paul, the blasphemous pretensions and persecuting deeds of the revived head of the Roman empire set forth in the prophecies of John all these are regarded by this futurist school as relating to a brief future period, immediately preceding the second advent. The futurist school denies the application of these important practical prophecies to the conflicts of the Church during the last eighteen centuries. It robs the Church of their practical guidance all through that period. This is the position taken by the Church of Rome, this is the position taken by the popes, cardinals, archbishops, bishops, and other great teachers of that apostate Church. This is the prophetic interpretation they have embodied in a thousand forms, and insisted upon with dogmatic authority. This has been the interpretation of proud Papal usurpers, of cruel persecutors, of merciless tyrants, of the Romanist enemies of the gospel and of the saints and servants of God.

We shall find, on the other hand, as we study the subject, that the historic interpretation of prophecy, the interpretation which condemns Rome, and which Rome consequently condemns, grew up gradually with the progress of events and the development of the apostasy of Latin Christianity; that it slowly modified its details under the illuminating influence of actual facts, but that it retained its principles unaltered from age to age; that it was defended by a multitude of earnest students and faithful expositors; and that it shaped the history of heroic struggles and of glorious revivals of spiritual life and testimony.

This is the interpretation whose history during fifteen centuries we propose to review this evening.

We shall divide these fifteen centuries into three periods:

I.      The period extending from apostolic times to the fall of the Roman empire in the fifth century.

II.     The period extending from the fall of the Roman empire and rise of the Papacy in the fifth century to its exaltation under the pontificate of Gregory VII (or Hildebrand), the founder of the Papal theocracy in the eleventh century.

III.    The period from Gregory VII to the Reformation.

First, then, let us glance at the history of prophetic interpretation in the interval extending from apostolic times to the fall of the Roman empire in the fifth century. This was the period of the so-called Fathers of the Christian Church. A multitude of their writings remain to us, containing, not only almost countless references to the prophecies in question, but complete commentaries on Daniel and the Apocalypse. It is boldly claimed by many that the Fathers of the first five centuries held the futurist interpretation of these books. We deny the correctness of this position, and assert that the Fathers of the first five centuries belonged to the historical school of interpretation. It was impossible for them, owing to the early position which they occupied, rightly to anticipate the manner and scale of the fulfillment of these wondrous prophecies; but as far as their circumstances permitted they correctly grasped their general significance, and adhered to that interpretation which regards prophecy as foretelling the whole course of the Church's warfare from the first century to the Second Advent.

It is impossible at this time to do more than present a brief summary of the view of the Fathers on this subject, and to name and refer you to their works.

**1.** The Fathers interpreted the four wild beasts of prophecy as representing the four empires, Babylon, Persia, Greece, and Rome. Here we have the foundation of the historical interpretation of prophecy. Take as an instance the words of Hippolytus on the great image and four wild beasts of Daniel: "The golden head of the image," he says, "is identical with the lioness, by which the Babylonians were represented; the shoulders and the arms of silver are the same with the bear, by which the Persians and Medes are meant; the belly and thighs of brass are the leopard, by which the Greeks who ruled from Alexander onwards are intended; the legs of iron are the dreadful and terrible beast, by which the Romans who hold the empire now are meant; the toes of clay and iron are the ten horns which are to be; the one other little horn springing up in their midst is the antichrist; the stone that smites the image and breaks it in pieces, and that filled the whole earth, is Christ, who comes from heaven and brings judgment on the world."1 This statement is remarkable for its clearness, correctness, and condensation, and expresses the view held still by the historic school.

Hippolytus says, in the treatise on "Christ and Antichrist": "Rejoice, blessed Daniel, thou hast not been in error; all these things have come to pass" (p. 19). "Already the iron rules; already it subdues and breaks all in pieces; already it brings all the unwilling into subjection; already we see these things ourselves. Now we glorify God, being instructed by thee." (p. 20).

**2.** The Fathers held that the ten-horned beasts of Daniel and John are the same. As an instance, Irenaeus, in his book "Against Heresies," chapter 26, says: "John, in the Apocalypse,..teaches us what the ten horns shall be which were seen by Daniel."

**3.** The Fathers held the historic interpretation of the Apocalypse. As Elliott says, none of the Fathers "entertained the idea of the apocalyptic prophecy overleaping the chronological interval, were it less or greater, antecedent to the consummation, and plunging at once into the times of the consummation."2 Here, for example, is the commentary of Victorinus on the Apocalypse of John, written towards the end of the third century. This is the earliest commentary extant on the Apocalypse as a whole. In this, the going forth of the white horse under the first seal, is interpreted as the victories of the gospel in the first century. This view, you will observe, involves the historical interpretation of the entire book of Revelation. Victorinus interprets the woman clothed with the sun, having the moon under her feet, and wearing a crown of twelve stars on her head, and travailing in her pains, as "the ancient Church of fathers, prophets, saints, and apostles"; in other words, the Judaeo-Christian body of saints. He could not, of course, point to fulfillments which were at his early date still future, but he recognizes the principle.

**4.** The Fathers held that the little horn of Daniel, the man of sin foretold by Paul, and the revived head of the Roman empire predicted by John, represent one and the same power; and they held that power to be the antichrist. For example, Origen, in his famous book, "Against Celsus," thus expresses himself (bk. 6., chapter 46.). After quoting nearly the whole of Paul's prophecy about the man of sin in 2 Thessalonians, which he interprets of the antichrist, he says: "Since Celsus rejects the statements concerning antichrist, as it is termed, having neither read what is said of him in the book of Daniel, nor in the writings of Paul, nor what the Savior in the gospels has predicted about his coming, we must make a few remarks on this subject..Paul speaks of him who is called antichrist, describing, though with a certain reserve, both the manner and time and cause of his coming..The prophecy also regarding antichrist is stated in the book of Daniel, and is fitted to make an intelligent and candid reader admire the words as truly divine and prophetic; for in them are mentioned the things relating to the coming kingdom, beginning with the times of Daniel, and continuing to the destruction of the world."

Jerome, in his commentary on the book of Daniel (chapter 7), says, with reference to the little horn which has a mouth speaking great things, that "it is the man of sin, the son of perdition, who dares to sit in the temple of God, making himself as God."3

**5.** The Fathers held that the Roman empire was the "let," or hindrance, referred to by Paul in 2 Thessalonians, which kept back the manifestation of the "man of sin." This point is of great importance. Paul distinctly tells us that he knew, and that the Thessalonians knew, what that hindrance was, and that it was then in existence. The early Church, through the writings of the Fathers, tells us what it knew upon the subject, and with remarkable unanimity affirms that this "let," or hindrance, was the Roman empire as governed by the Caesars; that while the Caesars held imperial power, it was impossible for the predicted antichrist to arise, and that on the fall of the Caesars he would arise. Here we have a point on which Paul affirms the existence of knowledge in the Christian Church. The early Church knew, he says, what this hindrance was. The early Church tells us what it did know upon the subject, and no one in these days can be in a position to contradict its testimony as to what Paul had, by word of mouth only, told the Thessalonians. It is a point on which ancient tradition alone can have any authority. Modern speculation is positively impertinent on such a subject.4

What then was the view of the early Church? Look at the words of Tertullian. Quoting Thessalonians, he says: "Now ye know what detaineth that he might be revealed in his time, for the mystery of iniquity doth already work; only he who now hinders must hinder until he be taken out of the way. What obstacle is there but the Roman state; the falling away of which, by being scattered into ten kingdoms, shall introduce antichrist..that the beast antichrist, with his false prophet, may wage war on the Church of God?"5

In his magnificent "Apology," addressed to the rulers of the Roman empire, Tertullian says that the Christian Church ù not himself, mark, but the Christian Church prayed for the emperors, and for the stability of the empire of Rome, because they knew "that a mighty shock impending over the whole earth ù in fact, the very end of all things, threatening dreadful woes ù was ONLY RETARDED by the continued existence of the Roman empire. " 6

Read the words of Chrysostom in his "Commentary on 2 Thessalonians": "One may first naturally inquire what is that which withholdeth, and after that would know why Paul expresses this so obscurely. . 'he who now letteth will let, until he be taken out of the way.' That is, when the Roman empire is taken out of the way, then he shall come; and naturally, for as long as the fear of this empire lasts, no one will readily exalt himself; but when that is dissolved, he will attack the anarchy, and endeavor to seize upon the government both of men and of God. For as the kingdoms before this were destroyed, that of the Medes by the Babylonians, that of the Babylonians by the Persians, that of the Persians by the Macedonians, that of the Macedonians by the Romans, so will this be by antichrist, and he by Christ."

Then, accounting for Paul's reserve in alluding to this point he adds: "Because he says this of the Roman empire, he naturally only glanced at it and spoke covertly, for he did not wish to bring upon himself superfluous enmities and useless dangers. For if he had said that, after a little while, the Roman empire would be dissolved, they would now immediately have even overwhelmed him as a pestilent person, and all the faithful as living and warring to this end." 7

From Irenaeus, who lived close to apostolic times, down to Chrysostom and Jerome, the Fathers taught that the power withholding the manifestation of the "man of sin" was the Roman empire as governed by the Caesars. The Fathers therefore belong to the historic, and not to the futurist school of interpretation; for futurists imagine that the hindrance to the manifestation of the man of sin is still in existence, though the Caesars have long since passed away.

6. The Fathers held that the fall of the Roman empire was imminent, and therefore the manifestation of antichrist close at hand Justin Martyr, for example, one of the earliest of the Fathers, in his "Dialogue with Trypho," chapter 22, says: "He whom Daniel foretells would have dominion for 'time and times and a half ' is already even at the door, about to speak his blasphemous and daring things against the Most High."

Cyprian, in his "Exhortation to Martyrdom," says: "Since..the hateful time of antichrist is already beginning to draw near, I would collect from the sacred Scriptures some exhortations for preparing and strengthening the minds of the brethren, whereby I might animate the soldiers of Christ for the heavenly and spiritual contest." 8

7. The Fathers held that the "man of sin" or antichrist, would be a ruler or head of the Roman empire. A striking illustration of this is the interpretation by Irenaeus and Hippolytus of the mysterious number 666, the number of the revived beast, or antichrist. Irenaeus gives as its interpretation the word Latinos. He says: "Latinos is the number 666, and it is a very probable (solution), this being the name of the last kingdom, for the LATINS are they who at present bear rule. " 9

Hippolytus gives the same solution in his treatise on "Christ and Antichrist."

8. The Fathers held that the Babylon of the Apocalypse means Rome. On this point they were all agreed and their unanimity is an important seal on the correctness of this interpretation. Tertullian, for example, in his answer to the Jews, says:

"Babylon, in our own John, is a figure of the city Rome, as being equally great and proud of her sway, and triumphant over the saints" (chapter 9.). Victorinus, who wrote the earliest commentary on the Apocalypse extant, says, on Revelation 17: "The seven heads are the seven hills on which the woman sitteth ù that is, the city of Rome."

Hippolytus says: "Tell me, blessed John, apostle and disciple of the Lord, what didst thou see and hear concerning Babylon? Arise and speak, for it sent thee also into banishment."10 You notice here the view that Rome which banished the Apostle John is the Babylon of the Apocalypse.

Augustine says, "Rome, the second Babylon, and the daughter of the first, to which it pleased God to subject the whole world, and bring it all under one sovereignty, was now founded."11 In chapter 28, he calls Rome "the western Babylon." In chapter 41 he says: "It has not been in vain that this city has received the mysterious name of Babylon; for Babylon is interpreted confusion, as we have said elsewhere."

It is clear from these quotations that the Fathers did not interpret the Babylon of the Apocalypse as meaning either the literal Babylon on the Euphrates, or some great city in France or England, but as meaning Rome. And this is still the interpretation of the historic school, though for the last 800 years events have proved Babylon to represent Rome, not in its pagan, but in its Papal form.

It should be noted that none of the Fathers held the futurist gap theory, the theory that the book of Revelation overleaps nearly eighteen centuries of Christian history, plunging at once into the distant future, and devoting itself entirely to predicting the events of the last few years of this dispensation. As to the subject of antichrist, there was a universal agreement among them concerning the general idea of the prophecy, while there were differences as to details, these differences arising chiefly from the notion that the antichrist would be in some way Jewish as well as Roman. It is true they thought that the antichrist would be an individual man. Their early position sufficiently accounts for this. They had no conception and could have no conception of the true nature and length of the tremendous apostasy which was to set in upon the Christian Church. They were not prophets, and could not foresee that the Church was to remain nineteen centuries in the wilderness, and to pass through prolonged and bitter persecution under a succession of nominally Christian but apostate rulers, filling the place of the ancient Caesars and emulating their antichristian deeds. Had they known these things, we may well believe their views would have completely harmonized with those of historic interpreters of later times. The Fathers went as far as they could go in the direction in which historical interpreters of these last days have traveled. Further, much that was dark to them in prophecy has become clear to their successors in the light of its accomplishment. Divine providence has thrown light, as it could not fail to do, on Divine prediction.

**II.** We come now, in the second place, very briefly to review the history of prophetic interpretation in the interval extending between the fall of the western empire of Rome and the development of the Papal theocracy in the eleventh century, under Gregory VII. The interpreters of this period belonged, like the Fathers, to the historic school. They interpreted the Apocalypse as a prophecy of the whole course of events from the first advent to the consummation.

The following authors living in this interval wrote commentaries on the entire Apocalypse: Primasius, the Venerable Bede, Anspert, Haymo, Andreas, Arethras, and Berengaud.

Primasius, who lived in the middle of the sixth century, interpreted the "hundred and forty-four thousand" sealed persons in the Apocalypse as the Christian Church. He held that antichrist would substitute himself for Christ and blasphemously assume His dignity, and that the seven-hilled city was Rome.

The Venerable Bede, who lived in the north of England at the close of the seventh century, was an historical interpreter of the Apocalypse. Here is a copy of his commentary. He takes the first seal to represent the triumphs of the primitive Church. He expounds the lamb-like beast of Revelation 13 as a pseudo-Christian false prophet.

Ambrose Anspert wrote a copious commentary on the Apocalypse in the middle of the eighth century. He expounds the second beast of Revelation 13 as meaning the preachers and ministers of antichrist, and teaches that antichrist will be "pro Christo," or in Christ's place. It is a remarkable fact that he expounds the grievous "sore," or ulcer, poured out under the first vial, as meaning infidelity. This is the general view at the present day among historical interpreters. They consider the infidelity of the French Revolution to be the fulfillment of this vial.

Haymo's commentary, written in the ninth century, is for the most part abridged from Anspert. Andreas, who was Bishop of Caesarea, states definitely that the Apocalypse was a prophecy of the things to happen from Christ's first coming to the consummation. He interprets the "hundred and forty-four thousand" as meaning true Christians, and antichrist to be a Roman king and "pseudo- Christ," or false Christ.

Arethras, who wrote in the ninth century, mainly follows Andreas.

Berengaud's commentary on the Apocalypse, written in the same century, is the least satisfactory of all. He was a Benedictine monk, and lived at a very dark period. His notion was that antichrist would be an avowed infidel and an open advocate of licentiousness. He was, as far as is known, the first interpreter to propound this view.

The interval during which these interpreters lived was marked by the steady rise, but not by the full manifestation of the Papacy. Two notions contributed powerfully to prevent their recognizing in the imperfectly developed Papacy the predicted "man of sin." They imagined that as the eastern empire of Rome, seated at Constantinople, still continued, the "let" or hindrance to the manifestation of antichrist remained, completely overlooking the fact that the antichristian power foretold in prophecy is definitely linked with the seven hills of Rome, and thus with the fall of the western empire, and the apostasy of the Latin or western Church.

Then they spiritualized and explained away a great deal of prophecy, and supposed that they were living in the millennium, and that the antichrist would not be manifested till the brief outbreak of evil at its close. This false notion had fatal consequences. While these interpreters, in common with the generality of Christians at their period, were looking for the advent of the "man of sin" in the distant future, he stole unperceived into their midst, and usurped the place of Christ over His unwatchful flock.

Before we leave this mediaeval period, there are three remarkable testimonies to which we must just refer. Gregory the Great, in the sixth century, declared before

Christendom that whosoever called himself universal bishop or universal priest was the precursor of antichrist. In this he was doubtless perfectly correct. When Boniface III, shortly after the death of Gregory, took this title in the year 607, he became the precursor of antichrist, as fully revealed under Boniface VIII.

Gherbert of Rheims, before the year 1000, said of the pope sitting on his lofty throne in gold and purple, that if destitute of charity, he was antichrist sitting in the temple of God.

Lastly, Berenger, in the eleventh century, referring to the pope's enforcement at that time of the doctrine of transubstantiation, affirmed the Roman see to be not the apostolic seat, but the seat of Satan.

Thus gradually did an understanding of the true character of the Papacy dawn upon the Christian church of this period.

**III.** We will now, in the third and last place, briefly consider the history of prophetic interpretation from the time of Gregory VII, in the eleventh century, to the Reformation, in the sixteenth.

The pontificate of Gregory VII was the era of the Papacy unveiled. At this date the pope dropped the mask of the shepherd, and exchanged the crook for the scepter and the sword. The accession of Gregory VII, or Hildebrand, as he was called, created, as we have before stated, the Papal theocracy. Do you know what this means? He claimed for himself, in the name of God, absolute and unlimited dominion over all the states of Christendom, as successor of St. Peter, and vicar of Christ upon earth. The popes who came after him pushed these claims to their utmost extent. At the end of the thirteenth century they assumed the proud title of masters of the world. Three names stand out conspicuously in the three middle centuries of this dark period, Gregory VII, Innocent III, and Boniface VIII. The historian of the middle ages well says, "As Gregory VII appears the most usurping of mankind till we read the history of Innocent III, so Innocent III is thrown into the shade by the supreme audacity of Boniface VIII."12 In those days lived the great Italian poet, Dante. He described his age with extraordinary power. Writing in the thirteenth century, and in Italy, he painted the Papacy as the world beheld it then. And what did the world see then? It saw in the Papacy the usurping "man of sin"; and in the Church of Rome the Babylon of the Apocalypse. Mark, even the world saw it. Hear a few lines from Dante's immortal poem on Hell, Purgatory, and Paradise:

"Woe to thee, Simon Magus! woe to you His wretched followers, who the things of God Which should be wedded unto goodness, them, Rapacious as ye are, do prostitute For gold and silver!"

"Your avarice O'ercasts the world with mourning, under foot Treading the good, and raising bad men up. Of shepherds like to you, the Evangelist Was ware, when her, who sits upon the waves, With kings in filthy whoredom he beheld, She who with seven heads towered at her birth, And from ten horns her proof of glory drew, Long as her spouse in virtue took delight. Of gold and silver ye have made

your god, Differing wherein from the idolater, But that he worships one, a hundred ye? Ah, Constantine, to how much ill gave birth, Not thy conversion, but that plenteous dower, Which the first wealthy Father gained from thee!" 13
In his poem on Paradise he says: "My place he who usurps on earth hath made A common sewer of puddle and of blood. No purpose was of ours that the keys Which were vouchsafed me should for ensigns serve Unto the banners that do levy war On the baptized: nor I for sigil mark Set upon sold and lying privileges, Which makes me oft to bicker and turn red. In shepherd's clothing greedy wolves below Range wide o'er all the pastures. Arm of God, Why longer sleepest thou?" In the end of his poem on Paradise, he refers to the Apostle John as ù "The seer That ere he died, saw all the grievous times Of the fair bride, who with the lance and nails Was won."

You will observe that these beautiful and touching words recognize the historical interpretation of the Apocalypse. The Apostle John, according to Dante, saw "all the grievous times" through which the Church was destined to pass.

And what Dante saw, the Albigenses saw, and the Waldenses. What wonder was there in this? Would not the wonder have been had the saints remained blind to a fulfillment of prophecy so plain and palpable that even the world recognized it? In the sunny south of France, in Provence and Catalonia, lived the Albigenses. They were a civilized and highly educated people. Among these people there sprang up an extensive revival of true religion, and one of its natural effects was a bold testimony against the abominations of apostate Rome. Here is Sismondi's History of the Albigenses. On page 7 he says of them and of the Vaudois: "All agreed in regarding the Church of Rome as having absolutely perverted Christianity, and in maintaining that it was she who was designated in the Apocalypse by the name of the whore of Babylon." Rome could not endure this testimony; she drew her deadly sword and waged war against those who bore it. In the year 1208 the Albigenses were murderously persecuted. Innocent III (what a mockery his name!) employed the crusaders in this dreadful work. The war of extermination was denominated sacred. The pope's soldiers prosecuted it with pious ardor; men, women, and children were all precipitated into the flames; whole cities were burned. In Beziers every soul was massacred; seven thousand dead bodies were counted in a single church, where the people had taken refuge; the whole country was laid waste; an entire people was slaughtered, and the eloquent witness of these early reformers was reduced to the silence of the sepulcher.

Thus began the tremendous war against the saints foretold in Daniel and the Apocalypse, and thenceforward it was murderously prosecuted from century to century. Early in the thirteenth century was founded the Inquisition, and full persecuting powers entrusted by the popes to the Dominicans.

A remnant of the Vaudois escaping from the south of France took refuge in the Alps, where the light of the Gospel had been preserved from the earliest times. I have visited the Waldensian valleys, and will try in a few words to bring them before you.

You doubtless remember the position of the city of Milan on the plain of Lombardy. From the top of the famous cathedral of Milan there is a magnificent view of the southern Alps. The plains of Lombardy and Piedmont extend to their base. The Alps are seen stretching to the east and west, as far as the eye can reach. There they stand in rugged, wild sublimity, their lower slopes mantled with dark forests, their summits crowned with glaciers and eternal snows.

To the west, among these, beyond the city of Turin, rises the vast white cone of Monte Viso. Among the mountains at its base lie the Waldensian valleys. They are five in numbers, and run up into narrow, elevated gorges, winding among fir-clad steeps, and climbing into the region of the clouds, which hover round the icy, alpine peaks. These valleys were the refuge of the "Israel of the Alps." Protestants long before the Reformation, these noble mountaineers resolutely refused to bow the knee to Baal; they were a faithful remnant of the early Church preserved all through the central ages of apostasy.

This folio volume is a faithful history of the Waldenses, written 217 years ago, by the Waldensian pastor Leger. It contains his portrait. I have often looked at it with interest. The countenance is scarred with suffering, but full of spiritual light. Leger tells with simple clearness the story of the Waldenses from the earliest times, quoting from ancient and authentic documents. He gives in full their confession of faith, and narrates the history of their martyrdoms, including the dreadful massacre in the vale of Lucerna, in 1655, of which he himself was an eye witness. This book was written only fourteen years after that massacre. It contains numerous depositions concerning it, rendered on oath, and long lists of the names of those who were its victims. It gives also plates depicting the dreadful ways in which they were slaughtered. These plates represent men, women, and children being dismembered, disemboweled, ripped up, run through with swords, impaled on stakes, torn limb from limb, flung from precipices, roasted in flames. They are almost too horrible to look at. And this was only one of a long series of massacres of the Waldenses extending through 600 painful years. Milton wrote of these Protestant sufferers his immortal sonnet:

"Avenge, O Lord, Thy slaughtered saints, whose bones Lie scattered on the Alpine mountains cold; Even them who kept Thy truth so pure of old, When all our fathers worshipped stocks and stones, Forget not: in Thy book record their groans Who were Thy sheep, and in their ancient fold Slain by the bloody Piedmontese, that rolled Mother with infant down the rocks. Their moans The vales redoubled to the hills, and they To heaven. Their martyred blood and ashes sow O'er all the Italian fields, where still doth sway The triple tyrant; that from these may grow A hundredfold, who, having learned Thy way, Early may fly the Babylonian woe."

The persecuted Waldenses were students of prophecy from the oldest times. How did they interpret the prophecies concerning "Babylon" and the "man of sin"? Here in this book of Leger's is their Treatise on Antichrist, written in the year 1120, or nearly 800 years ago. It is written in a language now extinct; Leger gives a French translation in parallel columns (here it is at p. 71). In simple, telling terms that treatise brands the Romish Church as the harlot Babylon, and the Papacy as the "man of sin" and antichrist. That was the faith and confession of the Waldenses. 14

Turn now for a few moments to Bohemia. You remember that it is an extensive province in the northwest of Austria. There a reformation sprang up more than a century before the time of Luther, and was quenched in seas of blood. What gave rise to it? The testimonies of John Huss and Jerome of Prague. What did these men hold as to the Church of Rome and the Papacy? That Rome is Babylon, and the Papacy the antichrist.15 Witness their testimony, quoted by Foxe the martyrologist. I have stood on the spot in Constance where these men were condemned to death. Rome burned them. Here is a history of "the Reformation and anti-reformation in Bohemia." The Bohemian brethren avowed the doctrines of John Huss, including his views on the anti-Papal prophecies. Rome exterminated the reformed Bohemians. The story is a dreadful one.16 But from their ashes rose new witnesses. From the persecuted Bohemians sprang the Moravians, who this day are missionaries throughout the world!

Turn lastly, for a moment, to England. Before the Reformation, 500 years ago, God raised up in this country John Wicliffe. Men called him "the morning star of the Reformation." He translated the Scriptures into the English tongue, and waged war against the errors and abominations of the Church of Rome. How did Wicliffe interpret these prophecies? Just as the Waldenses did. Here is one of his books filled with references to the pope as antichrist. He wrote a special treatise, entitled Speculum de Antichristo ("The Mirror of Antichrist"). From Wicliffe sprang the English Lollards. They numbered hundreds of thousands. What was their testimony? Let me give it to you in the words of one of them, Lord Cobham, that famous man of God, who lived just a century before Luther.

When brought before King Henry V and admonished to submit himself to the pope as an obedient child, this was his answer: "As touching the pope and his spirituality, I owe them neither suit nor service, forasmuch as I know him by the Scriptures to be the great antichrist, the son of perdition, the open adversary of God, and an abomination standing in the holy place."

Remaining firm in his rejection of Romish error and refusal to bow down to the Papacy, Lord Cobham was condemned to death as a heretic.

John Foxe tells us that on the day appointed for his death, in the year 1417, Lord Cobham was brought out of the Tower of London, "with his arms bound behind him, having a very cheerful countenance. Then he was laid upon a hurdle, and so drawn forth to St. Giles' Fields, where they had set up a new pair of gallows. As he was coming to the place of execution, and was taken from the hurdle, he fell down devoutly upon his knees, desiring Almighty God to forgive his enemies. Then stood he up and beheld the multitude, exhorting them in most godly manner to follow the laws of God written in the Scriptures, and in any wise to beware of such teachers as they see contrary to Christ in their conversation and living; with many other special counsels. Then he was hanged up there by the middle, in chains of iron, and so consumed alive in the fire, praising the name of God as long as his life lasted.

In other words, he was roasted to death. They were burned, burned, these blessed men of God! Huss was burned; Jerome was burned; Lord Cobham was burned. Even Wicliffe's bones were dug up, forty- one years after his death, and burned. Savonarola, who preached with trumpet tongue that Rome was Babylon, was burned. All these were burned before the Reformation, and thousands more. They were burned, but their words were not burned! Their testimony was not burned! It lived on! Fire could not scorch it; could not stifle it; swords could not slay it; naught could destroy it. Truth is immortal, truth is unconquerable. Imprison it, and it comes forth free; bury it, and it rises again; crush it to the earth, and it springs up victorious, purer for the conflict, nobler for the victory. The truth to which the confessors witnessed sprang up again a century later, and rolled over Europe the tremendous tide of the Reformation.

And whence came this testimony which no power could repress? Whence came this testimony, trumpet- tongued, that Rome, in all its myriad-handed might, was impotent to silence or arrest? Whence came it, but from that sacred volume, writ in gloomy prisons, in lands of captivity, in scenes of exile, for the guidance, the preservation, the support of God's suffering saints and faithful witnesses in every age! Daniel the captive, Paul the prisoner, John the exile ù such were its inspired authors; men whose piercing vision looked down the long vista of the Church's conflicts, marked her martyrdoms, and saw her triumphs from afar.

Oh, word of divinely given prophecy! Oh, wondrous volume, whose seven seals the Lamb has loosed and opened to meet the moral and spiritual needs of the suffering Church He loves so well! how have thy solemn utterances, thy mysterious symbols, been scanned and studied by earnest, saintly eyes! how hast thou been pondered in prisons, remembered on racks, repeated in the flames! Thy texts are windows through which the light shines from the third heaven down into the darkest depths of earth's conflicts, mysteries, and woes. Oh, sacred and sanctifying truth! how have thy words been watered with the tears of suffering saints, steeped in their griefs and sorrows, and dyed in the copious streaming of their blood! Precious are the lives which have sealed thee; precious the truth those lives have sealed! Thy words have been wings by which the persecuted Church has soared from the wilderness and the battlefield into the pure serene of everlasting love and peace! Like a bright angel, thou art heaven descended, and leadest to the skies. By thee has God guided to their glorious consummation the noble army of saints, confessors, martyrs, shining round His throne like the everlasting stars. They are gone into that worm of glory ù for ever gone; but the light which led them there remains behind! We cannot touch them; they have vanished from the sight of men like the prophet whose chariot to heaven was the winged flame! We cannot hear the music of their harpings, or the thunder of their song; but we still grasp the book they loved, which made them all they were, and all they are. Ye Waldenses, from the lonely, blood- stained Alps; ye nameless victims of the dreadful Inquisition; ye noble Protestants before the Reformation, Wicliffe, Huss, Jerome, Cobham, Savonarola ù we possess the holy pages which ye pondered, the words of truth and life ye sealed with martyr blood! Be those words to us what they were to you; let them be our inspiration and our testimony, afand the testimony of our children after us, till the hour when truth, emancipated from all trammels, shall shine through the world in its unclouded splendor, and error and superstition and falsehood from its presence shall for ever flee away!

## Notes

*1 Hippolytus: vol. 1., p. 447*
*2 Elliott: Hort, Apocalypticce, vol. 4., p. 299, 4th ed.*
*3 "Est enim homo peccati, filius perditionis, ita ut in templo Dei sedere audeat, faciens se quasi Deum." 4 As to the "let" or hindrance to the manifestation of the "man of sin" referred to in 2 Thessalonians 2, Mr. Elliott says: "We have the consenting testimony of the early Fathers, from Irenoeus, the disciple of the disciple of St. John, down to Chrysostom and Jerome, to the effect that it was understood to be the imperial power ruling and residing at Rome." ù Horae Apocalypticae, vol. 3., p. 92.*
*Irenaeus held that the division of the Roman empire into ten kingdoms would immediately precede the manifestation of antichrist. In his work, "Against Heresies," book 5, chapter 30, he says, "Let them await, in the first place, the division of the kingdom into ten; then, in the next place, when these kings are reigning, and beginning to set their affairs in order and advance their kingdom, (let them learn) to acknowledge that he who shall come claiming the kingdom for himself and shall terrify those sons of men of whom we have been speaking, having a name containing the aforesaid number (666), is truly the abomination of desolation." Thus, according to Irenaeus, the manifestation of antichrist required the previous overthrow of the then existing Roman empire.*
*"Tertullian's Apology" thus describes the habit of the Christian Church of the second century to pray for the security of the Roman empire, in the knowledge that its downfall would bring the catastrophe of the reign of antichrist and the ruin of the world. Addressing the "rulers of the Roman empire," he says: "We offer prayer for the safety of our princes to the eternal, the true, the living God, whose favor, beyond*

all others, they must themselves desire..Thither we lift our eyes, with hands outstretched, because free from sin; with head uncovered, for we have nothing whereof to be ashamed; finally, without a monitor, because it is from the heart we supplicate. And without ceasing for all our emperors we offer prayer. We pray for life prolonged; for security to the empire.. With our hands thus stretched out and up to God, rend us with your iron claws, hang us up on crosses, wrap us in flames, take our heads from us with the sword, let loose the wild beasts upon us ù the very attitude of a Christian praying is the preparation for all punishment. Let this, good rulers, be your work, wring from us the soul, beseeching God on the emperor's behalf. Upon the truth of God and devotion to His name put the brand of crime..There is also another and a greater necessity for our offering prayer in behalf of the emperors, nay, for the complete stability of the empire, and for Roman interests in general. For we know that a mighty shock impending over the whole earth ù in fact, the very end of all things, threatening dreadful woes ù is only retarded by the continued existence of the Roman empire. We have no desire then to be overtaken by these dire events; and in praying that their coming may be delayed, we are lending our aid to Rome's duration." - "Apology," Sections 30-32. (Est et alia maior necessitas nobis orandi pro imperatoribus, etiam pro omni statu imperii rebusque Romanis, qui vim maximam universo orbi imminentem ipsamque clausulam saeculi acerbitates horrendas comminantem Romani imperii commeatu scimus retardari." ù Tertullian: "Apologeticurn, " Section 32.)
Jerome writes to the same effect in his commentary on 2 Thessalonians 2: "He who now letteth, or hindreth." "Ut qui tenet nunc teneat, etc. Donec REGNUM QUOD NUNC TENET, de medeo auferatur, prius qua antichristus reveletur."
Monon o katecwm arti ewv ek mejsou genutai toutejstin h arch h Rwmai'kh otan arqh ejk mejsou, tote ejteinov hxei. . .Wsper gajr aij pro toutou katelqusan basileiai, oion h Madon hpo babulwniwn, h babulwniwn upo Perswn, h Perswn upo Makedonwn, h Makedonun upo Rwmaian J outw kaij auth uJpo tou Anticristou, kakeinov upo tou Cristou.  - Chrysostom:
"Homily on 2 Thessalonians 2:6-9."
5 Tertullian: "On the Resurrection," chaps, 24,25
6 Apology, Section 32
7 Chrysostom: Homily 4., "On 2 Thessalonians 2."
8 Treatise 11.
9 Irenoeus: "AgainstHeresies," book 5, chapter 30.
10 Treatise "On Christ and Antichrist," Section 36.
11 "City of God," book 18, chapter 22.
12 Hallam, "History of the Middle Ages," p. 384.
13"Di voi pastori s' accorse il Vangelista, Quando colei, che siede sovra l'acque Puttaneggiar co' Regi a lui fu vista: Quella che con le sette teste nacque, E dalle diece corna ebbe argomento, Fin che virtute al suo marito piacque. Fatto v'avete Dio d'oro e d'argento: E che altro e da voi all' idolatre, Se non ch'egli uno, e voi

96

n'orate cento? Ahi Costantin, di quanto mal fu matre, Non la tua conversion, ma quella dote Che da te prese il primo ricco patre!" Dante: "Inferno," canto 19.
**14** Extract from the Waldensian Treatise on Antichrist, dated A.D. 1120 (Histoire Generale des Eglises Evangeliques des Vallees de Piemont, ou Vaudoises, par Jean Leger, A.D. 1669, p. 71, etc.).

## LATIN

"ANTICHRIST..Ma meseima la falseta, pausa contra la verita quilli se quebre e se orna de belleza, e de pieta, de fora de la Gleisa de Christ, enaima de Christ, enaima de Nom, de Officies, de Scripturas, e de Sacramens, e de motas autras cosas. La iniquita d'aquesta maniera com li seo Ministre majors, e menors, com li seguent ley de maluas cor e cec, aital congregation ensemp presa es appela ANTICHRIST, o BABYLONIA, o QUARTA BESTIA, o MERETRIX, o HOME DE PECCA, Filli de perdition.
"Li seos Ministres son-appella FALS PROPHETAS, Maistres mesongers, Ministres de tenebras, Sperit d'error, MERETRIX APOCALYPTICA, maire de fornication, niolas senza aigua, arbres auctomnals, morts & arancas per doas vez, undas del crudel mar, stellas errans, balaamitiens, e Gissiptiens.
"El es dit Antichrist emperco ca cubert e orna sot specie de Christ, e de la Gleisa, e de li seo fidel membre, contraria a la salu faita per Christ, e aministra verament en la Gleisa de Christ."

## FRENCH

"L'ANTICHRIST..Mais c'est la faussete meme opposee a la verite, qui se couvre et s'orne de beaute, et de piete, hors de l'Eglise de Christ, comme des Noms, des Offices, des Ecritures et des Sacremens, et de plusieurs autres choses: l'iniquite laquelle est de cette maniere, avec tous ces Ministres grans et petis, avec tous ceux qui le ensuivent de mauvais coeur, et avengle, telle congregation prise ensemble est appelee ANTICHRIST, ou BABYLONE, ou QUATRIEME BETE, ou PAILLARDE, ou HOMME DE PECHE, FILS DE PERDITION.
"Ses Ministres sout appelez FAUX PROPHETES, Maitres mensongers, Ministres de tenebres, Esprit d'erreur, PAILLARDE APOCALYPTIQUE, Mere de fornication, nuees sans eau, arbres automnals morts et arrachez par deux fois, ondes de la cruelle mer, etoiles errantes, Balaamites, et Egyptiens. "Il est dit Antichrist, pour ce que couvert et orne de la Livre de Christ, et de son Elgise, et de ses fideles membres, il contrarie au salut fait par Christ, et administre vrayement en l'Eglise de Christ."
**15** "An epistle of John Huss to the people of Pragne:
"...The more circumspect ye ought to be, for that ANTICHRIST laboreth the more to trouble you. The last judgment is near at hand; death shall swallow up many, but to the elect children of God the kingdom of God draweth near..Know ye, well beloved,

that ANTICHRIST being stirred up against you deviseth divers persecutions." ù "Acts and Monuments," volume 3., pp. 497,498.

"A letter of John Huss to the Lord John de Clum:

"...By your letter which I received yesterday, I understand first, how the iniquity of the great strumpet, that is, of the malignant congregation, WHEREOF MENTION IS MADE IN THE APOCALYPSE, is detected, and shall be more detected; with which strumpet the kings of the earth do commit fornication, fornicating spiritually from Christ; and, as is there said, sliding back from the truth, and consenting to the lies of ANTICHRIST, through his seduction and through fear, or through hope of confederacy, for getting of worldly honor." "Acts and Monuments," volume 3, p. 499.

"Letter of John Huss, wherein he comforteth his friends and willeth them not to be troubled for the condemning of his books, and also declareth the wickedness of the clergy:

"Master John Huss, in hope, the servant of God, to all the faithful who love him and his statutes, wisheth the truth and grace of God..Surely even at this day is the malice, the abomination, and filthiness of ANTICHRIST revealed in the pope and others of this council..Oh how acceptable a thing should it be, if time would suffer me to disclose their wicked acts, which are now apparent; that the faithful servants of God might know them? I trust in God that He will send after me those that shall be more valiant; and there are alive at this day that shall make more manifest the malice of ANTICHRIST, and shall give their lives to the death for the truth of our Lord Jesus Christ, who shall give, both to you and me, the joys of life everlasting.

"This epistle was written upon St. John Baptist's Day, in prison and in cold irons; I having this meditation with myself, that John was beheaded in his prison and bonds for the word of God." ù "Acts and Monuments," volume 3, pp 502,503.

16 In the year 1421 the miseries of the Bohemians greatly increased.

Besides the executions by drowning, by fire, and by the sword, several thousands of the followers of Huss, especially the Taborires, of all ranks and both sexes, were thrown down the old mines and pits of Kuttenberg..In one pit were thrown 1,700, in another 1,308, and in a third 1,321 persons. Every year, on the 18th of April, a solemn meeting was held in a chapel built there, in memory of those martyrs, until the year 1613, when the mint-master Wrschesowetz endeavored to prevent it, yet it continued until the great persecution of 1621. A monument, it is said, still marks the place (Lasitius, 'Origo Fratrum,' volume 1, p. 69; Theobald's 'Hussite War,' p. 150, 1624; Reiger's 'History of the Bohemian Brethren,' vol. ii., p. 592; Regenvoscius, 'Systema Hist. Ecclesiastes Sclavonic.')." ù "The Reformation and Anti-Reformation in Bohemia," p. 13.

# Lecture Six -Interpretation and Use of These Prophecies in Reformation Times

The sixteenth century presents the spectacle of a stormy sunrise after a dismal night. Europe awoke from the long sleep of superstition. Nations shook off their chains. The dead arose. The witnesses to truth who had been silenced and slain stood up once more and renewed their testimony. The martyred confessors reappeared in the Reformers. There was a cleansing in the spiritual sanctuary. Civil and religious liberty were inaugurated. The discovery of printing and revival of learning accelerated the movement. There was progress everywhere. Columbus struck across the ocean and opened a new hemisphere to view. Rome was shaken on her seven hills, and lost one-half of her dominions. Protestant nations were created. The modern world was called into existence.

The sixteenth century was the age of the Reformation. The Church had become frightfully deformed; it needed to be thoroughly reformed It had departed from the faith; it needed to be brought back to it. It needed a restoration of non-apostate Christianity. A reassertion was required of rights Divine and human. The Papacy had subverted both the government of God and the liberties of man. Its central principle involves the expulsion from the worm of its rightful Ruler and Savior, and substitutes for Him a dynasty of blasphemous usurpers. And it involves equally the destruction of all man's noblest rights. It denies to him his lawful access to his Maker. A fellow mortal, a pretended priest, stands in the way, and blocks the path of eternal life. He stands across the sunshine of God's love, and casts upon the trembling human spirit a deadly shade. He claims to have the keys of heaven and hell. He thunders lying anathemas, and forbids mankind to approach the throne of infinite mercy save through him, and then only just so far as he permits. Thus Christ is eclipsed, salvation is stolen; the Papal priest is substituted for the Savior of sinners, the mystery of iniquity for the mystery of godliness, the proud pope of Rome for the holy Prince of Peace, poison for food; and Satan himself is palmed upon the Church of Jesus Christ as her head and husband. What a cursed system! Thought can scarcely fathom the abyss of evil which it creates! It arrests the flowing of heaven's waters in the wilderness, and turns the streams of life to stagnant, putrid blood. It arrests the shining of heaven's holy light, the illuminating influence of gospel truth, and plunges the world in gloom and darkness so gross that they may be felt. It arrests the healing hand of Divine grace and forgiveness, and substitutes for it the polluting touch of priestly fingers, stained and contaminated with lust, hypocrisy, and blood. It changes grace, that sweet and sacred mystery, spiritual, holy, not of the earth, free, oh, how free, and how Divine! for it is the Spirit's influence ù it changes this into a mystical abomination, an insufferable compound, a something manipulated by the fingers of hypocrites, "ministered," as they say, through sacraments, and sacraments of their own invention and management. Seven sacraments, forsooth! A something transmitted, too, through a generation of pretended vicars of Jesus Christ, and their agents, and doled out by them to a dying worm for pecuniary considerations! Do they not blush to perpetuate such damnable deceptions? Have the eternal interests of men no value in their eyes? Is the grace of God to be transmuted to a vile currency, that it may be deposited in the pockets of priests, and circulated by them as base coin is by rogues and vagabonds? Is conscience utterly dead within them? Dead? It is as good as dead; "seared with a hot iron," till it has lost the sense of fight and wrong, and can no longer feel the infamy of doctrines and deeds which would have made the men of Sodom blush with shame. A system which travesties the truth, hardens the conscience, enslaves the mind, corrupts the heart, which buries the Bible, prostitutes the ministry, profanes the sacraments, persecutes the saints, betrays and butchers the flock of Christ, and outrages all that is sacred and all that is Divine ù deserves and demands to be exposed, detested, judged, destroyed, and swept out of an injured world.

And God raised up the Reformation to do this work of protest, exposure, condemnation, and deliverance. To restore to men His word, to restore to them their rights, to open the eyes of nations, to raise them and make them stand upon their feet as responsible and free, to roll off their spirits the dark incubus, the eternal nightmare of priestly imposture and tyranny, to reestablish the ordinances and privileges of pure and primitive religion; such was the work of the Reformation which God wrought in Europe three centuries ago.

He who had raised up the prophets and apostles in olden times, He who raised up confessors and witnesses in the middle ages, raised up reformers in the sixteenth century, lionlike men, to undertake this mighty enterprise and accomplish this glorious work. There was that lion Luther, who shook Rome and Europe with his roar; and that lion Tyndale, who wrenched the Bible from the priests and gave it to us here in England in our own mother tongue, though it cost him his life to do it; and that Swiss lion Zwingle, who fell on the battlefield; and that lion of Picardy, John Calvin, who rose in his strength and majesty when Zwingle fell; and that lion John Knox of Scotland, who feared not the face of man, and turned not aside for any: these, and such as these, were the men through whom God overthrew in Germany, in Switzerland, in France, in England, Scotland, and Holland, the diabolical power and dominion of the Papacy.

We wish to invite your special attention to the fact that the convictions of the Reformers with reference to the character of the Papal Church, and the duty of separation from it, were largely derived from their study and interpretation of the prophetic Scriptures. We invite you to consider the manner in which the

Reformers interpreted the prophecies bearing upon the Papal apostasy, the practical use which they made of them, and the power which these prophecies exerted in directing and sustaining the great work of the Reformation. To the Reformers Rome was the "Babylon" of the Apocalypse, and the Papal pontiff the predicted "man of sin." Separation from the Church of Rome and from its pontifical head was regarded by them as a sacred duty. They urged on all Christian persons within the Church of Rome the apocalyptic command, "Come out of her, My people, that ye be not partakers of her sins, and that ye receive not of her plagues." To them separation from Rome was not separation from Christ, but from antichrist. This was the principle upon which they began and prosecuted the work of the Reformation, the principle which directed and supported them, and rendered them invincible.

Take first the case of the reformer Luther. Early in the year 1520, he wrote to Spalatinus thus: "I am extremely distressed in my mind. I have not much doubt but the pope is the real antichrist. The lives and conversation of the popes, their actions, their decrees, all agree most wonderfully to the descriptions of him in Holy Writ."

In the autumn of the same year he printed a treatise on the "Babylonish Captivity of the Church." Such was the title. In this he exposed the imposture of indulgences; he showed that their object is to rob men of money by the perversion of the gospel. In this animated production Luther called the Papacy "the kingdom of Babylon." Meanwhile Leo X. published his famous damnatory bull against Luther, containing extracts from his works, and forbidding all persons to read his writings on pain of excommunication; commanding those who possessed his works to burn them; excommunicating Luther as an obstinate heretic delivered to Satan for the destruction of his flesh, and commanding all secular princes, under pain of incurring the same censures and forfeiting all their dignities, to seize his person, that he might be punished as his crimes deserved. In October of the same year, Luther wrote to Spalatinus: "At last the Roman bull is come, and Eckius is the bearer of it. I treat it with contempt. You see that the expressed doctrines of Christ Himself are here condemned. I feel myself now more at liberty, being assured that the popedom is antichristian and the seat of Satan."

On December 1st he published two tracts in answer to the bull, one of which was entitled, "Martin Luther against the Execrable Bull of Antichrist." In its conclusion he admonishes the pope and his cardinals no longer to persevere in madness, "no longer to act the undoubted part of the antichrist of Scriptures." On December 10th in the same year, 1520, Luther called together the professors and students in the town of Wittemberg, and publicly burned the Papal bull. Along with it he burned the canon law, the decretals, the Clementines, and the extravagants of the popes.

The die was now cast. Luther had declared war against the Roman pontiff. He had "boldly denominated him the man of sin, and exhorted all Christian princes to shake off his usurpations." In this manner was the Reformation inaugurated. In order to justify his action, Luther selected thirty articles from the code of Papal laws, as illustrating the contents of the books he had consumed. These he printed with pointed remarks, calling on the people to use their own judgment with reference to them. He sums up by saying that on comparing the different parts of the canon law, its language simply amounts to this: "that the pope is God on earth above all that is earthly, temporal, or spiritual; that all things belong to the pope, and that no one must venture to say, What doest thou?"

Here is an old black-letter copy of Luther's "Commentary on the epistle to the Galatians." Under the expression in the second verse, "the Churches of Galatia," he says, "Wheresoever the substance of the holy sacraments remaineth, there is the holy Church, although antichrist there reigns, who, as the Scripture witnesseth, sitteth not in a stable of fiends, or in a swine-sty, or in a company of infidels, but in the highest and holiest place of all, namely, in the temple of God." Again he exclaims: "Is not this to sit in the temple of God, to profess himself to be ruler in the whole Church? What is the temple of God? Is it stones and wood? Did not Paul say, The temple of God is holy, which temple ye are? To sit ù what is it but to reign, to teach, and to judge? Who from the beginning of the Church has dared to call himself master of the whole Church but the pope alone? None of the saints, none of the heretics hath ever uttered so horrible a word of pride." 1 Elsewhere again he says, 2 that when Daniel "saw the terrible wild beast which had ten horns, which by the consent of all is the Roman empire, he also beheld another small horn come up in the middle of them. This is the Papal power, which rose up in the middle of the Roman empire."

Thus did Luther interpret prophecy; and under the influence of these interpretations of the prophetic teachings of Daniel, Paul, and John sprang up and advanced the glorious Reformation of the sixteenth century.

One of the witnesses of Luther's disputation at Leipsic in the year 1519 was Philip Melanchthon, the learned professor of Greek at Wittemberg. Melanchthon was a man of wonderful ability and application. The treatment of the most difficult subjects became simple in his hands. He was one of the greatest theologians of his age, and composed the celebrated Confession of Augsburg in 1530, the foundation of the reformed German faith. As this Confession was intended to be publicly read to the hostile Roman Catholic emperor Charles V, in the presence of princes and ecclesiastical dignitaries, Melanchthon toned it down as far as possible, avoiding all judgments of the Roman Catholic Church which would cause offense. Luther complained of this omission. "Satan sees clearly," said he, "that your apology has passed lightly over the articles of purgatory, the worship of saints, and above all of the pope and of antichrist. " 3

Melanchthon lacked the bold spirit of Luther, but he shared most of his sentiments. He was clear in his convictions that Rome is the Babylon of the Apocalypse, and the pope the man of sin. 4 In his disputation on marriage, referring to the first Epistle to Timothy, he says, "Since it is most certain that the pontiffs and the monks have forbidden marriage, it is most manifest, and without any doubt true, that the Roman pontiff, with his whole order and kingdom, is the very antichrist." 5 He adds: "Likewise in 2 Thessalonians 2, Paul clearly says that the man of sin shall rule in the Church, exalting himself against the worship of God, etc. But it is manifest that the popes do rule in the Church, and under title of the Church in defending idols. Wherefore I affirm that no heresy hath arisen, nor indeed shall be, with which these descriptions of Paul can more truly and certainly accord and agree than to this Papal kingdom." 6

He further adds in the same disputation (article 25): "The prophet Daniel also attributes these two things to antichrist; viz., that he shall place an idol in the temple, and honor it with gold and silver, and that he shall not honor women. That both these things belong to the Roman pontiff, who does not clearly see? The idols are clearly the impious mass, the worship of saints, and the statues which are exhibited in gold and silver that they may be worshipped."

The Reformation begun in Switzerland by Zwingle, who was previously canon and priest of Zurich, and carried on by Oecolampadius, Bullinger, and others, produced the Helvetic Confession, drawn up at Basle by reformed Swiss theologians, in 1536. This Confession, after being accepted and signed by the reformed cantons and towns, was sent to the Lutheran divines assembled at Smalkald in 1537. In both the Helvetic and Smalkald Confessions the Papacy is condemned as the predicted antichristian power. 7

The same great doctrine is taught in the valuable Bohemian Confession of 1573, which was composed of four Confessions of more ancient date.

John Calvin, that mighty theologian and reformer, whose works are published in fifty volumes, uttered upon this subject no uncertain sound. In his letter to the emperor Charles V, on the necessity of reforming the Church, he wrote as follows: "The arrogance of antichrist of which Paul speaks is, that he as God sitteth in the temple of God, showing himself that he is God. For where is the incomparable majesty of God after mortal man has been exalted to such a height that his laws take precedence of God's eternal decrees? I omit that the apostle describes the prohibitions of meats and of marriage as a doctrine of devils; that is surely bad enough: but the crowning impiety is to set man in a higher rank than God. If they deny the truth of my statement, I appeal to fact." He goes on, "What are those two laws of celibacy and auricular confession but dire murderers of souls?" At the conclusion of this letter to the emperor he says: "I deny that see to be apostolical wherein naught is seen but a shocking apostasy; I deny him to be the vicar of Christ who in furiously persecuting the gospel demonstrates by his conduct that he is antichrist; I deny him to be the successor of Peter who is doing his utmost to demolish every edifice that Peter built; and I deny him to be the head of the Church who by his tyranny lacerates and dismembers the Church, after dissevering her from Christ, her true and only head."

In his "Institutes of the Christian Religion" 8 Calvin again defends the view that the Roman pontiff is antichrist. "To some," he says, "we seem slanderous and petulant when we call the Roman pontiff antichrist; but those who think so perceive not that they are bringing a charge of intemperance against Paul, after whom we speak, nay, in whose very words we speak..Paul says that antichrist would sit in the temple of God. ..Hence we infer that his tyranny is more over souls than bodies, a tyranny set up in opposition to the spiritual kingdom of God..When he adds that in his own time the mystery of iniquity, which was afterwards to be openly manifested, had begun to work in secret, we thereby understand that this calamity was neither to be introduced by one man, nor to terminate in one man. Moreover, when the mark by which he distinguishes antichrist is that he would rob God of his honor and take it to himself, he gives the leading feature which we ought to follow in searching out antichrist, especially when pride of this description proceeds to the open devastation of the Church. Seeing then it is certain that the Roman pontiff has impudently transferred to himself the most peculiar properties of God and Christ, there cannot be a doubt that he is the leader and standard bearer of an impious and abominable kingdom."

Take now the testimony of William Tyndale. Here are several volumes containing the doctrines and treatises of that famous minister, reformer, and martyr, who first translated the New Testament from Greek into English. See how plainly this learned and honest man spoke out on the antichristian character of the Papacy. "Antichrist," he says, "in another manner hath sent forth his disciples, those false anointed of which Christ warneth us before, that they should come and show miracles and wonders, even to bring the very elect out of the way, if it were possible. ..A bishop must be faultless, the husband of one wife. Nay, saith the pope, the husband of no wife, but the holder of as many women as he listeth. What saith the pope? I command to read the gospel in Latin..It is verily as good to preach to swine as to men, if thou preach it in a tongue they understand not..Well, saith the pope, if they will not be ruled, cite them to appear, and pose them sharply what they hold of the pope's power, of his pardons, his bulls, of purgatory, of ceremonies, of confessions..If they miss in any point, make heretics of them and burn them..The emperors and kings are no other nowadays but even hangmen unto the popes and bishops, to kill whomsoever they condemn, without any more ado; as Pilate was unto the scribes and Pharisees and high bishops, to hang Christ..What signifieth that the prelates are so bloody, and clothed in red? That they be ready every hour to suffer martyrdom for the testimony of God's word? Is that also not a false sign, when no man dare [before] them once open his mouth to ask a question of God's word, because they are ready to bum him?. .

Is not that shepherd's hook, the bishop's crosier, a false sign? Is not that white rochet that the bishops and canons wear, so like a nun and so effeminately, a false sign? What other things are their sandals, gloves, miters, and all the whole pomp of their disguising, than false signs, in which Paul prophesies that they should come? And as Christ warned us to beware of wolves in lambs' skins, and bade us look rather unto their fruits and deeds than to wonder at their disguisings. Run throughout all our holy religions, and thou shalt find them likewise all clothed in falsehood."

In his exposition of the famous passage about antichrist in the First Epistle of John, Tyndale says: "Though the Bishop of Rome and his sects give Christ these names (His rightful names), yet in that they rob Him of the effect, and take the signification of His names unto themselves, and make of Him but a hypocrite, as they themselves be, they be the right antichrists, and deny both the Father and the Son; for they deny the witness that the Father bore unto His Son, and deprive the Son of all the power and glory that His Father gave Him. For 'whosoever denieth the Son, the same hath not the Father,' for 'no man knoweth the Father but the Son, and to whom the Son showeth Him.' Moreover, if thou know not the mercy that God hath showed thee in Christ, thou canst not know Him as a Father. Thou mayest well, apart from Christ, know Him as a tyrant, and thou mayest know Him by His works as the old philosophers did, that there is a God; but thou canst neither believe in His mercy nor love His laws ù which is the only worship in the spirit save by Christ."

All the other English reformers, including Latimer, Ridley, Cranmer, Bradford, and Jewell, held the pope of Rome to be the man of sin. So did John Knox in Scotland; and he sounded out his testimony on this subject as with a trumpet. Here is an old copy of Knox's "History of the Reformation." Its contents are thus described on the title page: "The manner, and by what persons, the light of Christ's gospel has been manifested into this realm after that horrible and universal defection from the truth which has come by the means of that Roman antichrist."

Knox begins his history by giving a list of the articles of faith attributed to the Lollards of Kyle, taken from the register of Glasgow. Of these the thirty-second article runs thus: That the pope is the head of the Kirk of antichrist." After describing the affecting martyrdom of Patrick Hamilton ù whose dying words were, "Lord Jesus, receive my spirit! how long shall darkness overwhelm this realm? how long wilt Thou suffer this tyranny of men?" he tells how he himself was led to undertake the public preaching of God's word. In the year 1547 Knox, wearied of removing from place to place by reason of persecution, came to the Castle of St. Andrews, resolved to leave Scotland for Germany. Here he took the part of a godly preacher named John Rough against Dean Annan, a Romanist. Knox wielded his pen with such effect that Annan was beaten from all his defenses, and was compelled to take shelter under the authority of the Church, which authority, he said, "damned all Lutherans and heretics, and therefore he needed no further disputation." To this Knox answered: "Before we hold ourselves, or that ye can prove us, sufficiently convinced, we must define the Church by the right notes given to us in God's Scripture of the true Church; we must discern the immaculate spouse of Jesus Christ from the mother of confusion, spiritual Babylon, lest that impudently we embrace a harlot instead of the chaste spouse; yea, to speak in plain words, lest that we submit ourselves to Satan, thinking that we submit ourselves to Jesus Christ. For, as your Roman Church, as it is now corrupted,...I no more doubt but that it is the synagogue of Satan, and the head thereof called the pope, to be the man of sin of whom the apostle speaketh, than that I doubt that Jesus Christ suffered by the procurement of the visible Church of Jerusalem. Yea, I offer myself by word or writing to prove the Roman Church this day further degenerate from the purity which was in the days of the apostles, than was the Church of the Jews from the ordinances given by Moses when they consented to the innocent death of Jesus Christ."

Knox tells us that these words were "spoken in the open audience of the parish church of St. Andrews," after Dean Annan's delivery. The people, hearing the offer, urged Knox to lay his proofs before them in a public speech, saying that if Knox was right, they had been miserably deceived.

Knox consented, and was appointed to preach the following Sunday. On that day, he tells us, he preached his first sermon, taking his text from the seventh chapter of Daniel. He gives us an outline of its contents. It opened with a "short discourse" on the four empires the Babylonian, Persian, Grecian, and Roman ù as set forth by the four wild beasts of the seventh chapter of Daniel, and then showed that the persecuting "little horn" of the fourth empire was identical with the man of sin and antichrist, and signified the Roman Papacy. For this sermon Knox was called to account before a convention of "gray friars and black fiends," as he calls them. Nine articles were laid against him. Of these the first was that he had taught that "no mortal man can be head of the Church"; and the second that "the pope is an antichrist, and so is no member of Christ's mystical body." Knox gives an account of his argument with the friars on this occasion, in which he evidently had the best of it. Thus was launched the Reformation in Scotland, and Knox's sermon in St. Andrews on the "little horn" of prophecy struck its keynote and started its testimony.

The English reformers were no less clear in their views and emphatic in their teachings. Ridley thus expresses himself: "The see of Rome is the seat of Satan, and the bishop of the same, that maintaineth the abominations thereof is antichrist himself indeed; and for the same causes this see at this day is the same that St. John calls, in his Revelation, Babylon, or the whore of Babylon, and spiritual Sodom and Egypt, the mother of fornications and abominations upon earth."

Latimer, when examined by the commissioners on his trial, said: "I confess there is a Catholic Church, to the determination of which I stand, but not the Church which you call Catholic, which sooner might be called diabolic." In his second conference with Ridley he says: "Yea, what fellowship hath Christ with antichrist? therefore it is not lawful to bear the yoke with Papists. 'Come forth from among them, and separate yourselves from them, saith the Lord.'"

Bishop Jewell wrote a most masterly and powerful commentary on Thessalonians, proving the pope of Rome to be the man of sin. Here is a copy of it. Take as a specimen the following sentences about antichrist: "Some say that he should be Jew of the tribe of Dan; some that he should be born in Babylon;...some that Mohammed is antichrist;...some that Nero was antichrist; some that he should be born of a friar and a nun; some that he should continue but three years and a half; some that he should turn trees upside down with the tops to the ground, and should force the roots to grow upwards, and then should flee up into heaven and fall down and break his neck. These tales have been craftily devised to beguile our eyes, that whilst we think upon these guesses, and so occupy ourselves in beholding a shadow, or probable conjecture of antichrist, he which is antichrist indeed may unawares deceive us.

"He will come in the name of Christ, yet will he do all things against Christ and under pretense and color of serving Christ; he shall devour the sheep and people of Christ; he shall deface whatsoever Christ hath taught; he shall quench that fire which Christ hath kindled; those plants which Christ hath planted he shall root up; he shall undermine that house which Christ hath built; he shall be contrary to Christ, his faith contrary to the faith of Christ, and his life contrary to the life of Christ.."

"Christ was humble and lowly. The prophet, in his own person, speaks of Him, Psalm 22: 'I am a worm, and not a man; a shame of men, and the contempt of the people.'

And the apostle saith, Philippians 2: 'He humbled Himself, and became obedient unto death, even the death of the cross.'

Behold His parents, His birth, His cradle; behold His life, His disciples, His doctrine, and His death; all were witnesses unto His humility. He saith of Himself, 'The Son of man hath not where to rest His head'; and to His disciples He saith, 'The kings of the Gentiles reign over them, and they that bear rule over them are called gracious lords; but ye shall not be so.' And again, 'Learn of Me; for I am meek and lowly in heart, and ye shall find rest unto your souls.'"

"Now, on the other part, take view of antichrist. Behold his birth, his place, his chair, his estate, his doctrine, his disciples; and all his life you shall see nothing but pomp and glory. Gregory calls him the king of pride. He is proud in life, proud in doctrine, proud in word, and proud in deeds; he is like Lucifer, and sets himself before his brethren, and over nations and kingdoms."

"He makes every knee to bow down to him and worship him; he makes kings to bring him water, to carry his train, to hold his cup, to bear his dish, to lead his bridle, and to hold his stirrup; he claims power over heaven and earth; he saith he is lord over all the world, the lord of lords and the king of kings; that his authority reaches up into heaven and down into hell; that he can command the angels of God; that he condemns whom he will condemn; that he makes saints at his pleasure; that whatsoever he blesses is blessed, and that whatsoever he curses is cursed."

"He sells merits, the forgiveness of sins, the sacrifice for the quick and the dead; he makes merchandise of the souls of men; he lays filthy hands upon the Lord's anointed; he removes kings and deposes the states and princes of the world. This is antichrist; this is his power. Thus shall he work and make himself. So shall he sit in the temple of God. The people shall wonder at him, and shall have him in reverence; they shall say, Who is like unto the beast? who is so wise, so mighty, so godly, so virtuous, so holy, so like unto God? ù so intolerable and monstrous shall be his pride."

Listen now to the dying testimony upon this subject of the well-known reformer Archbishop Cranmer. Let me read you the words he spoke just before his martyrdom: "Forasmuch as I am come to the last end of my life, whereupon all hangeth of my life past and of my life to come, either to live with my master Christ for ever in joy, or else to be in pain for ever with wicked devils in hell, and I see before mine eyes presently either heaven ready to receive me, or else hell ready to swallow me up, I shall therefore declare unto you my very faith, how I believe, without any color or dissimulation; for now it is not time to dissemble, whatsoever I have said or written in time past." Having briefly expressed the chief articles of his faith, he refers to his previous recantation in the following terms: "And now I come to the great thing that so much troubleth my conscience more than anything I ever did or said in my whole life, and that is the setting abroad of a writing contrary to the truth, which now here I renounce and refuse, as things written with my hand contrary to the truth which I thought in my heart, and which was written for fear of death, and to save my life if it might be; and that is all such bills and papers which I have written or signed with my hand since my degradation, wherein I have written many things untrue. And forasmuch as my hand offended, writing contrary to my heart, my hand shall first be punished therefore; for, may I come to the fire, it shall first be burned; and as for the pope, I refuse him as Christ's enemy, and antichrist, with all his false doctrines."

On uttering this, Cranmer was pulled down from the stage and led to the fire. Having put off his outer garments, he stood there in a shirt which hung down to his feet. His beard was long and thick, and covered his bosom. Then was an iron chain tied about him, and the fire set to the faggots. When these were kindled, and the fire began to burn near him, stretching out his arm he put his right hand into the flame, holding it there immovable. Thus did he stand, moving no more than the stake to which he was bound. His eyes were lifted to heaven and often he repeated, "This hand hath offended; oh, this unworthy right hand!" At last, in the greatness of the flame, he cried, "Lord Jesus, receive my spirit!" and gave up the ghost.

"Antichrist, which now by the will of God doth rage for the trial of our faith, doth nothing else but procure us a ready horse to bring us to heaven." So said that holy man John Bradford; "brother Bradford," as Ridley called him. And he too was burned. When led to the stake, he took a faggot in his hand and kissed it, rejoicing to suffer death in the cause of Christ. Standing then by the stake, with both hands uplifted, he cried, "O England, England! repent thee of thy sins; repent thee of thy sins; beware of idolatry; beware of the false antichrists; take heed they do not deceive thee."

Cranmer, Ridley, Latimer, and Bradford were burned for their testimony against the Papal antichrist, just as Huss and Jerome and Cobham had been before. Thousands of martyrdoms have sealed this testimony, and on this testimony rests the Reformation. To reject this testimony is to reject the foundation of that work; it is to reject the foundation of the noblest and divinest work which has been wrought in this world since the day of Pentecost.

Do not misunderstand me. I do not say that the teachings of Scripture prophecy form the sole foundation of the Reformation. The doctrinal and practical truths of Scripture guided the action of the reformers as well as the prophetic. They opposed the Church of Rome, as condemned alike by the doctrines, the precepts, and the prophecies of the word of God. It might be difficult to say which of the three weighed with them most. On each they were clear and emphatic. These three elements cannot be separated in estimating the springs of the Reformation. From the first, and throughout, that movement was energized and guided by the prophetic word. Luther never felt strong and free to war against the Papal apostasy till he recognized the pope as antichrist. It was then he burned the Papal bull. Knox's first sermon, the sermon which launched him on his mission as a reformer, was on the prophecies concerning the Papacy. The reformers embodied their interpretations of prophecy in their confessions of faith, and Calvin in his "Institutes." All the reformers were unanimous in the matter; even the mild and cautious Melanchthon was as assured of the antipapal meaning of these prophecies as was Luther himself. And their interpretation of these prophecies determined their reforming action. It led them to protest against Rome with extraordinary strength and undaunted courage. It nerved them to resist the claims of that apostate Church to the uttermost. It made them martyrs; it sustained them at the stake. And the views of the reformers were shared by thousands, by hundreds of thousands. They were adopted by princes and peoples. Under their influence nations abjured their allegiance to the false priest of Rome. In the reaction which followed, all the powers of hell seemed to be let loose upon the adherents of the Reformation. War followed war: tortures, burnings, and massacres were multiplied. Yet the Reformation stood undefeated and unconquerable. God's word upheld it, and the energies of His almighty spirit. It was the work of Christ as truly as the founding of the Church eighteen centuries ago; and the revelation of the future which He gave from heaven ù that prophetic book with which the Scripture closes ù was one of the mightiest instruments employed in its accomplishment.

To resist the use to which Scripture prophecy was put by the reformers is no light or unimportant matter. The system of prophetic interpretation known as Futurism does resist this use. It condemns the interpretation of the reformers. It condemns the views of all these men, and of all the martyrs, and of all the confessors and faithful witnesses of Christ for long centuries. It condemns the Albigenses, the Waldenses, the Wicliffites, the Hussites, the Lollards, the Lutherans, the Calvinists; it condemns them all, and upon a point upon which they are all agreed, an interpretation of Scripture which they embodied in their solemn confessions and sealed with their blood. It condemns the spring of their action, the foundation of the structure they erected. How daring is this act, and how destitute of justification! What an opposition to the pillars of a work most manifestly diviner for it is no less than this, for Futurism asserts that Luther and all the reformers were wrong in this fundamental point. And whose interpretation of prophecy does it justify and approve? That of the Romanists. Let this be clearly seen. Rome felt the force of these prophecies, and sought to evade it. It had no way but to deny their applicability. It could not deny their existence in Scripture. They were there plainly enough. But it denied that these prophecies referred to the Romish Church and its head. It pushed them aside. It shifted them from the entire field of mediaeval and modern history. As to Babylon the Great, it asserted that it meant Rome pagan, not Rome Papal. Rome pagan shed all the blood referred to in Revelation 17,18. Rome Christian had shed none of it. Prophecy was eloquent about the deeds of the Caesars, but silent as to those of the popes; and this though the persecutions perpetrated by the popes had exceeded those of the Caesars. Prophecy expended its strength in warning the Church of the perils from heathenism which it perfectly understood, and was speechless as to the far greater perils arising from the Christian apostasy on which it needed the fullest warning and instruction. It was eagle-eyed as to dangers from without, but blind to dangers from within. It guided and guarded the Church of the three first centuries, but left the Church of the next thousand years and more without a lamp to light its footsteps. As to the prophecies of the man of sin, or antichrist, these had nothing to do with the middle ages, or with the Roman popes, or the long central centuries of the Church's sorest conflicts; they only referred to a diminutive interval in the far off future, at the end of the world. The man of sin was only an ephemeral persecutor. His whole power was to continue but three and a half years. He was to be a cunning Jew of the tribe of Dan; a clever infidel who was to call himself God and set himself up in a Jewish temple at Jerusalem. Christians had nothing to do with him as such. A Jew was to do all the mischief. The whole evil was but a Jewish infidel spasm in the very last hour of history before the Second Advent. Therefore the reformers were all wrong in their denunciations of the Papacy. They were foolish, misguided, unreasonable, fanatical, and the popes were uncondemned by the voices of the prophets. Daniel and John said nothing about them. They were not the predicted apostates. What though they did shed the blood of heretics like water, and drink it like wine, and make themselves drunken with it, and exalt themselves above kings, and above the world, and clothe themselves with wealth and splendor, with purple and scarlet, gold and peats! what though they did sit supreme upon the seven hills, and ride and rule the Roman empire in its divided Gothic state, and use its powers for the persecution of heretics, and the suppression of what some presumed to call the gospel of Jesus Christ! The prophecies which those contemptible reformers and miserable so-called martyrs said applied to them did nothing of the sort; it was folly to suppose they did. They applied to other people and to other circumstances.

The thunders of prophecy were not directed against them, but against those dead Caesars, and that unborn Jew. And so they puffed at the reformers, and scoffed at the martyrs, and scorned and derided and despised them, and went on in their proud tyranny, and abated nothing of their blasphemous pretensions and blood persecutions.

Which think you were right in their interpretations of Scripture? Those proud popes, those cruel inquisitors, those inhuman monsters who mangled the bodies of holy men and women in their torture chambers, those sanctimonious murderers who stirred up all the might of Christendom, from century to century, against the gospel and against the faithful witnesses of Jesus; or those pure and persecuted saints, those faithful Waldenses and Wicliffites, those earnest Hussites and Lollards, those self-sacrificing Lutherans and Huguenots, those noble confessors, reformers, and martyrs? With one mind and mouth all these Protestants agreed in the substance of their protest. To them Rome was Babylon, and its proud head the antichrist. Were they all mistaken, deluded, and their cruel, tyrannical oppressors and persecutors correct? What think you?

Perhaps you say, But was Rome right in nothing? Must a doctrine be wrong because Rome holds it? Does not Rome hold the truth as to the divinity of Christ, and as to some other points of importance? I grant Rome holds some truths. It would have no moral power unless it did. Even the Mohammedans hold some great truths, and the heathen also. But mark, this is a question of Rome's judgment concerning herself and the bearing of prophecy on her own history and character. It is here in this judgment that the Futurist claims that Rome was right, and the reformers in the wrong. And the consequences are most serious, for we are living in an age of revived Papal activity. Not only is the Papacy exerting an enormous influence in the outside world, not only has it formulated and decreed its own infallibility, not only is it attacking Protestantism in its strongholds with every weapon in its reach, political, civil, religious, but the principles and practices of the system it guides and governs have been introduced into the bosom of the Protestant Church, and planted securely within its walls, and are working most disastrously for its corruption and overthrow. Never was there a time in the Church's history when she more needed the barriers which prophecy has erected for her protection. And now when they are so sorely needed, they are not to be found. Futurism has crept into the Protestant Church, and broken down these sacred walls. Romanists, Ritualists, and Protestant Futurists are all agreed as to the non- applicability of Scripture prophecies to the Church of Rome and the Papacy. The Romanists are two hundred millions, the Ritualists are hundreds of thousands, and Protestant Futurists are many thousands in number. They all deny these prophecies their place and office. They remove these barriers. What then is to keep out the incoming Papal flood? The word of prophecy in its solemn warnings of the dangers the Church has to encounter, the foes it has to resist, is asserted to be silent as to this. Why then should this be feared? The reformers were mistaken; the popes were right. Charles V and Charles IX, Philip of Spain and Mary of England, the Duke of Alva and Louis XIV, and all the tribe of Innocents and Leos, Gregories and Clements, Pius IV and Pius IX ù all these were right in rejecting the fundamental position that Papal Rome is Babylon, and its head antichrist; and all the reformers, without an exception, were wrong in maintaining it; they were foolish interpreters of the "sure word of prophecy," and utterly in error as to the real testimony of Scripture concerning the Church of Rome.

Is this the position you adopt? Is this the conclusion you defend? Are these the views you advocate? You, a Protestant, and this after all that has been written upon the subject, and all the blaze of light which history and experience have poured upon it? If it is, look to it that you be not found fighting against the truth, warring against the word of God, resisting the testimony of the prophetic Spirit; hindering the work of the Reformation, promoting the progress of the apostasy, opposing Christ, and helping antichrist.

Even the Romanists themselves shame you in their clear-sighted comprehension of the issues of this question. Cardinal Manning says, "The Catholic Church is either the masterpiece of Satan or the kingdom of the Son of God." Cardinal Newman says, "A sacerdotal order is historically the essence of the Church of Rome; if not divinely appointed, it is doctrinally the essence of antichrist." In both these statements, the issue is clear, and it is the same. Rome herself admits, openly admits, that if she is not the very kingdom of Christ, she is that of antichrist. Rome declares she is one or the other. She herself propounds and urges this solemn alternative. You shrink from it, do you? I accept it. Conscience constrains me. History compels me. The past, the awful past rises before me. I see THE GREAT APOSTASY, I see the desolation of Christendom, I see the smoking rains, I see the reign of monsters; I see those vice-gods, that Gregory VII, that Innocent III, that Boniface VIII, that Alexander VI, that Gregory XIII, that Pius IX; I see their long succession, I hear their insufferable blasphemies, I see their abominable lives; I see them worshipped by blinded generations, bestowing hollow benedictions, bartering lying indulgences, creating a paganized Christianity; I see their liveried slaves, their shaven priests, their celibate confessors; I see the infamous confessional, the mined women, the murdered innocents; I hear the lying absolutions, the dying groans; I hear the cries of the victims; I hear the anathemas, the curses, the thunders of the interdicts; I see the racks, the dungeons, the stakes; I see that inhuman Inquisition, those fires of Smithfield, those butcheries of St. Bartholomew, that Spanish armada, those unspeakable dragonnades, that endless train of wars, that dreadful multitude of massacres. I see it all, and in the name of the ruin it has wrought in the Church and in the world, in the name of the truth it has denied, the temple it has defiled, the God it has blasphemed, the souls it has destroyed; in the name of the millions it has deluded, the millions it has slaughtered, the millions it has damned; with holy confessors, with noble reformers, with innumerable martyrs, with the saints of ages, I denounce it as the masterpiece of Satan, as the body and soul and essence of antichrist.

## *Notes*

1. *"Works," volume 2, p. 385*
2. *Ibid., volume 2, p. 386.*
3. *See D'Aubigne's "History of the Reformation," book 14, chapter 8.*
4. *"Works," volume 4, p. 537.*
5. *"Quod Romanus pontifex, cum universo ordine suo et regno, sit ipsissimus antichristus," etc. ù "Works," volume 4, p. 537.*
6. *"Quare affirmo, nullam, unquam extitisse haeresin, neque adeo futuram esse, cui verius et certius hae Pauli descriptiones, convenire ac competere queant atque huic pontificio regno." ù "Works," volume 4, p. 537.*
7. *"Art. Smalc S. 347: Constat, Romanos pontifices cum suis membris defendere impiam doctrinam et impios cultus. Ac plane notae ANTICHRISTI competunt in regnum papae et sua membra Paulus enim ad Thessalonicenses describens ANTICHRISTUM, vocat eum adversarium Christi, extollentem se super omne, quod dicitur aut colitur Deus, sedentem in templo Dei, tanquam Deum. Loquitur igitur de aliquo regnante in ecclesia, non de regibus ethnicis: et hunc vocat adversarium Christi, quia doctrinam pugnantem cum evangelio excogitaturus sit, et is arrogabit sibi auctoritatem divinam. Primum autem constat, papam regnare in ecclesia,*

*et praetextu ecclesiasticae auctoritatis et ministerii sibi hoc regnum constituisse. "..Deinde doctrina papae multipliciter pugnat cum evangelio, et afrogat sibi papa auctoritatem divinam tripliciter: primum quia..,secunda quia..,tertio quia..Hoc autem est se Deum facere, nolle, ab ecclesia aut ab ullo judicari..Haec quum ita sint, cavere omnes Christiani debent, ne fiant participes impiae doctrinae, blasphemiarum et injustae crudelitatis papae. Ideo papam cum suis membris, tanquam regnum ANTICHRISTI, deserere et exsecrari debent."*

# Lecture Seven - Interpretation and Use of These Prophecies in Post-Reformation Times

Three centuries have rolled by since the accomplishment of the glorious Reformation. These centuries have a double aspect ù a Protestant, and a Papal. On the one hand, they present the spectacle of an era of liberty and light; and, on the other hand, of reaction and revolution. In the history of Protestantism these centuries have been an era of liberty, civil and religious. In A.D. 1500 there was not a free nation in Europe; all were subject to the tyrannical government of Rome. Now half Europe and America are free from that intolerable yoke. In the year 1500 there was hardly a Protestant to be found in the world; Rome had exterminated them all by prolonged and cruel persecution. At the present day Protestants are 150,000,000 in number.

And the last three centuries have been an era of light. At their commencement the human mind experienced an emancipation, and was furnished with new instruments. Learning was revived, and the art of printing discovered. Since then the Word of God has been multiplied, translated, and expounded as never before. And the understanding of prophecy has shared the general advance. During this time libraries have been written on the prophetic Scriptures. Mighty interpreters have been raised up, men such as Mede, Sir Isaac Newton, Elliott, whose investigations have drawn back the veil of long continued ignorance, and let in new light upon some of the darkest obscurities of the theme. Interpreters have risen in groups like constellations of stars, and knowledge has increased.

On the other hand, post-Reformation times have been times of Papal reaction and revolution. In the first place, the Protestant Reformation was encountered by a tremendous Papal reaction, the rising wave of life and liberty was met by a counterwave of resistance. Hardly was the ship of a Protestant Church set free and launched upon the deep than there arose a mighty tempest. The resurrection of the slain "witnesses" of Christ in the person of the reformers was answered by a resurrection of all the powers of the pit. The awakening of men's souls brought war, ecclesiastical and civil, a war of anathemas and a war of extermination. Swords flashed forth, flames were kindled; Rome rose in its anger and its might, and did wondrously. She thundered excommunications, she slaughtered millions; not without an awful struggle would the prince of darkness give up his kingdom. No! Look to it, ye brave reformers; ye will need the armory of heaven and its help, for the hosts of hell are roused against you. Ye may conquer, but it shall be through strife and anguish, and seas of blood.

Draw up your confessions of faith, ye blessed restorers of a pure gospel; dare to give them to the world if ye will, but ye shall be stoutly answered. Against your Confession of Augsburg Rome shall erect her Council of Trent: she shall formulate her canons and decrees; she shall impose her Creed of Pius IV, and utter her chorus of anathemas.

Rise up, O Luther! cry out concerning "the Babylonian captivity of the Church," burn the Papal bull, rouse Germany; but you shall have your match. Satan shall bring forth his Loyola, and Loyola his Jesuits ù subtle, learned, saintly in garb and name, protean in form, infinite in disguises, innumerable, scholars, teachers, theologians, confessors of princes, politicians, rhetoricians, casuists; instruments keen, unscrupulous, double-edged; men fitted to every sphere and every enterprise ù they shall swarm against the Church of the Reformation, each one wise in the wisdom and strong in the strength which are not from above but from beneath.

Rise up, Zwingle, thou lion of Zurich! lead forth thy brave Swiss against the enemies of liberty and truth! but ye must perish on the field of battle ere your cause succeed.

Ride forth, fair flower of France! strive, ye brave Huguenots, for your country's freedom and the faith of the gospel! But Paris shall run with your blood; ye shall fall like leaves from a tree shaken by tempest; ye shall lie in heaps, like rubbish in the streets; your bodies shall choke the streams, they shall rot in rivers, they shall hang in chains, they shall be shoveled into cemeteries, or buried in dung-heaps. Rome shall ring her joy- bells and sing her Te Deums, and fill her cathedrals and palaces with acclamations because the massacre of St. Bartholomew has overthrown, for a time, the work of the Reformation in France.

Stand up, ye Hollanders! stand up, William the Silent! stand up, ye men of Haarlem and Rotterdam, of Amsterdam and Leyden, ye brave burghers and earnest theologians. Ye dare to contend for civil liberty and sacred truth: your land shall groan beneath the tread of Alva's troops; your fortresses shall fall, your citizens shall be thrust through with Spanish swords, your possessions shall be plundered, your wives and your daughters shall be dishonored and foully murdered, your children trampled beneath horse-hoofs, and trodden down like mire in the streets.

Break thy chains, O England! Rome shall find means to rivet them again; thou shalt have thy bloody Mary, and thy fires of Smithfield. Protestant bishops shall burn for it; against thy seagirt isle Spain shall send her proud armada; a fleet of one hundred and thirty great ships of war shall come across the seas, twelve of them named after the twelve apostles; they shall be laden with seamen and troops, with swords and guns, with priests and Jesuits; the pope shall bless the banners. Woe to thee, O England, if Heaven help thee not, if its winds forsake thy cause!

Combine yourselves together, ye Protestant states of Germany: claim your rights of conscience; stand for the truth; establish your Protestant liberties: but you shall have your desolating war of thirty years! From Bohemia to the broad waters of the Scheldt, from the banks of the Po to the shores of the Baltic, whole countries shall be devastated, harvests destroyed, cities and villages reduced to ruins! half Europe shall be set on fire, and civilization shall be buried for a season in bloodshed and barbarism.

The apostate Church commands the swords of Latin Christendom ù the harlot rides the beast, and the beast has claws and great iron teeth, and sharp, strong horns, and inhuman ferocity: she sits proudly upon it, and it obeys her, grasping, rending, and crushing whom she will. But what if the beast should grow weary of carrying her? What if the beast should take a dislike to her usurping ways? What if it should resist her, and cast her off and turn its power against her, and serve her as she had served others? Ah! that would be a different story, but not an experience unforetold. John foresaw it would be thus eighteen centuries ago, and history has fulfilled his predictions: for Romish reaction was followed by democratic revolution; 1572 was followed by 1793, the Massacre of St. Bartholomew by the Reign of Terror. France Papal crushed France Protestant, and was crushed in its turn by France infidel. Have you not heard of Voltaire, of Rousseau, of Robespierre, of Danton, of the execution of Louis XVI and Marie Antoinette, of the massacres in Paris in 1793, of the guillotine, of the noyades or wholesale drownings, of how the river Loire was choked with corpses, of the war in La Vendee, of the worship of the goddess of reason, of the turning cathedrals into stables, of the forty thousand churches, chapels, and oratories tom down by the revolutionists, of the massacre and banishment of priests and Jesuits, of the burning of palaces, the beggaring of princes, the overthrow of monarchy and government and aristocracy and corrupt religion, as by the heavings of a social earthquake, or the outburstings of an irresistible volcano? Have you not heard of how the infidel democracy rose in its might, struck down the powers which had deceived and oppressed it, confiscated all the vast revenues of the Church, the domains of the Crown, the estates of the nobles, "slaughtered one million and twenty-two thousand persons, of all ranks and ages, and both sexes, till the streets of Paris ran with blood, and the guillotines could not overtake their work"? And have you not heard how a little later on the Papal States were conquered by Napoleon, and converted into a Roman republic; how the Papacy was extinguished, the Vatican plundered, ecclesiastical property confiscated, and the pope dragged from the altar, and sent as a prisoner to die in exile? Are not these matters of history, and of recent history? Here is Thiers' "History of the French Revolution"; here is Alison's history of that revolution, in twelve volumes; and here is Carlyle's history of the same, written as with a pen of fire. It is but a century since these things were accomplished, and the after-waves of that mighty revolution are rolling still.

These two great movements which have followed the Reformation, the Papal reaction of the 16th and 17th centuries, and the Revolution of the 18th century, have mightily helped to open men's eyes to the true character of Romanism, and to the fulfillment of the prophetic Scriptures. The last three centuries have consequently witnessed a great advance in the comprehension of prophecy, and we are this evening to study the expositions which have resulted.

First, note the fact that Rome's reply to the Reformation in the 16th century included an answer to the prophetic teachings of the Reformers. Through the Jesuits Ribera and Bellarmine, Rome put forth her futurist interpretation of prophecy. Ribera was a Jesuit priest of Salamanca. In 1585 he published a commentary on the Apocalypse, denying the application of the prophecies concerning antichrist to the existing Church of Rome. He was followed by Cardinal Bellarmine, a nephew of Pope Marcellus II, who was born in Tuscany in 1542, and died in Rome in 1621. Bellarmine was not only a man of great learning, but "the most powerful controversialist in defense of Popery that the Roman Church ever produced."

Clement VIII used these remarkable words on his nomination: "We choose him, because the Church of God does not possess his equal in learning." Bellarmine, like Ribera, advocated the futurist interpretation of prophecy. He taught that antichrist would be one particular man, that he would be a Jew, that he would be preceded by the reappearance of the literal Enoch and Elias, that he would rebuild the Jewish temple at Jerusalem, compel circumcision, abolish the Christian sacraments, abolish every other form of religion, would manifestly and avowedly deny Christ, would assume to be Christ, and would be received by the Jews as their Messiah, would pretend to be God, would make a literal image speak, would feign himself dead and rise again, and would conquer the whole world ù Christian, Mohammedan, and heathen; and all this in the space of three and a half years. He insisted that the prophecies of Daniel, Paul and John, with reference to the antichrist, had no application whatever to the Papal power.

The futurist writings of Ribera and Bellarmine were ably answered by Brightman, of whose work on the Apocalypse, published about the year 1600, this is a copy; and they have been answered since his time in a succession of learned works which I cannot stop to enumerate: for I desire to dwell upon another, and, as I regard it, a more important phase of prophetic interpretation marking the last three centuries, a phase not of a negative but of a positive character. Protestant interpreters have done more than answer the false futurism of the Church of Rome. They have built up the true historic interpretation of prophecy; they have built up a solid and symmetrical system, a system which has developed slowly, which has progressed constantly, which has been born not of diligent investigation only, but of profound experience; a system whose truth has been sealed and demonstrated by its ever-growing correspondence with the actual course of events. True theology, like true science,

118

is slow in development. The growth of astronomy, for example, has extended through six thousand years. The system of Ptolemy was corrected by that of Copernicus; that of Copernicus was advanced by the laws of Kepler and the wonderful discoveries of Newton; and then further perfected by the Herschels and many others in recent times.

Keeping strictly to the prophecies relating to Romanism and the Reformation, I will now endeavor to show you some of the analogous progress which has been made in their comprehension during the last 250 years. The following names represent a complete pillar of prophetic interpretation: Joseph Mede, Sir Isaac Newton, Jurieu, Vitringa, Daubuz, Fleming, De Chesaux, Bishop Newton, Faber, Cunninghame, Keith, Bickersteth, Wordsworth, Elliott, and Birks. Their principal works are on this table, and I will now briefly trace the progress they exhibit in prophetic interpretation made in the last two and a half centuries.

Joseph Mede was a fellow of Christ's College in Cambridge, and lived in the first half of the 17th century, the century immediately succeeding that of the Reformation. He was a man of great learning and diligence, and deep insight into the Divine word, and made prophecy his special study. Dr. Twisse, who was prolocutor in the Westminster Assembly of Divines, wrote a preface to Mede's work on the Apocalypse, in which he says that "as it is written of the virtuous woman in the Proverbs of Solomon, 'many daughters have done virtuously, but thou surmountest them all,' so it may be said of Mede's exposition of Revelation: many interpreters have done excellently, but he surmounteth them all." Mede's key to the Apocalypse, written in Latin, was translated into English by Richard More, one of the burgesses in the English Parliament; and the House of Commons published that translation in 1641, the year of the great massacre of Protestants in Ireland. Here is a copy of that work published by the House of Commons. The Puritan Parliament set its seal thus upon the historical antipapal interpretation of prophecy, and upon this valuable work of Joseph Mede. Mede did what no interpreter had previously done; he laid down the important principle, that, for the correct understanding of the Apocalypse, it is necessary, in the first place, to fix the order of its principal visions apart from the question of their interpretation. Accordingly Mede sought to exhibit the synchronism and the succession of these visions, or the order of the prophecies contained in the Apocalypse. Setting aside and ignoring for the time all question of the meaning of these prophecies, he endeavored to demonstrate from the visions themselves the position they occupy with reference to one another. Their mutual relations once proved serve as a most valuable clue to their significance. Mede prefaces his work with the prayer: "Thou who sittest upon the throne, and Thou, O Lamb, Root of David, who wast only worthy to take and open this book, open the eyes of Thy servant, and direct his hand and mind, that in these Thy mysteries he may discern and produce something which may tend to the glory of Thy name and profit of the Church."

The first synchronism which Mede establishes is that of what he calls a "noble quaternion of prophecies," remarkable by reason of the equality of their times. First, of the woman remaining in the wilderness for three and a half times, or as it is declared in the prophecy, 1,260 days; second, of the beast whose deadly wound was healed ruling forty-two months; third, of the outer court of the temple trodden underfoot by the Gentiles for the same number of months; fourth, of the witnesses prophesying in sackcloth 1,260 days. Mede points out that not only are these times equal, but they begin at the same period and end together, and must therefore synchronize throughout their course. The events of the last 250 years have confirmed Mede's interpretation as to the general synchronism of these times, but they have also shown that these periods should be reckoned from an era rather than from a point of time; and that they terminate in a corresponding era. The three and a half times of prophecy date from the era of the rise of the Papal and Mohammedan powers, and extend to the era of the overthrow of those powers; in which era we are living at the present day. Let me refer you to a work on this subject which I published a year ago, entitled "Light for the Last Days," tracing these prophetic times, and the eras of their commencement and close. Mede established several other synchronisms; as, for example, one between the revived Roman head of Revelation 13, and the two-horned, lamb-like beast, which John calls elsewhere "the false prophet," which acts for the revived head. He shows that the two are inseparable companions; that they are together alike in their rising and in their ruin, that the one exercises the power of the other, and thus, whatever be their meaning, that they are necessarily synchronous. He then traces the position of the remaining visions of the Apocalypse as they stand related to these, showing which precede these central visions, which synchronize with them, and which succeed them; thus making out and establishing the connection and order of the entire series of visions; and this, as I have already stated, apart from all question of interpretation. Having gone through the book of Revelation thus, Mede next proceeds to expound and demonstrate its fulfillment in the events of history. I have said that Mede's work on Revelation was approved and printed by the Puritan Parliament. Just at that time the Westminster Assembly of Divines drew up its most valuable Confession of Faith, a Confession subsequently accepted by the national Presbyterian Church of Scotland. Here is a copy containing a list of the hundred Puritan divines who met in the Westminster Assembly, headed by the name of Dr. William Twisse, the prolocutor, who wrote the preface to Mede's work to which I have already referred. The Westminster Confession of Faith endorsed the historical interpretation of prophecy, and declared the Roman pontiff to be the predicted "man of sin." Weigh well the following words of the Westminster divines upon this subject, embodied in the 25th chapter of their solemn declaration of the things they held and taught on the authority of Scripture. "There is no other head of the Church but the Lord Jesus Christ, nor can the Pope of Rome in any sense be head thereof but is that antichrist, that man of sin and son of perdition, that exalteth himself in the Church against Christ and all that is called God."

One of the divines who put his hand to this statement was the famous Puritan writer, Dr. Thomas Goodwin, of London, and he has left us an exposition of the book of Revelation of which this is a copy. It belongs, I need hardly say, to the historical school, and describes the Apocalypse as "the story of Christ's kingdom."

Sir Isaac Newton followed Mede and the Puritan writers and further advanced the comprehension of prophecy. He was a Christian as well as a philosopher, and took delight in studying and comparing the works and word of God. The vastness of his genius led him to the most extensive views of things natural and Divine. He studied nature as a whole, history as a whole, chronology as a whole, and, in connection with these, prophecy as a whole. While Mede directed his attention especially to the Apocalypse, Newton investigated both it and the book of Daniel, tracing out their connections with the course of history and chronology, utilizing in the latter his unrivaled astronomical skill. Here is a copy of his "Observations on the Prophecies of Daniel and the Apocalypse of John," printed in the year 1733, six years after his death. In the first chapter Newton says: "Among the old prophets Daniel is most distinct in order of time, and easiest to be understood, and therefore in those things which relate to the last times he must be made the key to the rest. In the third chapter he says: "The prophecies of Daniel are all of them related to one another as if they were but several parts of one general prophecy given at several times. The first is the easiest to be understood, and every following prophecy adds something new to the former." "In the vision of the image composed of four metals the foundation of all Daniel's prophecies is laid. It represents a body of four great nations which should reign over the earth successively, viz. the people of Babylonia, the Persians, the Greeks, and Romans; and by a stone cut out without hands which fell upon the feet of the image and brake all the four metals to pieces and became a great mountain and filled the whole earth, it further represents that a new kingdom should arise after the four, and conquer all those nations, and grow very great, and last till the end of all ages." In chapter 4 he says: "In the next vision, which is of the four beasts, the prophecy of the four empires is repeated with several new additions, such as are the two wings of the lion, the three ribs in the mouth of the bear, the four wings and four heads of the leopard, the eleven horns of the fourth beast, and the Son of man coming in the clouds of heaven to the Ancient of days sitting in judgment."

In chapter 7 he expounds the "little horn" of the fourth beast, with eyes as a seer and a mouth speaking great things, and changing times and laws; and shows it to represent a power both prophetic and kingly, and that such a seer, a prophet, and a king is the Roman Papacy. He traces its rise, and the contemporaneous rise of the ten horns at the fall of the western Roman empire. He traces also its dominion, and anticipates its doom at the close of the foretold period. He interprets the days of prophecy as years, reckoning, to use his own words, a prophetic day for a solar year. He shows the futurity in his time, and proximity of the worldwide overthrow of the Papal power. He says that the time had not then come perfectly to understand these mysterious prophecies, "because the main revolution predicted in them had not yet come to pass. In the days of the voice of the seventh angel, when he shall begin to sound, the mystery of God shall be finished, as He hath declared to His servants the prophets; and then the kingdoms of this world shall become the kingdoms of our Lord and His Christ, and He shall reign for ever." Till then, he says, "we must content ourselves with interpreting what hath been already fulfilled." He adds: "Amongst the interpreters of the last age there is scarce one of note who hath not made some discovery worth knowing, and thence I seem to gather that God is about opening these mysteries."

He points out that an angel must fly through the midst of heaven with the everlasting gospel to preach to all nations before Babylon falls and the Son of man reaps His harvest, and says: "If the general preaching of the gospel be approaching, it is to us and our posterity that those words mainly belong, 'In the time of the end the wise shall understand, but none of the wicked shall understand.' 'Blessed is he that readeth, and they that hear the words of this prophecy, and keep those things which are written therein.'"

How marvelously has Sir Isaac Newton's anticipation of a general preaching of the gospel been accomplished in the glorious evangelization of the world during the last century!

This judicious writer expressed it as his opinion to Whiston, his learned successor, that the Church of Rome was destined to be overthrown by a tremendous infidel revolution; in other words, that superstition would be trodden down by infidelity. Remembering that Sir Isaac Newton died half a century before the French Revolution, this was a very remarkable anticipation!

One of the most important features of Sir Isaac Newton's work is its exposition of the use of symbolic language in prophecy. He lays it down as a principle, that "for understanding the prophecies we are in the first place to acquaint ourselves with the figurative language of the prophets.

This language is taken from the analogy between the world natural, and an empire or kingdom considered as a world politic." The prophecies of Daniel and the Apocalypse being symbolic in their language are not to be interpreted literally. In these books the sun, moon, stars, earth, fire, meteors, winds, storms, lightning, hail, rain, waters, sea, rivers, floods, dry land, overflowing of waters, drying up of waters, fountains, islands, trees, mountains, wilderness, beasts, as the lion, bear, leopard, goat, with their horns, heads, feet, wings, teeth, etc., are all symbolic; they are symbols of things of a different nature, though things analogous to these, or in some sense resembling them. On this principle, for example, the two witnesses of Revelation 11 are symbolic, and do not represent two actual men from whose mouth literal fire proceeds, and who literally shut heaven, and literally turn waters to blood, and smite the earth with literal plagues, and who are slain and lie dead for three and a half literal days, and then literally rise from the dead, and literally and visibly ascend to heaven in a cloud; nor is their ascension followed by a literal earthquake, and a literal fall of the tenth part of a literal city, and by literal lightnings, voices, thunderings, and hail. All these are symbols of other things, and their literal interpretation is an absurdity. Futurists utterly degrade these solemn and majestic predictions by their pernicious attempts to expound them on the principle of a literal fulfillment. The first step in the direction of the comprehension of these prophecies is the consistent recognition of their symbolic character. A sufficient number of these symbols are divinely interpreted for us, to serve as a clue to all the rest, as when a beast is explained to represent a kingdom, and a candlestick a local Church. The second step to a comprehension of symbolic prophecy is the settlement of the meaning of the various symbols which they employ. Contemporaneous with Sir Isaac Newton there were several great Huguenot expositors of prophecy. Among these I may name Jurieu and Daubuz. Both these were exiled Huguenots, and belonged to the five hundred thousand Protestants who were compelled to leave France by the persecuting action of Louis XIV in revoking the Edict of Nantes. Their sufferings under the Papal power turned their attention to the prophetic word, and in it they found support and consolation. Jurieu, for example, begins his prophetic work with the sentence: "The afflicted Church seeks for consolation. Where can she find it but in the promises of God?" Here is a copy of this work by Jurieu, published in 1687, entitled, "The Accomplishment of the Scripture Prophecies; or, The Approaching Deliverance of the Church," "proving that the Papacy is the antichristian kingdom, and that that kingdom is not far from its ruin; that the present persecution may end in three years and a half, after which the destruction of antichrist shall begin, which shall be finished in the beginning of the next age, and then the kingdom of Christ shall come upon the earth."

Here is another work published at the same period by one of the exiled Huguenot ministers. Its title runs thus: "A New System of the Apocalypse: written by a French Minister in the year 1685, and finished but two days before the dragoons plundered him of all except this Treatise." The author anticipated that the reformed religion overthrown by the revocation of the Edict of Nantes would be again reestablished in three and a half years; which it was in the most remarkable manner, though not just as he expected. The great English Revolution, which brought about the re- establishment of Protestantism, followed three and a half years after the revocation of the Edict of Nantes, and these men lived to see it, and to rejoice in it. The author of this little work points out the futurity at that time of the vials on Papal Rome, in which he was evidently correct. Here is another Huguenot work of the same period, written by an exiled minister, describing the way in which all Protestants throughout France had been forbidden, under the severest penalties, to assemble for the worship of God; and also forbidden to leave the country under pain of the galleys or even condemnation to death. This work traces in a very remarkable way the similarity of the experience of the reformed Church in this last great Papal persecution, to that of the Jews under Antiochus Epiphanes in the time of the Maccabees. It contains in an appendix the famous bull of Pope Clement XI, condemning a hundred Jansenist propositions as "false, pernicious, injurious, outrageous, seditious, impious, blasphemous," etc. The hundred propositions taken from the works of the Jansenists are given here, and they are all most excellent and in perfect harmony with the teachings of Scripture. Among them are the following: "Proposition 79. It is useful and necessary at all times, in all places, and for all sorts of persons, to study the Scripture, and to understand its spirit, piety, and mysteries."

"Proposition 84. It is to close to Christian people the mouth of Jesus Christ to take from their hands the holy word of God, or to keep it shut in taking from them the means of understanding it." In other words, to take the Bible out of the hand of Christian people, or to take away from them the means of understanding the Scripture, is to shut the mouth of Christ Himself as far as they are concerned.

"Proposition 85. To forbid the reading of Scripture, and particularly of the gospel, to Christians is to forbid the use of light to the children of light." Which proposition also the pope condemns as an insufferable and abominable doctrine, and adds: "We forbid to all the faithful of both sexes to think, teach, or speak on these propositions in any other way than as we lay down in this constitution or bull; and whoever shall teach, understand, or expound these propositions, or any of them, in public or private in any other way than is laid down by the pope, subjects himself to the severest censures and condemnations of the Church, and incurs the indignation of Almighty God, and of the holy apostles Peter and Paul." All the propositions cited by Clement XI in this bull, and condemned by him as "scandalous, impious, blasphemous," are as scriptural as those we have quoted.

I have mentioned Daubuz among these exiled Huguenots. He was the author of a large and learned commentary upon the Apocalypse of considerable value, with which I must associate, as belonging to the same period, the "Commentary on Revelation" published by the learned Dutch professor, Vitringa. Here are copies of these two works. Vitringa's was published in 1695, and the commentary by Daubuz in 1720. They both belong to the historical school, and exhibit an erudition of the widest range, both secular and ecclesiastical, embracing Hebrew, Greek, and other literature bearing on the interpretation of prophecy.

The well-known prophetic student Robert Fleming lived at the time of Vitringa and Daubuz. He published, in the year 1701, a small but remarkable work, of which this is a copy, entitled, "The Rise and Fall of Rome Papal." Its theme is the relation of Papal and prophetic chronology. Fleming shows, as others had done for many centuries, that the 1,260 days of prophecy represent 1,260 years, and advocates their interpretation upon the intermediate or calendar scale, which would shorten the whole period by eighteen years. Reckoning from the most important dates in the rise of the Papacy, and guided by the prophetic times, Fleming indicated two years then future which would be marked in all probability by crises in the overthrow of the Papal power, the years 1794 and 1848; he also mentions 1866. Now it should be remembered that Fleming published this work in 1701, and that the French Revolution fell out at the first of the dates which he indicated the Reign of Terror took place, as you will remember, in 1793; and that the year 1848 brought another tremendous crisis in Papal history. The revolution that year broke out in Paris on February 23rd, and before March 5th every country lying between the Atlantic and the Vistula had in a greater or less degree been revolutionized. On March 15th, a fortnight after the fall of Louis Philippe, a constitution was proclaimed at Rome, and the pope fled to Gaeta, and was subsequently formally deposed from his temporal authority, and an Italian republic proclaimed. The year 1866 was equally or even more important, as introducing the series of Papal defeats which culminated four years later, in 1870, in the overthrow of the Papal monarchy in France, and the fall of the Papal temporal power in Italy.

"Is it not a proof that this historical expositor Fleming was working on right lines, and had seized the true clue, that he should have fixed, nearly a century beforehand, on the close of the eighteenth century as the commencement of the era of Divine vengeance on the Papal power, and have pointed out, within a single year, the very central period of that signal judgment; 1 and that he should have similarly indicated the years 1848 and 1866 as years of Papal overthrow, saying, with reference to the former, "We are not to imagine that this vial will totally destroy the Papacy, though it will exceedingly weaken it, for we find it still in being and alive when the next vial is poured out"? The vial which succeeds he interprets as the judgment on the Mohammedan power, especially as existing in Turkey; and by the vial which follows that again, the seventh vial, he understands the final destruction of Rome or mystical Babylon. He says: "As Christ concluded ' His sufferings on the cross with this voice, 'It is finished,' so the Church's sufferings are concluded with a voice out of the temple of heaven, and from the throne of God and Christ there, saying, 'It is done.' And therefore with this doth the blessed millennium of Christ's spiritual reign on earth begin." 2

About fifty years later than the time of Fleming, or in the middle of the last century, was published a work by a Swiss astronomer named De Cheseaux, entitled "Historical, Chronological, and Astronomical Remarks on Certain Parts of the Book of Daniel." A copy of this book exists in the British Museum. It demonstrates the astronomic character of the prophetic times. It proves, in the clearest and most conclusive way, that the 1,260 years of prophecy, and the

2,300 years of prophecy, and also the period of 1,040 years which is their difference are astronomic cycles of one and the same character, luni-solar cycles, or cycles harmonizing the revolutions of sun and moon, and affecting the order of time dealt with in the calendar. These discoveries are of the deepest interest. As M. de Cheseaux says: For many ages the book of Daniel, and especially these passages of it, have been quoted and commented on by numerous and varied authors, so that it is impossible for a moment to call in question their antiquity. Who can have taught their author the marvelous relation of the periods he selected with soli-lunar revolutions? Is it possible, considering all these points, to fail to recognize in the author of the book of Daniel the Creator of the heavens and of their hosts, of the earth and the things that are therein?

I cannot enlarge at the present time on De Cheseaux's discoveries. If you desire to know more about them, you will find a chapter on the subject in my work on the "Approaching End of the Age."

I must notice one more writer of the last century, the excellent Bishop Newton, whose deservedly popular work on prophecy has gone through so many editions. Newton acted on Lord Bacon's suggestion, expressed in his "Advancement of Learning," that a history of prophecy was wanted, in which every prophecy of the Scripture should be compared with the event fulfilling it. The twenty- sixth dissertation of Newton's work recapitulates his exposition of the prophecies relating to Romanism. In it he says: "The prophecies relating to Popery are the greatest and most essential, and the most striking part of the revelation. Whatever difficulty and perplexity there may be in other passages, yet here the application is obvious and easy. Popery being the great corruption of Christianity, there are indeed more prophecies relating to that than to almost any other distant event. It is a great object of Daniel's, and the principal object of St. Paul's, as well of St. John's prophecies; and these considered and compared together will mutually receive and reflect light from, and upon, each other."

Bishop Newton considered that the sounding of the seventh trumpet, or pouring out of the third woe, the woe of the vials, upon the Papacy was still future in his day, and he was evidently correct, as he lived before the time of the French Revolution. He held also that at the fall of the Ottoman empire and the Christian antichrist the Jews would turn to the Lord and be restored to their own land, and says that the prophecies relating to the conversion and restoration of the Jewish people are simply innumerable. 3

We must now, in the last place, briefly consider the progress made in prophetic interpretation during the present century. I have already said that the French Revolution cast a flood of light upon the whole question of prophetic interpretation. It strongly confirmed the historic view, including its leading feature, the year-day chronology of the prophetic times.

Faber and Cunninghame wrote very fully upon this subject during the first twenty years of the century, showing the true measure and position of the "seven times" of prophecy, as extending from the rise of the four monarchies to the fall of the fourth, in the days in which we live; and of the three-and-a-half times as reaching from the rise to the fall of the Papal power.

Among the most valuable expositors who have succeeded these I may mention Keith, who deals mainly with the evidential side of prophetic interpretation. One of his most important works is entitled, "History and Destiny of the World and the Church according to Scripture; or, The Four Monarchies and the Papacy." He quotes throughout, from first to last, the testimony of the Romanists themselves, in confirmation of his assertions. His work is an unanswerable argument for the Protestant interpretation of prophecy.

The time would fail me to speak of the works of the well-known Bickersteth, or to refer in detail to the many able writers in England, Scotland, Switzerland, Germany, Holland, and America, who within the last fifty years have expounded Scripture prophecy on the historic principle. I can do no more than say a few sentences in closing about three of the greatest of these writers, Bishop Wordsworth, Revelation E. B. Elliott, and Professor Birks, of Cambridge.

The works of the late Bishop Wordsworth, that learned and eloquent commentator, demonstrate with perfect conclusiveness that Rome Papal is the Babylon of the Apocalypse. Wordsworth understood the Church of Rome better than any commentator, Elliott excepted, in recent times; and he was familiar also with the entire history and literature of the Christian Church. His testimony on the fulfillment of prophecy in Papal Rome is such as to settle the question finally for all intelligent and unbiased minds.

The learned commentator, Dean Alford, who was a semi-futurist, says: "I do not hesitate..to maintain that interpretation which regards Papal and not Pagan Rome as pointed out by the harlot of this vision (Revelation 17). The subject has been amply discussed by many expositors. I would especially mention Vitringa and Dr. Wordsworth."

While quoting Dean Alford, I would warn you against the snare into which many have fallen, of trusting themselves implicitly to the guidance of Greek scholars such as Alford, Tregelles, and Ellicott, in the study of prophecy. These students of the letter of sacred writ have their place and value, and should stand high in our estimation; but their special work did not qualify them for the comprehension of the far-reaching system of prophetic truth. The instrument they employ in their researches is the microscope, not the telescope. You cannot scan the starry heavens, or the breadth of the earth, with a microscope; you need a telescope for that.Greek scholars of such eminence are naturally short-sighted. They pore over manuscripts, words, letters, points. They seldom grasp the meaning of history of prophecy as a whole. They generally neglect the philosophy of history, and the light which astronomy has cast on the chronology both of history and prophecy. Besides this, they are too much influenced by traditional testimony, by the views of antiquity. The notions of the Fathers as to an individual, short-lived antichrist, notions which grew up in the twilight of early times, weigh more with them than the teachings of ages of subsequent experience. Wedded to the past, they are blind to the progressiveness of prophetic interpretation. They do not grasp the simple principle that the true interpreter of prophecy is neither tradition nor speculation, but ever-evolving history; that prophecy must be studied in the light of its fulfillment, and the future in the light of the past. Prophecy is vast, mountainous, and far- reaching sight is needed for its elucidation. A Christian philosopher like Sir Isaac Newton, accustomed to the study of the facts and laws of nature, and the entire course of history and chronology, is a far safer guide in this extensive subject than a Greek scholar whose whole business is the study of words. The man with the microscope sees small points uncommonly well, but he fails to perceive great general relations. As he does not steadily contemplate these relations, they produce no vivid impression upon him, and he is often led to conclusions totally at variance with the whole course of experience, and even with the teachings of common sense.

Not that all scholars however are shortsighted. Occasionally scholars are met with like Revelation E.B. Elliott and Professor Birks, both fellows of Trinity College, Cambridge, equally able to use the microscope and the telescope. Unquestionably the most learned and able work ever written upon the book of Revelation is Mr. Elliott's "Horae Apocalypticae." The late Dr. Candlish, of Edinburgh, no mean judge, describes Elliott as "among the most learned profound and able expositors any of the books of Scripture ever had." 4 Elliott's commentary on the Apocalypse is to historic interpretation what Butler's "Analogy" or Paley's famous work is to the evidence of Christianity ù a solid foundation. It is learned, candid, and conclusive. It assumes nothing without ground. It deals with unquestionable facts, and that too with great fullness. It compares history with prophecy in a more elaborate way, at all points, than any work which preceded it. In style it is somewhat involved and overloaded, and its ten thousand references repel the superficial reader; but it will remain a masterpiece of exposition while the study of the sure word of prophecy endures. Professor Birks, of Cambridge, while equal to Elliott as a scholar, and nearly equal to him in painstaking research, was his superior in philosophic grasp and logical ability. He was a comprehensive synthesist, a keen analyst, a convincing reasoner, an eloquent writer. He was accurate, clear-headed, patient in investigation, fair in statement, ripe in judgment. His works are an intellectual feast, as well as full of spiritual instruction. One of his books, that for example on "The Earlier Visions of Daniel," is worth more than all the futurists ever wrote on prophecy put together. His work on the "First Elements of Sacred Prophecy" is an overwhelming answer to futurism. Dealing with the most learned and masterly works in exposition and defense of that system which have ever appeared, those by Maitland, Tyso, Burgh, and Dr. Todd, without an effort it shivers them to fragments, and scatters them to the winds. It is a pity that this work has long been out of print, and that futurism is left to flourish in certain quarters in ignorance of this able demonstration of its error and absurdity.

I shall ever esteem it as a great privilege to have known Professor Birks. To him I communicated the earliest discoveries I made on the astronomic nature of the prophetic times ù discoveries afterwards embodied in my work entitled "The Approaching End of the Age," now in its tenth edition. Of my subsequent investigations on the same line I will say nothing here, save that I have partially published, and hope yet more fully to publish, the evidence that the whole of revealed chronology ù Historic, Levitical, and Prophetic ù is so related to natural chronology, or the time order of nature, as to form with it a single system, united and harmonious in all its parts. This is an important department of the connection of the natural and revealed; a connection involving the unity of their authorship. Nature and Scripture are not the works of two minds, or of many, but of one. They are two testaments, but one book, and as such are the work of the same Divine Author.

And now in conclusion. We have traced in these last three lectures the antiquity, the practical use, and the systematic development of the historical interpretation of prophecy ù the interpretation which regards Rome as the Babylon of the Apocalypse, and the Roman pontiff as "the man of sin." We have shown that the historical interpretation was the earliest adopted in the Christian Church; that it developed with the course of history; that it sustained the Church through the long central ages of apostasy; that it gave birth to the Reformation; that it has been since confirmed by the events of several centuries, and elaborated and defended by an unbroken series of learned and unanswerable works. In vain do the waves of controversy rage against this stately rock. It has stood for ages, and is destined to remain till the light of eternity shall break upon the scene. The historic interpretation is no dream of ignorant enthusiasts. It is no speculation of fanciful, ill-balanced minds. It has grown with the growth of generations; it has been built up by the labors of men of many nations and ages. It has been embodied in solemn confessions of the Protestant Church. It forms a leading element in the testimony of martyrs and reformers. Like the prophets of old, these holy men bore a double testimony ù a testimony for the truth of God, and a testimony against the apostasy of His professing people. The providential position which they occupied, the work they accomplished, gave singular and special importance to their testimony; and this was their testimony, and nothing less, that Papal Rome is the Babylon of prophecy, drunken with the blood of saints and martyrs; and that its head, the Roman pontiff, is the predicted "man of sin," or antichrist.

To reject this testimony of God's providential witnesses on a matter of such fundamental import, and to prefer it to the counter-doctrine advocated by the apostate, persecuting Church of Rome, is the error and guilt of modern futurism.

And that futurism is self-condemned. Futurism is literalism, and literalism in the interpretation of symbols is a denial of their symbolic character. It is an abuse and degradation of the prophetic word, and a destruction of its influence. It substitutes the imaginary for the real, the grotesque and monstrous for the sober and reasonable. It quenches the precious light which has guided the saints for ages, and kindles a wild, delusive marsh-fire in its place. It obscures the wisdom of Divine prophecy; it denies the true character of the days in which we live; and while it asserts the nearness of the advent of Christ in the power and glory of His kingdom, it at the same time destroys the only substantial foundation for the assertion, which is prophetic chronology, and the stage now reached in the fulfillment of the predictions of the apostasy.

But in spite of the injurious effects of these false interpretations, "the foundation of God standeth sure"; none can cancel the prophecies which He has written in His holy word, and none can deny or destroy the mighty and far-reaching results which their true interpretation has already accomplished in the world. It has given us, and this is its glory, it has given us the REFORMATION. It has broken the iron chains of superstition and despotism, and lifted nations from the depths of their abasement. It has reared a temple whose walls no enemy can ruin. It has reopened, it has given back to the world, that book whose teachings have led millions into the way of life and peace.

And the sacred light of these prophecies is still guiding the Church of God across the wide ocean of her dangerous way. Those steadfast stars of prophecy which lighted of old the persecuted Waldenses through the darkness of the middle ages, which lighted the progress of the Lollards and the Bohemians before the Reformation, which lighted the noble reformers through gloom and tempest three hundred years ago, and which have since lighted watchful saints through troubled centuries, are shining still in that high and holy firmament, whence no mortal hand can pluck them down; and they shall shine on ù those thousand glittering stars of prophecy till they have fulfilled their glorious mission, till they have guided the Church in safety to her celestial haven, and their long-enduring radiance melts at last in the rising splendors of eternal day.

## Notes

1. "Approaching End of the Age," p. 476.
2. Fleming, "Decline and Fall of Rome Papal," p. 83.
3. Bishop Newton: "Dissertation on the Prophecies," pp. 682,696.
4. Robert S. Candlish, D.D.: Lecture on "The Pope, the Antichrist of Scripture."

# Lecture Eight - Double Foreview of the Reformation

In our previous lectures we have considered from the standpoint of prophecy the great Papal system of Latin Christianity, and it now remains for us to show you, in this closing one, that the same mirror of the future which so fully reflected the coming Roman apostasy reflects as clearly that Reformation movement of the sixteenth century which emancipated from it myriads of mankind.

This could hardly be otherwise. As prophecy traces the entire story of Roman rule, in both its pagan and Papal forms, and carries it on to a point even now future, it would not, of course, pass by unnoticed the most remarkable and noteworthy incident in the later section of history. It could not omit from its anticipative record an episode so distinctly providential as that Protestant exodus, which split western Christendom into two halves, and severed from the communion of Rome Norway, Sweden, Denmark, Germany, Holland, and Great Britain.

It might well be omitted from Daniel's very distant foreview, but scarcely from the latter prophecy of John, when the incipient workings of the apostasy had already commenced. Neither the story of the apostate Church nor that of the true would be complete without it; for it was an episode of stupendous importance to the welfare of hundreds of millions of mankind through nine or ten generations, both to those whom it liberated from the superstitions and tyrannies of Rome, and to those on whom by a counter movement ù it riveted her fetters more strongly then ever.

What! should the ruin wrought by Romanism be plainly portrayed in advance on the prophetic page, and the revival produced by the Spirit of God and the word of His mouth be left altogether out of view? Should the work of Satan, his corruption and defilement of the professing Church, be reflected in the Divine mirror, and not the work of the glorious Head of the true Church through His faithful witnesses in the restoration to the world of the primitive Christianity it had lost? Never! A true mirror reflects everything alike, and Scripture prophecy anticipates the entire outline of Church history. Just as there were no events in the history of Israel which were not foretold before they came to pass, so in the history of the Church. The Reformation of the sixteenth century, and its glad and glorious results, are as clearly foreshadowed and foretold as the Romanism of the dark ages.

You will naturally inquire, Where and how? Before replying, let me remind you that there are two kinds of prophecy in Scripture ù the acted, and the spoken or written; the type and the prediction. In the Levitical sacrifices, for instance, we have acted prophecies of the atonement; in Isaiah 53 we have verbal predictions of it. The whole history of the natural Israel is typical of that of the spiritual Israel, or Christian Church. Both are delivered from Egypt, both are redeemed by the blood of the Lamb, both are led through a desert, both are sustained by bread from heaven, both journey towards a rest that remains for the people of God. This broad analogy descends in a wonderful way to details. The Apostle Paul in 1 Corinthians 10 shows this, and states that, not only was Israel's history typical, but that it was divinely ordered that it might be so; in other words, it was intentionally prophetic. "These things," he says, "happened unto them for ensamples (or types, ?????), and are written for our instruction." Not only are they recorded for our warning, but they occurred in the providence of God in order that they might foreshadow the experiences of the Christian Church, and that she might learn from them solemn and needed lessons.

The incidents of Jewish history actually happened, that they might be types of Christian history; and Divine foreknowledge is as much exemplified in this correspondence between type and antitype as in that between prediction and fulfillment.

I am to show you this evening, then, two sets of predictions of the Reformation, one acted in Jewish history, the other symbolized in apocalyptic prophecy; the one embodied in the story of the Old Testament, the other in the symbolic predictions of the New.

Before I can do this, you must allow me to remind you with some degree of accuracy what the Reformation was, as to its broad historical characteristics. It was not the formation of the Church, but its re-formation after its ruin by Romanism. It was not a first beginning, but a second. Pentecost formed the Church; Popery deformed it; Protestantism reformed it. Pentecost occurred in the first century, and is associated with the work of the apostles themselves. The Reformation did not occur till the sixteenth century, and was not completed till the seventeenth, and is associated with such names as Luther and Calvin, Zwingle and Knox, Cranmer and Latimer. The first belongs to ancient history, the last to modern times. A great chronological gap of nearly fifteen hundred years lies between the two. There were the early ages of first love, apostolic zeal, rapid extension, martyr suffering, noble confessions and apologies; followed by other centuries of imperial Christianity, growing corruption, of bitter strife and ambitious rivalries; and these again by a thousand years of Papal domination and ever- deepening moral darkness before the glad light of the Reformation broke over the earth. It is a late episode of Church history, not an early one.

And further. When it did take place, its results were very partial. It has affected but a portion of apostate Christendom. It has not brought back to the faith of Christ Austria, Italy, Spain, Portugal, France, or Belgium. The reformed nations may be the mightiest, the wealthiest, and the most progressive; but they constitute only a fraction of Roman Christendom. The greater part of it remains involved still in the Papal apostasy.

Moreover Protestantism priceless as have been the benefits it has conferred on those who have joined its ranks ù is yet very far from being a perfect recovery of primitive Christianity. It has risen out of the gross ignorance and superstition of mediaeval Romanism; it has altogether abandoned the idolatry of image worship, virgin worship, saint worship, and the adoration of the priest-made wafer deity of the Latin mass; it has recovered a purer faith and a simpler ritual, and secured for the Church a measure of liberty and independence; above all, it has circulated the Scriptures in the vulgar tongues of the nations of Christendom, and has adopted as its motto, "The Bible, the whole Bible, and nothing but the Bible": but it has never completely purified itself from Romish doctrine and practice, it has never regained complete independence of secular domination, it has never got clear of union with the world. It has rejected the claim of the Church to rule the State, it has not as clearly refused the pretension of the State to rule the Church; it has suffered worldly ambition, priestcraft, simony, and abuses of many kinds; and it has developed two strong tendencies, one to a return to the Romish apostasy, and the other to rationalism and infidelity. The true spiritual Church of Christ is still, even in Protestant lands, but a small part of the professing Church. I want you clearly to bear in mind from the outset then, first, that, in point of time, Protestantism is a late or modern movement; secondly, that it is, in point of sphere, a limited one; and thirdly, that it is, in point of character, a very imperfect return to primitive Christianity.

One more introductory remark before I pass on. May we not safely conclude that Protestantism will last till the end of the age and the second advent of Christ? The reformed Churches will never be darkened by a universal apostasy, as was the early Church. The innumerable millions of Bibles read and studied all over the world, the countless human minds enlightened by their contents, and human hearts regenerated by their revelation of God in Christ, and linked by faith and love and eternal life to the Savior, forbid the fear that the recovered gospel will ever again be lost to the world. The chronology of the Papacy shows us that the coming of the Lord is at hand; and hence we may rest assured that the Reformation is, not only a late incident in Church history, but that it is the last great movement. The next will be the final change from the militant to the triumphant condition of the Church, when the fourth empire shall pass away, and be succeeded by the kingdom of the Son of man and of the saints. We have entered on that phase of Church history which will exist at the second advent; nothing remains unfulfilled of the predictions concerning Romanism, except her sudden destruction at the end of this age.

As regards the history of the Reformation, I want you to remember that it took place in stages during a period extending over about half a century. Its commencement is reckoned from the year when Luther published his theses against indulgences, A.D. 1517; and its close, in Germany at least, may be placed in A.D. 1555, when the celebrated Peace of Augsburg confirmed the Protestants of Germany in all their rights and possessions, and recognized their complete national and ecclesiastical independence of the popes. The close of the anti-Reformation Council of Trent and the full establishment of the Protestant Church in England were in A.D. 1563, forty-six years from the initial date of the Reformation. The struggle to maintain the position gained, in face of the murderous Papal reaction, which dates from the Council of Trent, occupied a much longer period, and was not over even at the Peace of Westphalia, at the end of the thirty years' religious war, in A.D. 1648, when a basis was laid for the settlement of the long struggle in Central Europe.

It extended however in France and England still further, nearly up to the close of the seventeenth century, when it was finally settled in favor of Popery in France by the revocation of the Edict of Nantes, and in favor of Protestantism in England by the glorious Revolution, which placed William of Orange on the throne, and passed the act of succession excluding Popish monarchs for the future. Not without so severe and long-continued a struggle did the reformed religion establish itself, even in the countries where it did take root, nor did Protestantism cease to resist, even in the countries where it was ultimately crushed.

As to the various aspects of this great Reformation movement, you must distinguish especially between three.

**1.** It was first and mainly, as we have said, a return from gross and long-continued apostasy to primitive Christianity; it was a revival of spiritual religion in the hearts of men. As at the first promulgation of the gospel in Europe the pagan people "turned from idols to serve the living and true God, and to wait for His Son from heaven," so in the sixteenth century. Men turned once more from the idols of Papal instead of pagan Rome which they had been worshipping, and they turned to GOD. They turned from the doctrines of demons to the gospel of Christ; they began once more to rejoice in the belief that Jesus had delivered them from the wrath to come; they received the doctrines proclaimed by the reformers not as the word of men, but as it was in truth, the word of God. It worked in them effectually, so that they took joyfully the spoiling of their goods, and all the other sufferings which came upon them from their enemies, and from them sounded out everywhere the word of the Lord. They received the word in much affliction, but in the joy of the Holy Ghost, and in power and assurance. The Reformers were like the apostles, holy, self-denying, Bible-loving, hard-working preachers of the gospel. In its first and primary aspect the Reformation was a spiritual work. Its germ was the work of the Holy Ghost in the soul of Luther, convincing him of sin, of righteousness, and of judgment, leading him to repentance and to belief of the gospel of God's grace, and convincing him that salvation was "not of works." It was what we should in these days call a spiritual revival, traceable to the sovereign grace of God in the first place, and to the republication of His Word in the second.

**2.** But the Reformation did more than produce a spiritual revival. As a matter of history, it gave also to the world a new ecclesiastical system. It established reformed Churches in separation from the Church of Rome, national Churches, with secular monarchs in some cases at their head. This was the case in England, where Henry VIII made himself head of the Church in these lands. Whether this was for evil or for good we must not here consider, but simply note the fact that the Reformation movement built up a new outward organization of an ecclesiastical character, with new articles and rubrics, new ceremonies and practices, and a new fountain head of authority. This new organization was not only distinct from, but antagonistic to Romanism, and because of its being so was called Protestant. It has grown with enormous rapidity during the last three centuries, and has already attained proportions not far short of those of the ancient and apostate Church against which it protests. It is characterized by the circulation of the Bible, and the reference to it as to a standard of all controversies; by the recognition that ministers of Christ should not be "sacrificing priests" but gospel preachers, preachers of the word, heralds of the great salvation; and by an acknowledgment of the right of private judgment in the interpretation of Scripture.

**3.** And lastly, the Reformation produced Protestant kingdoms ù nations which severed all the links that bound them to Rome, and asserted their own absolute independence of the popes.

In a word, the movement was one of renovation and liberation, which spread in successive and ever- widening circles, from the individual to the Church, and from the Church to the nation. It was one founded on a recovered Bible, extended by a renewal of the long-disused practice of preaching, and issuing in the largely improved but still imperfect state of things which we see around us this day. It emancipated the minds of men from long and bitter bondage; it gave an impetus to arts and sciences, to enterprise and culture, to freedom and liberty. It was naturally hailed as a glad deliverance by all who came under its influence; but it brought upon them long struggles and cruel sufferings under the terrible and mighty Roman wild beast. The world reeled under the fierceness of his wrath on the escape of so many of his victims, his thunderous roar rent the air, his mad passion caused the blood of saints to flow in torrents, his cruel claws dragged thousands into his dens of torture in dark Inquisition dungeons; and so horrible was the sacrifice of human life resulting from his rage, that the world turned on him at last and bade him be still; bound, and beat him into silence, drew his claws and his teeth, deprived him of dominion and the power to do further damage, and left him feeble and defenseless, albeit as fierce as ever.

We stated just now that this great Reformation movement was doubly foretold in the Bible. It is foreshadowed in the typical history of Israel in the Old Testament, and its story forms one act of the prophetic drama of the Apocalypse in the New.

## 1. IT WAS FORESHADOWED IN THE HISTORY OF ISRAEL.

Just as the exodus of Israel from Egypt after the passover and their crossing of the Red Sea foreshadowed the redemption of the Church by the death and resurrection of "Christ our Passover," just as the murmurings and rebellions of Israel in the wilderness prefigured the similar incidents in Church history ù so the idolatries of Israel foreshadowed the idolatry which early crept into the Church, and which soon corrupted it altogether. Even in the desert Israel fell into idolatry, and worshipped the golden calf; and perhaps the most salient feature of their history is the constant tendency to relapse into this degrading iniquity. No sooner were Moses and Joshua and their contemporaries dead and gone than declensions into idolatry became frequent. Various tyrants were allowed to conquer and oppress the people as a chastisement for this sin; and when they cried to God in their trouble, and He sent judges and deliverers, they perhaps served Jehovah as long as the judge lived, but quickly afterwards relapsed again. Six times over they were given up to their enemies, and the united servitudes they endured extended to a hundred and eleven years. Still they did evil "in the sight of the Lord, and served Baalim, and Ashtaroth, and the gods of Syria and Zidon, the gods of Moab and Ammon, and the gods of the Philistines, and forsook the Lord, and served not Him" (#Jud 10:6):

Hardly had the Jews reached the zenith of their national prosperity under David and Solomon than again there set in a process of declension. Solomon himself built idol temples for his heathen wives, and after the schism between Israel and Judah, idolatry became the State religion among the ten tribes, who worshipped the golden calves set up by Jeroboam the son of Nebat at Dan and at Bethel, and adopted besides all the idolatries of the heathen around them.

Israel built, as we read in Kings, "high places in all their cities, from the tower of the watchmen to the fenced city. And they set them up images and groves in every high hill, and under every green tree: and there they burnt incense in all the high places, as did the heathen whom the Lord carried away before them; and wrought wicked things to provoke the Lord to anger: for they served idols, whereof the Lord had said unto them, Ye shall not do this thing..And they left all the commandments of the Lord their God, and made them molten images, even two calves, and made a grove, and worshipped all the host of heaven, and served Baal" (#2Ki 17:9-16).

So general did this worship of Baal become in Israel, that in the days of Elijah it was all but universal, and there were but seven thousand left who had not bowed the knee to Baal. Jeremiah exclaims in the Lord's name, "Hath a nation changed their gods, which are yet no gods? but My people have changed their glory for that which doth not profit. Be astonished, O ye heavens, at this, and be horribly afraid, be ye very desolate, saith the Lord. For My people have committed two evils; they have forsaken Me the fountain of living waters, and hewed them out cisterns, broken cisterns, that can hold no water" (#Jer 2:11-13).

Isaiah cries, "How is the faithful city become a harlot!..They have forsaken the Lord, they have provoked the Holy One of Israel unto anger, they are gone away backward."

Ezekiel describes the idolatry of Jerusalem and Samaria under the figure of the grossest and most abominable harlotry.

Hosea said, "Israel hath forgotten his Maker, and buildeth temples" (Hosea 8:14). "Ephraim is joined to idols: let him alone" (Hosea 4:17).

Amos accused Israel, saying, "Ye have borne the tabernacle of your Moloch and Chiun your images, the star of your god, which ye made to yourselves" (#Amos 5:26).

Speaking by the mouth of Jeremiah, the Lord exhorts His people "Trust ye not in lying words, saying, The temple of the Lord, The temple of the Lord, The temple of the Lord, are these..Will ye steal, murder, and commit adultery, and swear falsely, and burn incense unto Baal, and walk after other gods whom ye know not; and come and stand before Me in this house, which is called by My name, and say, We are delivered to do all these abominations? Is this house, which is called by My name, become a den of robbers in your eyes? (Jer 7:4-11).

The ancient prophets are full of this subject, as you will remember; expostulations, appeals, threats, irony, indignant remonstrance are all employed in turn; but the people were obdurate. "We will not hearken unto thee," said they to Jeremiah "we will certainly..burn incense unto the queen of heaven, and pour out drink offerings unto her" (#Jer 44:16,17).

The enormity of this sin was enhanced by the fact that the very object of Israel's existence as a nation was that they might be a holy nation, a peculiar people to Jehovah. They were the sole witnesses to the true God in the world, and yet they seemed obstinately resolved to sink back to the level of their heathen neighbors. The relapse of Israel and Judah into heathen idol worship was punished in the providence of God by their captivity in the lands of the heathen: Israel was carried captive into Assyria, and Judah into Babylon. The heathenism of Jerusalem and of Babylon were substantially the same; each was marked by gross idolatry, and accompanied by the cruel persecution of all who resisted it. Manasseh filled Jerusalem with the blood of the faithful whom he slew. In Babylon, however, both idolatry and persecution found their most complete development. Nebuchadnezzar set up his golden image, issued his persecuting edict, and kindled his fiery furnace; and Belshazzar made his impious feast, and brought the vessels of God's house to his table, that he and his lords, his wives and his concubines, might drink wine in them; and praise "the gods of silver, and

gold, of brass, iron, wood, and stone, which see not, nor hear, nor know"; and Daniel said, addressing the doomed man,
"The God in whose hand thy breath is, and whose are all thy ways, hast thou not glorified" (#Dan 5:23)
Jeremiah cries concerning Babylon: "Behold, the days come, saith the Lord, that I will do judgment upon her graven images" (#Jer 51:52).
"A drought is upon her waters; and they shall be dried up: for it is the land of graven images, and they are mad upon their idols" (#Jer 1:38).
The climax of apostasy and rebellion was reached at last; and when Judah had practically sunk to the level of idolatrous Babylon, God suffered her to be conquered and carried captive by one Babylonian tyrant after another, and His own temple at Jerusalem, which had been so desecrated and profaned, He permitted to be captured and burned. The visible existence of the Jewish nation ceased for a time. The daughters of Jerusalem hung their harps upon the willows by the rivers of Babylon, and Judah lay desolate.
Then, about five hundred years before the first advent of Christ, there came suddenly and unexpectedly deliverance and restoration. Ezra and Nehemiah were raised up to lead back and reorganize in the land a remnant of the people. The temple of God rose from its ashes once more on Mount Moriah. Jerusalem was rebuilt, and its civil and religious polity restored; it was surrounded with walls and towers; the long forgotten word of God was recovered, and read in the audience of the people; and as the language had become somewhat obsolete during the seventy years of the Babylonish captivity, the Jewish reformers, we are told, not only "read in the book in the law of God distinctly," but they also "gave the sense, and caused them to understand the reading" (#Neh 8:8).
The restoration from Babylon inaugurated a blessed era of civil and religious liberty. The restored remnant were not without severe trials; it was by no means easy for them to accomplish their task in face of the persistent and successful opposition of Sanballat the Horonite and his confederates and companions. Again and again the work had to cease, and the people would have given up in despair but for the encouraging and stimulating words of Haggai, Zechariah, and other prophets. The joint ministry of Ezra and Nehemiah seems to have lasted about half a century, and they were permitted to see the work accomplished, the Jewish people liberated from their long exile, and, better still, from all tendency to heathenism and idolatry. They never fell back into that sin after the return from Babylon. The long suspended worship of God was restored; magistrates, judges, and teachers of the law were appointed over the land. The people entered into a solemn covenant to separate themselves from all idolaters, and even, painful as it was, from the heathen wives some of them had taken; and before Ezra and Nehemiah passed to their rest the people, the worship, the temple, and the city were all restored, and the canon of Old Testament Scripture was arranged and closed.

Many political and military troubles arose afterwards, but no such overthrow and restoration. It was to that second temple that Christ came, thus making the glory of the latter house greater than that of the former.

Need I interpret all this true and yet typical history? Does it not apply itself to the later antitypical history? Have you not seen the Reformation of the sixteenth century as I have described the return from Babylon? Is not Jerusalem the true Church, and Babylon the false? and is not Babylon, Rome? Scripture distinctly states this. "The woman which thou sawest" (whose brow was branded "Babylon") "is that great city which reigneth over the kings of the earth." The angel said this to John. In John's days no other great city than Rome ruled over the kings of the earth. Babylon represents Rome. The captive Jews represent God's people oppressed in and by Rome. Their deliverance and restoration, under Ezra and Nehemiah, represent the Reformation under Luther and Calvin and other reformers. Their repentance and abandonment of idolatry, their reading of the word of God and re-establishment of the worship of God, all this had its parallel in the movement we have described. Their rebuilding of Jerusalem and reorganization of Jewish polity and national life foreshadowed the constitution of reformed Protestant communities and nations; the duration of the two movements was the same, about half a century; the results of the two movements were similar; in spite of much bitter but futile opposition; the proportion of the restored remnant was the same, representatives of only two tribes out of the twelve returned to Jerusalem.

Protestantism is growing now with amazing rapidity; but at the end of the sixteenth century it was small, compared with the hosts of Romanism. Both movements consisted of a spiritual work, an ecclesiastical work, and a political work. Both are connected with a recovered Bible, and both "gave the sense" of the original documents to the common people, or made them understand the word of God. Luther, Tyndale, and others translated the Bible into the vulgar tongues of Europe. The close and wonderful parallel extends to many particulars, which I have no time to indicate. Both movements occur late in the stories to which they respectively belong; and if the first advent belongs to the days of the restored temple, we have every reason to believe that the second will take place in this Protestant era, for, as I will show you presently, a chronological prediction occurs in the prophecy of it in Revelation.

But I must revert to the point of Israel's idolatry for a moment, and ask you to glance at the remarkable development of this same sin in the apostasy in the Romish Church.

All through its history idolatry has been the most marked characteristic of the Papal system. Romanism is simply the old Roman paganism revived under Christian names. Romanism and paganism bear to each other the most exact and extraordinary resemblance.

Had paganism its temples and altars, its pictures and images? So has Popery. Had paganism its use of holy water and its burning of incense? So has Popery. Had paganism its tonsured priests, presided over by a pontifex maximus, or sovereign pontiff? So has Popery; and it stamps this very name, which is purely heathen in origin, upon the coins, medals, and documents of the arrogant priest by whom it is governed. Had paganism its claim of sacerdotal infallibility? So has Popery. Had paganism its adoration of a visible representative of Deity carried in state on men's shoulders? So has Popery. Had paganism its ceremony of kissing the feet of the sovereign pontiff? So has Popery. Had paganism its college of pontiffs? So has Popery, in the college of cardinals. Had paganism its religious orders? So has Popery. Had paganism its stately robes, its crowns and crosiers of office? So has Popery. Had paganism its adoration of idols, its worship of the queen of heaven, its votive offerings? So has Popery. Had paganism its rural shrines and processions? So has Popery. Had paganism its pretended miracles, its speaking images, and weeping images, and bleeding images? So has Popery. Had paganism its canonization of saints, as in the deification of the dead Caesars? So has Popery. Had paganism its idolatrous calendar and numerous festivals? So has Popery. Had paganism its enforced celibacy, its mystic signs, its worship of relics? So has Popery. Had paganism its cruel persecution of those who opposed idolatry? So has Popery. Was paganism satanically inspired? So is Popery. God overthrew paganism; Satan revived it under Christian names: but God shall yet destroy it, and sweep its hateful presence from the earth.

And further, just as there never failed in Israel...

## A LINE OF FAITHFUL WITNESSES

...to testify against the idolatry of the people of God, so also in the case of Romanism. All the prophets testified against Jewish idolatry. Isaiah, Jeremiah, and Ezekiel, Hosea and Amos were burning witnesses against it; but perhaps the most typical witness of all was Elijah the Tishbite. This holy and earnest man was one who feared God, and consequently feared not the face of his fellow man. Though Jezebel had slain the prophets of the Lord, he hesitates not to startle Ahab with the bold accusation that his idolatries were the cause of the famine that was desolating the land. "I have not troubled Israel; but thou, and thy father's house, in that ye have forsaken the commandments of the Lord, and thou has followed Baalim."

Forced to flee to the wilderness when Jezebel seeks his life, hear him plead with God that he had been jealous for His name, "because the children of Israel have forsaken Thy covenant, thrown down Thine altars, and slain Thy prophets with the sword; and I, even I only, am left; and they seek my life, to take it away."

Like these Jewish witnesses, the Christian witnesses of later days were very jealous for the Lord, grieved and indignant at the desecration of His name and cause. Like the prophets they were opposed, despised, denounced, persecuted, exiled, and slain. Who were these Christian witnesses? They were, to use the words of one of them, an exiled Huguenot, "those who since the birth of anti-Christianity have cried against its errors and idolatries." If you wish to know their names this Huguenot will tell you. He says in his "Commentary on the Apocalypse," "they were called Berengarians, Stercorists, Waldenses, Albigenses, Leonists, Petrobrusians, Henricians, Wicliffites, Lollards, etc.; as they are now styled Lutherans, Zwinglians, Calvinists, Sacramentarians, Huguenots, heretics, schismatics, etc; and to these reproachful names their enemies added fines, confiscations, imprisonments, banishments, and condemnations to death."[1] Read Foxe's "Acts and Monuments of the Martyrs" if you desire a fuller account of the lives and testimony of these faithful witnesses against antichrist and his abominable idolatries, and of the sufferings they endured in the cause of truth through weary centuries. God never left Himself without a witness. All through the dark ages there were bold and holy men who stood aloof from Rome's corruptions, as we have seen, who denounced her idolatries, who endured her malice, who dared the fury of the wild beast, who resisted unto blood striving against sin. We shall have to speak again of these witnesses in connection with the New Testament prophecy of the Reformation.

Meantime let me remind you that from the existence of this analogy it follows that the moral judgments which are applicable to the Jewish apostasy and reformation are equally so to the Christian. To justify the Christian apostasy is in principle to justify that Jewish apostasy so signally condemned in the Word of God; and to condemn the Christian reformation is in principle to condemn that Jewish reformation so evidently sealed with divine approval. To approve the apostasy, whether Jewish or Christian, is to approve the work of sin and Satan; and to condemn the Reformation, whether Jewish or Christian, is to condemn the work of divine providence and grace. The enemies of the Reformation are the enemies of God. Those who would pull down the sanctuary which the Reformation reared would have pulled down the second temple built by the exiles restored from Babylonish bondage. But what said the promise of God as to that second temple? "Be strong, saith the Lord, and work: for I am with you..I will shake all nations, and the desire of all nations shall come: and I will fill this house with glory, saith the Lord of hosts..The glory of this latter house shall be greater than that of the former, saith the Lord of hosts: and in this place will I give peace." [2] And again, "The Lord whom ye seek, shall suddenly come to His temple." [3]

## NEW TESTAMENT PROPHECY OF THE REFORMATION

We turn now, in the second place, to THE PROPHECIES OF THE REFORMATION in the last book of the Bible. Here again the prediction is an acted one; but instead of being acted in real history, it is acted as on a stage. The whole drama of the Apocalypse is thus acted. Symbolic beings perform symbolic actions. The dramatis personae seen in vision by St. John include heavenly, earthly, and satanic beings, all of whom are representative, symbolical. Christ is represented by "a lamb as it had been slain," or by a mighty, cloud-clothed angel; Satan, as inspiring the Re-man empire, by "a great red dragon"; and so on. In no other way could so vivid a foreview of the events of ages have been presented in so small a compass. The book of Revelation consists of John's descriptions of the living, moving, acting hieroglyphs he saw. He uses constantly the words, "and I saw," "and I heard." In reading it we should try first to realize accurately what the hieroglyph which John saw and describes was, and then consider what it signified. Other Scripture use of similar figures will in most cases give the clue to the meaning.

John also takes part in the drama himself. He speaks and is spoken to, and when he does so he represents the true witnesses of Christ at the time and in the circumstances prefigured. He is himself a hieroglyph, as it were, and stands as the representative of the true servants of God who would be living in the successive periods the events of which are predicted.

The drama as a whole foreshadows the external and internal history of the Church from John's own day to the second advent. As its outward history depends largely on the mere political history, many purely secular events, such as the overthrow of the Roman empire, have their place in this prophetic drama. For just as, if a traveler takes a voyage in a ship, the history of the ship becomes for the time his history, just as the story of an individual cannot be told without taking into account his environment, so the story of the Church cannot be told without a consideration of the contemporary state of the world in which it exists. Moreover Providence employs outward events in the government of the Church itself; wars and invasions are judgments; so are revolutions and insurrections, famines and pestilences. They have therefore properly their place in Church history.

But the Church has also an inward spiritual history, which depends, not on earthly events, but on heavenly and satanic action. If she is sustained, revived, increased, and rendered spiritually victorious, it is because her glorious Head is acting in her and on her behalf. If she is betrayed, corrupted, misled, or persecuted and oppressed, it is because Satan is acting against her in and by her enemies. In the Apocalypse these spiritual agencies are symbolized, as well as material historical events. They are seen acting, but always indirectly through outward agents. Thus earthly material events are continually linked in this wonderful prophecy with their hidden spiritual causes. The Father, the Son, and the Holy Ghost, angels and archangels, and the spirits of the just, are all seen in action under various symbols; and so also are the devil and his agents. Under the symbols of the dragon and the wild beasts, they are seen opposing and counterworking Christ, and persecuting and slaughtering His faithful witnesses. The visions of this holy and sanctifying book, to the study of which a special blessing is attached, constitute a prophetic history of the Church and of the world from apostolic days to the present day, and on to the end of this age. They are, as you know, arranged in order in three groups of seven: first seven seals, then seven trumpets, and then seven vials. Speaking broadly (for I have no time to do more, nor is it needful to our subject), the first six seals represent events extending from John's own day to the fall of paganism and the establishment of Christianity in the Roman earth; while the seventh contains the seven trumpets and all that follows. The first four trumpets depict the Gothic invasions and the overthrow of the old Roman empire in the fifth century. The next two trumpets give events in the East instead of the West, the fifth predicting the Saracenic conquests of the seventh and eighth centuries (symbolized as the ravages of an army of locusts), and the sixth the Turkish invasions of eastern Europe, which extended from the middle of the eleventh century to the middle of the fifteenth. These, and the intolerable misery they occasioned to the Greek Churches of the East, are symbolized under the sixth trumpet by the career of the Euphratean horsemen in the ninth chapter of the book. This vision brings down the prophetic history to the fall of Constantinople, the capital of the eastern empire of Rome, before the Turks in A.D. 1453; and the remainder of the fifteenth century seems covered in the prophecy by the statement that "the rest of the men who were not killed by these plagues, yet repented not of the works of their hands, that they should not worship devils, and idols of gold, and silver, and brass, and stone, and wood." This description of continued obdurate and inveterate apostasy and idolatry applies both to eastern and western Christendom at that time. Thus we are brought down chronologically to the end of the fifteenth century; and then there is a break and a great change in the series of visions!

And what is the next scene that attracts the eye of the holy seer? It is a vision symbolic of the Reformation movement of the sixteenth century, coupled with a retrospective narrative of the history of Christ's true witnesses against idolatry, from the beginning of the apostasy to the close of the Protestant Reformation. You will find this most interesting prophecy in the tenth and first thirteen verses of the eleventh chapters of Revelation. Study it carefully at your leisure, and you will see that the vision consists of the manifestation of a glorious mighty angel, who evidently symbolizes Christ Himself, and of the bestowal by Him on John (in his representative character) of three things:

1.  Of a little open book which he was to eat;
2.  Of a great commission which he was to execute; and
3.  Of a reed with which he was to measure the temple of God.

There follows the story of Christ's "two witnesses," symbolized as two olive trees and two candlesticks; the narrative of their doings and sufferings, of their persecution and slaughter by their enemies, of their brief, trance-like death, and of their speedy resurrection and exaltation. Lastly, there is a great earthquake or revolution, and the fall of a tenth part of the city, or a tenth part of Roman Christendom.

Do you ask my grounds for asserting that the "mighty Angel" of this vision is no other than Christ Himself? I will give you them! His power and glory, the rainbow encircling His head, the sun-like brightness of His countenance, and the resemblance of His feet to pillars of fire ù all these features identify Him with the Son of man seen by John in the first vision of this book. His position and his words identify him also with the one whom Daniel in his last chapter calls "my Lord." No mere angel is cloud-clothed and rainbow-crowned, resplendent as the sun, or speaks with a voice full of majesty, or assumes an attitude which implies the lordship of earth and sea, setting "his right foot on the sea, and his left foot on the earth." No angel would talk of "my two witnesses," or claim to give to men power and authority. There is a loftiness of tone and a sublimity of appearance and action about this Angel that distinguishes Him from all the other lowly servant angels of the book as widely as heaven is distinguished from earth. It is the Lord of angels and of men alike who is manifested in action at this point in the apocalyptic drama; and the very manifestation prepares us for events of the first magnitude, events like those which succeeded Christ's actual manifestation on earth, events like the first promulgation of the gospel in the apostolic age. The manifestation is of course only symbolic. The prediction is not that Christ would visibly appear at the juncture in question. He would act, but indirectly. His action would be the cause of human action. His glorious influence and interference would become visible in the course of mundane events. He would reveal His power in His providence.

This glorious Being holds in His hand, not seven stars, as in the first vision, but a little book ù open. At a command from heaven, John asks the Angel for this little book and receives it with the injunction, "Take it, and eat it up; and it shall make thy belly bitter, but it shall be in thy mouth sweet as honey." It is immediately added, "Thou must prophesy (or preach) again before many peoples, and nations, and tongues, and kings." Now the same remarkable figure of eating a book, and then going forth to proclaim to others its contents, does not occur here for the first time. We meet it in the Old Testament, where Ezekiel is commanded to eat a roll, and go and speak to the house of Israel; and the action is thus explained. Ezekiel says: "I did eat it; and it was in my mouth as honey for sweetness. And He said unto me, Son of man, go, get thee unto the house of Israel, and speak with My words unto them..All my words that I shall speak unto thee receive in thine heart, and hear with thine ears. And go, get thee..unto the children of thy people, and speak unto them, and tell them, Thus saith the Lord

God; whether they will hear, or whether they will forbear." We have no question therefore as to the meaning of this emblematic action in the vision. John was first to appropriate and digest the contents of the little book, and then to go forth and proclaim its messages to others as the word of the Lord.

Now what is this little book? What can it be but the Bible ù that blessed word of God, His own word? It is here seen given afresh, a second time, to the Church. And indeed, so long had the Bible been buried in Latin, so long withheld from the people, so long made void by the traditions of men, that it was as a new book given afresh to the Church when it was, as it were, rediscovered, restudied, and republished by the reformers at the close of the dark ages.

When Martin Luther, then a student of about twenty years of age, in the University of Erfurt, first accidentally found a Latin Bible, he was amazed. One day he opens several books of the library, one after the other, to see who their authors were. One of the volumes which he opens in its turn attracts his attention. He has never before seen one like it. He reads the title..It is a Bible! a rare book, at that time unknown. His interest is strongly excited; he is perfectly astonished to find in this volume anything more than those fragments of gospels and epistles which the Church has selected to be read publicly in the churches every sabbath day. Hitherto he had believed that these formed the whole word of God. But here are so many pages, chapters, and books of which he had no idea. His heart beats as he holds in his hand all this divinely inspired Scripture, and he turns over all the leaves with feelings which cannot be described. The first page on which he fixes his attention tells him the history of Hannah and young Samuel. He reads, and his soul is filled with joy to overflowing. The child whom his parents lend to Jehovah for all the days of his life; the song of Hannah, in which she declares that the Lord lifts up the poor from the dust, and the needy from the dunghill, that He may set him with princes; young Samuel growing up in the presence of the Lord: the whole of this history, the whole of the volume which he has discovered, make him feel in a way he has never done before. He returns home, his heart full. "Oh!" thinks he, "would it please God one day to give me such a book for my own!" Luther as yet did not know either Greek or Hebrew, for it is not probable that he studied these languages during the first two or three years of his residence at the university. The Bible which had so overjoyed him was in Latin. Soon returning to his treasure in the library, he reads and re-reads, and in his astonishment and joy returns to read again. The first rays of a new truth were then dawning upon him. In this way God put him in possession of His word. He has discovered the book which he is one day to give his countrymen in that admirable translation in which Germany has now for three centuries perused the oracles of God. It was perhaps the first time that any hand had taken down this precious volume from the place which it occupied in the library of Erfurt. This book lying on the unknown shelves of an obscure chamber, is to become the book of life to a whole people. The Reformation was hid in that Bible. 4

Later on, when soul agony had driven the young student from his loved university into a Benedictine convent, to seek the salvation for which he longed, it was the same blessed book, with its glorious doctrines of the forgiveness of sins and justification by faith alone, that calmed his storm-tossed spirit, and quickened his soul to new spiritual life. Staupitz, the vicar-general of his order, who proved himself a true pastor to the poor young monk, gave him a Bible of his own. His joy was great. He soon knew where to find any passage he needed. With intense earnestness he studied its pages, and especially the epistles of St. Paul. Right valiantly did the young reformer use the sword of the Spirit thus placed in his hand.

The Reformation, which commenced with the struggles of a humble soul in the cell of a convent at Erfurt, has never ceased to advance. An obscure individual, with the word of life in his hand, had stood erect in presence of worldly grandeur, and made it tremble. This word he had opposed, first, to Tetzel and his numerous host; and these avaricious merchants, after a momentary resistance, had taken flight. Next, he had opposed it to the legate of Rome at Augsburg; and the legate, paralyzed, had allowed his prey to escape. At a later period he had opposed it to the champions of learning in the halls of Leipsic, and the astonished theologians had seen their syllogistic weapons broken to pieces in their hands. At last he had opposed it to the pope, who, disturbed in his sleep, has risen up upon his throne, and thundered at the troublesome monk; but the whole power of the head of Christendom this word had paralyzed. The word had still a last struggle to maintain. It behooved to triumph over the emperor of the West, over the kings and princes of the earth, and then, victorious over all the powers of the world, take its place in the Church, to reign in it as the pure word of God. 5

"Let us believe the gospel, let us believe St. Paul, and not the letters and decretals of the pope," Luther was wont to say. "Are you the man that undertakes to reform the Papacy?" said an officer to him one day. "Yes," replied Luther; "I am the man. I confide in Almighty God, whose WORD I have before me." "Sooner sacrifice my body and my life, better allow my arms and legs to be cut off," said he to the archbishop, who tried to persuade him to retract his writings, "than abandon the clear and genuine WORD OF GOD."

From his lonely, Patmos-like prison in the castle of Wartburg, in the forests of Thuringia, Luther gave this priceless treasure, the word of God, to his country in a translation which is still in use in Germany. He felt that the Bible which had liberated him could alone liberate his people. "It was necessary that a mighty hand should throw back the ponderous gates of that arsenal of the word of God in which Luther himself had found his armor, and that those vaults and ancient halls which no foot had traversed for ages should be again opened wide to the Christian people for the day of battle." "Let this single book," he exclaims, "be in all tongues, in all lands, before all eyes, in all ears, in all hearts"; and again, "The Scripture, without any commentary, is the sun from which all teachers must receive light."

And not Luther only, but all the reformers ù like the apostles ù held up the word of God alone for light, just as they held up the sacrifice of Christ alone for salvation. They gave to the world the book which Christ had given to them, which they had found sweet to their souls, though it subsequently brought on them bitter trouble. It was an established principle of the Reformation to reject nothing but what was opposed to "some clear and formal declaration of the Holy Scriptures." "Here only is found the true food of the soul," said Luther, familiar as he was with the writings of the philosophers and schoolmen ù "here only." "You say, Oh if I could only hear God! Listen then, O man, my brother. God, the Creator of heaven and earth, is speaking to you."

The New Testament once printed and published did more to spread the revival of primitive Christianity than all the other efforts of the reformers. The translation was a splendid one; as a literary work it charmed all classes. It was sold for so moderate a sum that all could procure it, and it soon established the Reformation on an immovable basis. Scores of editions were printed in an incredibly short time. The Old Testament from the same hand soon followed, and both were diffused through a population, familiar till then only with the unprofitable writings of the schoolmen. The Bible was received with the utmost avidity. "You have preached Christ to us," said the people to the reformer; "you enable us now to hear His own voice." In vain Rome kindled her fires and burnt the book. It only increased the demand, and ere long the Papal theologians, finding it impossible to suppress Luther's translation, were constrained to print a rival translation of their own.

Once the Bible was thus read in the households of Christendom, the great change could not be averted. A new life, new thoughts, new standards, a new courage sprang up. God's own words were heard at the firesides of the people, and the power of the priest was gone. "The effect produced was immense. The Christianity of the primitive Church, brought forth by the publication of the Holy Scriptures from the oblivion into which it had fallen for ages, was thus presented to the eyes of the nation; and this was sufficient to justify the attacks which had been made upon Rome. The humblest individuals, provided they knew the German alphabet, women, and mechanics (this is the account given by a contemporary), read the New Testament with avidity. Carrying it about with them, they soon knew it by heart, while its pages gave full demonstration of the perfect accordance between the Reformation of Luther and the Revelation of God." 6

It was the same in France. In 1522 a translation of the four Gospels was published in France by one Lefevre, and soon after the whole New Testament. Then followed a version of the Psalms. In France, as in Germany, the effect was immense. Both the learned and noble and the common people were moved. "In many," says a chronicler of the sixteenth century, "was engendered so ardent a desire to know the way of salvation, that artisans, carders, spinners, and combers employed themselves, while engaged in manual labor, in conversing on the word of God, and deriving comfort from it. In particular, Sundays and festivals were employed in reading the Scriptures and inquiring after the goodwill of the Lord." The pious Briconnet, Bishop of Meaux, sent a copy to the sister of Francis I, urging her to present it to her brother "This from your hands," added he, "cannot but be agreeable. It is a royal dish," continued the good bishop, "nourishing without corrupting, and curing all diseases. The more we taste it, the more we hunger for it, with uncloying and insatiable appetite." "The gospel," wrote LeFevre in his old age, "is already gaining the hearts of all the grandees and people, and soon, diffusing itself over all France, it will everywhere bring down the inventions of men." The old doctor had become animated; his eyes, which had grown dim, sparkled; his trembling voice was again full toned. It was like old Simeon thanking the Lord for having seen His Salvation. Farel, the French reformer, maintained the sole sufficiency of the word of God as a rule of faith, and the duty of returning to its use. In the great Protestant Confession of Augsburg it is by a simple reference to Scripture that the new doctrines of the Reformation are justified. From first to last, from its incipient germ in the soul of Luther to the crowning day of the Reformation, the Bible was the very heart and core of the movement; and Protestantism has since deluged the world with Bibles. Do you wonder then that prophecy makes the giving of a "little book open" to the representative of the Church at that time a leading feature of its prefiguration?

But you must note that this was not the only thing given to John by the mighty Angel. There follows a great commission, which he was to execute.

He who of old had said to His disciples, "Go ye into all the world, and proclaim the glad tidings to every creature," renews this commission to John in his representative character, and says to him, "Thou must prophesy (or preach) again, before many peoples, and nations, and tongues, and kings." It is a second sending to the world of the gospel message, a second appointment of witnesses to proclaim the glad tidings.

And this was needed, for the fundamental ordinance of gospel preaching had long fallen into entire disuse among Romanists; the preacher had been lost in the sacrificing priest; the people had for ages had none to break to them the bread of life. Luther shrank at first from the office of a preacher, but it was forced on him by circumstances. After he had finished his translation of the book, and returned from his seclusion in the Wartburg, he began to publish the truth from the pulpit as well as through the press. "It is not from men," he wrote to the Elector, "that I received the gospel, but from heaven, from the Lord Jesus; and henceforth I wish to reckon myself simply His servant, and to take the title of evangelist." He began to preach in an old wooden hall in Wittemberg, and soon the largest churches were thronged to hear him. Within two or three years the gospel was being preached as well as read all over Germany, and in Sweden, Denmark, Pomerania, Livonia, France, Belgium, Spain, and Italy, and also in our own isle. Bilney had procured a copy of Erasmus' New Testament, and found comfort and saving light in its study. "Then," he says, "the Scriptures became to me sweeter than honey or the honeycomb"; adding, "as soon as, by the grace of God, I began to taste the sweets of that heavenly lesson which no man can teach but God alone, I begged the Lord to increase my faith, and at last desired nothing more than that I being so comforted of Him might be strengthened by His Spirit to teach sinners His ways."

Renouncing the Romish title of "priest" and that of doctor, Luther, in a treatise against Papal orders, styles himself simply, "the preacher," and the reformed Churches provided for a continuance, not of sacrificing priests, but of gospel preachers. "In the Popedom," says Luther in his "Table Talk," "they invest priests not for the office of preaching and teaching God's word; for when a bishop ordaineth one he saith, 'Take to thee power to celebrate mass, and to offer for the living and the dead.' But we ordain ministers, according to the command of Christ,...to preach the pure gospel and the word of God." So in the reformed Swedish Church it was enacted that none should be ordained who did not approve themselves both able and willing to preach the gospel. Instead of putting into the hands of the newly ordained the chalice and the patten, the reformers presented them with "a little book" ù the New Testament ù saying, 'Wake thou authority to read and to preach the gospel." If a recovered Bible be the first and greatest feature of the Reformation, most assuredly a renewal of gospel preaching stands next.

But a third thing was also given to John (in his representative character). In the vision, it was "a reed like unto a rod," with which he was to measure "the temple of God, and the altar, and them that worship therein," omitting, or casting out, the outer court, which was given up to the Gentile enemies who were treading down the holy city. It was a measuring reed in the first place, but it looked like a rod of princely or ecclesiastical authority ù "a reed like a rod." This measuring of "the temple of God" ù the symbol of the outward, visible Church in the world ù and this command to define and measure out its boundaries and dimensions, including one portion, and excluding another, looks like a direction to give attention and definition to the ecclesiastical foundations and boundaries, or limits, of the new reformed Churches, and to separate them in a formal public manner from the apostate Church of Rome.

If Protestant Christianity owed its birth to the Bible, and its early growth to revived gospel preaching, it owed its continued existence to its definite constitution as a separate ecclesiastical organization from Romanism. This came in due course. At first the reformers had to attend to the core and kernel of the movement; its spiritual side claimed all their efforts. A reformation of creed, of doctrine, of life and manners, of worship, of ordinances ù all this came first. But there followed ù and if the change was to be permanent there had to follow ù something additional and of a different character. When the child was born, it had to be dressed and named; life first, organization afterwards.

There had to come an embodiment of the new life in a new Church organization, and ù a definite separation from Rome. It was not merely that Rome on her part excommunicated and anathematized those whom she called heretics. The reformers felt that they had a solemn duty to perform. They had to justify their own separation from the apostasy by a public denunciation of it as such. They had to cast it out as any part of the true Church of Christ. They had to constitute a new evangelical and Protestant Church, to provide it with schools and colleges, with ministers, services, and buildings, and all the outward requirements of a fully organized system of religion.

This accordingly was the next stage of the Reformation movement, both in Germany and elsewhere. And this could not be done effectually without the concurrence of the governments of the respective countries. If Romish authority was to be thrown off, if public property was to be converted to Protestant uses, if Papal ordination was to be rejected and Papal bishops refused, the governments must evidently take part, and sanction the great change. Hence the need of the "rod" of authority; nor was it lacking when the time came for its use.

I have not time to trace the story. The Elector John, assuming to himself, like our own Henry VIII, the supremacy of the Church as a natural right of the Crown, "exercised it with resolution and activity, by forming new ecclesiastical constitutions, modeled on the principles of the great reformer." "Come, let us build the wall, that we be no more a reproach," said Nehemiah to the Jews. And so Luther and Melanchthon and other reformers urged the introduction into the reformed Churches of new formularies of public worship, the appropriation of the ecclesiastical revenues to the reformed parochial clergy and schools, and the ordination of a fresh supply of ministers independently of Rome. A general visitation of the churches was made by the prince's desire, to see to the execution of the new system, and complete what might be wanting to the establishment throughout Saxony of a...

## SEPARATE EVANGELIC CHURCH

In this feature the Reformation differed from all the earlier movements of a kindred nature, such as that of the Lollards in England or of Huss in Bohemia. As Schlegel remarks in his "Philosophy of History," "It was by the influence Luther acquired by asserting the king's authority, as well as by the sanction of the civil power, that the Reformation was promoted and consolidated. Without this, Protestantism would have sunk into the lawless anarchy that marked the proceedings of the Hussites." This change took place in all the reformed States, the measuring reed like a rod being given by the civil authorities to the founders of the new communions, that they might solidly construct them on a permanent basis.

The outer court, representing the apostate Church, they on the other hand formally cast out. It was insisted on at the Diet of Augsburg that "the Roman pope, cardinals, and clergy did not constitute the Church of Christ, though there existed among them some that were real members of that Church, and opposed the reigning errors. That the true Church consists of none but the faithful, who had the word of God, and were by it sanctified and cleansed; while, on the other hand, what Paul had predicted of antichrist's coming and sitting in the temple of God had had its fulfillment in the Papacy; and that the reformed Churches were not guilty of schism in separating themselves, and casting out Romish superstitions." In his answer to the pope, Luther writes: "Rome has cut herself off from the universal Church; if ye reform not, I and all that worship Christ do account your seat to be possessed and oppressed by Satan himself, to be the damned seat of antichrist, which we will not be subject to nor incorporate with, but do detest and abhor the same."

This formal separation of the reformers from the apostate Church, and this formal organization of the new Churches, holding evangelic faith, and using a pure ritual, is the fulfillment of this part of the symbolic prophecy of the Reformation; but we must not pause to justify this interpretation, as a most important and interesting section of our subject lies still before us. Thus far we have seen that the Reformation is predicted as first the result of the action and interference on her behalf of the glorious Head of the Church, that it was produced instrumentally by a recovered Bible and by a renewed gospel testimony in all lands, and that it issued in the development of a new ecclesiastical organization.

A retrospective narrative of the history of Christ's two witnesses is then given, which time forbids my fully expounding now. These witnesses unquestionably represent the faithful evangelic Churches, which held fast the gospel all through the dark ages of Roman apostasy. They are called candlesticks; and we are told in the first chapter of the book that CANDLESTICKS SYMBOLIZE CHURCHES. They are also called olive trees, and this figure is used in Zechariah (where two such trees are seen supplying the candlestick with oil) to represent faithful ministers. The double symbol seems to predict, that all through the darkest period of antichristian apostasy, faithful Churches, ministered to by faithful pastors, should exist. They might be few and feeble, persecuted and hidden, small in numbers, and inconspicuous in status; yet acting as Christ's faithful witnesses, and holding forth the word of life, they would keep alight amid the darkness the lamp of truth.

The number two is used apparently in compliance with the law of testimony. "In the mouth of two or three witnesses shall every word be established." These witnesses are not individuals, but Churches, and their prophesying or preaching lasts all through the dark ages, through the entire period of Papal domination, with the exception of one brief interval, during which they are to all appearance killed ù extinct.

In addition to witnessing for Christ and to His gospel, these evangelical Churches would also witness against the Roman antichrist and his assumptions. And the result would naturally be intense opposition on his part. When their testimony reached this point, he would make war with them, until at last he would overcome and kill them; that is, he would silence their witness completely. He would so exterminate Bible Christians wherever they were found in Christendom, by persecution unto death, that as witnessing Churches, maintaining a public testimony to the truth, they would cease to exist. Individuals, of course, would still ù like the seven thousand in Israel who had not bowed the knee to Baal ù hold fast their integrity; but such would be the power of the oppressor, that they would have to hide their heads and hold their peace, in face of a mighty and triumphant and universal idolatry. This state of things would however be of very brief duration; for at the end of three years and a half the death-like silence would be broken, the voice of true testimony would once more be publicly heard, the witnessing Churches would experience a wonderful and startling resurrection, which would greatly alarm the enemies who witnessed it; and instead of being oppressed and extinguished, the faithful Churches would thenceforth be exalted and established. Such is the prediction of Revelation 11 translated from symbolic into plain language.

Now to those who are familiar with the Church history of the middle ages all this reads like history. It is a sketch from nature, in which all the leading features of a well-known landscape are clearly discernible, though laid down only in a small miniature. All came to pass precisely as here foretold. As superstitions and apostasy darkened down over Christendom, and an ever- increasing multitude faithlessly bowed the knee to Baal; as the man of sin gradually developed his power and his false pretensions at Rome ù protests arose here and there, and witnesses for Christ sprang up whose records remain with us to this day. In the East there were the Paulicians, who arose about the middle of the seventh century, and whom we know principally through the writings of their foes, who brand them as heretics. Already, even at that date, the priests withheld the Testament from the laity as too mysterious for the comprehension of common people, and a sort of paganized Christianity had begun to prevail, when a man named Constantine, who had come into possession of the gospels and of the epistles of St. Paul, and received their teachings into his heart, set himself like the great apostle himself to propagate the truth by extensive missionary labors. He pledged his followers to read no other book, and hold no other doctrines than those of Scripture, and his thirty years of labor produced what his enemies called a sect, but what seems to have been in reality a true Christian Church. A persecuting edict was issued against it; Constantine himself was stoned to death, his successor burned alive, with other leaders of the party. A subsequent president of the sect, one Sergius, writes, "From East to West and from North to South, I have run, preaching the gospel of Christ, and toiling with these my knees." His faithful ministry lasted for thirty-four years, and tended to the large extension of the Church, which was bitterly persecuted by the eastern emperors of Rome. He too sealed his testimony with his blood, urging his followers to "resist not evil." The Empress Theodora slaughtered and drowned one hundred thousand of these Paulician Christians, without extinguishing them. Her cruelties, however, at last drove them to resistance, and they lost to some extent the purity and godliness which had marked their earlier days. They spread into Thrace and as far as Philippopolis, and even as late as the twelfth century it was found impossible to reconcile them to the Catholic faith.

In the West, the confessors of Christ were similarly raised up in the early part of the seventh century, just when Gregory the Great was founding at Rome the distinctive system of Latin Christianity. Serenus, Bishop of Marseilles, protested both by word and deed against image worship ù one of the most characteristic features of Romanism. In the great Council of Frankfort, A.D. 794, under Charlemagne, a protest was made by the emperor and three hundred bishops of the West, in opposition to the popes, on this subject of image worship; and the Council of Paris, in A.D. 825, accompanied its decrees against the practice with an express rebuke to the pope. In fact, the Gallican Churches at this time held many views which we should now call Protestant, in opposition to the doctrines already prevalent at Rome; such as the sufficiency of the Scriptures, prayers in the vulgar tongue, the nature of the eucharist, and the truth as to justification and repentance, the folly of relics and pretended miracles, and other similar practices. Claude, the good Bishop of Turin, has been called "the Protestant of the West." He was a contemporary of Sergius ù "the Protestant of the East" ù in the ninth century. He was a true, fearless, enlightened witness for Christ, though men called him a "heretic." He took Scriptures as his guide, and protested against all the Romish innovations. He delighted, like Augustine, to set forth Christ and Divine grace through Him as the all in all in man's salvation. "With the utmost fullness, unreserve, and precision he asserts the great doctrine of man's forgiveness and justification in all ages through faith alone in Christ's merits, and not by any works of the law, ceremonial or moral."

Claude of Turin, though thus faithful, was not martyred, for the Papacy had not at that time established its supremacy in Savoy; but he was sorely persecuted, and his prophesying or preaching was "in sackcloth," like the emblematic witnesses. "If the Lord had not helped me, they would have swallowed me up quick," he writes. "They who see us do not only scoff but point at us." His diocese was a wide one, and his influence great, nor did it soon pass away. Traces of its effects may be found long after his departure; faithful witnesses continued to hold and teach the truth, as the corruptions around them increased. A sect who are mentioned by their enemies as "prophets" in the tenth century seem to have been spiritually descended from this good Bishop of Turin, and his sphere continued in Papal estimation to be a hotbed of heretics.

Later on, in the eleventh and twelfth centuries, we have numerous accounts of "heretics," who were brought before the Councils of Orleans, Arras, Toulouse, Oxford, and Lombers. The accounts still extant of the examinations of these so-called heretics show that, so far from being such, they were men who witnessed a good confession, and held fast the doctrines of the apostles. They denied all the distinctive teachings and practices of Popery, and were blameless and godly in their lives, even by the admission of their foes. Berenger, in the middle of the eleventh century, was the founder of a fresh witnessing Church, or, as his enemies put it, a fresh set of heretics. He was principal of a public school, and afterwards Archdeacon of Angers, and began by contending against the dogma of transubstantiation. He was a brilliantly clever, learned, and good man, and much venerated by the people. His doctrines were condemned by Papal councils; he was deprived of his benefice: but he had not the fortitude of a martyr, and was at last driven to retract through fear. Still he employed poor scholars to disseminate his doctrine, and died a penitent for his own want of courage and fidelity in A.D. 1088.

Time would fail me to tell of Peter de Bruys and his disciple Henry ù the Whitefield of his age and country ù who, after having almost overthrown the Papal system in Languedoc and Provence, was seized, convicted, imprisoned, and some say burned; of the heretics of Cologne, in 1147, who "bare the torment of the fire, not only with patience, but with joy and gladness"; of the thirty poor publicani, as they were called, tried at Oxford in 1160, who, convicted of holding the truth of Christ and denying the errors of Rome, were "branded on their foreheads, beaten with rods before the eyes of the populace,...publicly scourged, and with the sounding of whips cast out of the city."

A prohibition having been previously made that none should succor or shelter them, these poor, persecuted witnesses for Jesus, whose garments had been cut down to the girdle ù though the weather was cold and inclement ù perished in helpless wretchedness, yet singing, "Blessed are ye, when men hate you and persecute you!"

Nor can I pause to speak of the Henricians, who were condemned in 1165 for their noble testimony to the truth, and against the errors of the wolves in sheep's clothing who were called priests; nor of others who formed links in the long chain of witnesses which extended from the seventh to the twelfth centuries. One and all they endured privations and sufferings, which bear out the emblem of being clothed in sackcloth; and one and all they exhibited a self-denial, an unwearied zeal, and a degree of consistency and fortitude which show they were sustained by the power of Christ, according to this prediction: "I will give power unto My two witnesses, and they shall prophesy, clothed in sackcloth."

But I must pass on to the great witnessing Church of the Waldenses. Would that I could tell its thrilling story! Read it for yourselves; it deserves to be restudied in these dangerous days of latitudinarian indifference to truth or falsehood in doctrine. This far-famed "sect," or true Church of Christ, arose in A.D. 1179; some of its members were present at the third Lateran Council, with their books. Pope Alexander III showed them some favor, but they and their writings were condemned and anathematized by his successors, and persecution forthwith arose against them. They had a powerful missionary spirit, however, and their views soon spread in every direction; Provence, Languedoc, Arragon, Dauphine, and Lombardy were speedily permeated with the gospel, as preached by them. Their doctrine, as illustrated in their ancient poem called "The Noble Lesson," was scriptural and spiritual; and they protested against the Romish system, as one of soul- destroying error, against the confessional, against purgatory, against masses for the dead and the assumption of power to forgive sin, and against the love of money which marked the whole system. They denounced the Papacy as antichrist in a separate treatise. These Waldenses united all their communities into the bond of one Church, cultivated learning, eschewed mere ignorant fanaticism, and were filled with zeal and prudence. Their motto was, "The light shineth in darkness"; and their symbol or crest, a lighted candle in a candlestick the very symbol employed in this prediction of them and their fellow witnesses.

But we must now recall that the prophecy not only presents the whole line of faithful witnesses as sufferers and mourners by the sackcloth emblem, but that it predicts that at a certain stage in their history the Roman wild beast would in some specially definite way make war against them, conquer them, and kill them. This part of the prophecy began to receive its fulfillment at the end of the twelfth century, when, at the third Lateran Council (A.D. 1179), the Popedom roused itself collectively to a war of extermination against heretics. Previously to this, separate members of the system, acting alone and independently, had opposed the truth by force and cruelty. But in the thirteenth, fourteenth, and fifteenth centuries, Romanism, then in the plenitude of its power, gathered itself together for a great, determined, united, and persistent effort to crush out all that opposed its supremacy, and to clear Christendom of heresy.

This deadly onslaught against the saints was predicted, as you will remember, both by Daniel and by John in their foreviews of the Roman antichrist. He was to wear out the saints of the Most High, and prevail against them. Here the same fierce and fatal antagonism comes in as an incident in the career of the two representative "witnesses," who symbolize the succession of evangelical Churches, which kept up the testimony of Jesus during the dark ages. During the three centuries we have just mentioned the furnace was heated seven times hotter than it was wont to be heated. Persecution raged systematically. The fourth Lateran Council, in 1215, sanctioned all former plans for the extirpation of heresy, urged their adoption with renewed vigor, and subordinated secular authority to spiritual powers for the purpose. If kings would not clear their dominions of heresy, their subjects were to be absolved from all allegiance to them. Crusades against heretics were to be organized, and to secure the same privileges and rewards as crusades against the Turks. The Holy Scriptures were to be interdicted to the laity; even children were to be forced to denounce their own relatives.

All sorts of methods were to be used for the detection of heretics; bishops were to gird themselves for the work of ferreting out and exterminating them; and all the Franciscan and Dominican monks were to supply instruments for carrying out this process of inquisition and blood. The Waldenses and Albigenses were, of course, especially singled out for extermination. A crusade was proclaimed against them, and plenary absolution promised to all who should perish in the holy war. Never was a more merciless spirit of murder exhibited than by these terrible crusaders against the meek and lowly and Christian-spirited Vaudois. The Inquisition ù that invention of Dominic, or rather Gregory IX ù established its horrid tribunal for making inquest after unseen, secret "heresy"; and wherever any revival of true religion took place, or any confessors of Christ could be found, there they were hunted, if possible, to death. Genuine disciples of Christ, under whatever name they might pass, whether called Petrobrusians, Catharists, Waldenses, Albigenses, Wicliffites, Lollards, Hussites, Bohemians, or any other name, it mattered not ù to the torture and the stake with them if they held fast the gospel of Christ! Savonarola, one of the wisest and worthiest of the age, was burnt at the stake in 1498. Seven years of cruel war raged against the Hussites, and a civil persecution yet more bitter followed. Eighteen thousand soldiers were sent into the valleys of Piedmont, towards the end of the fourteenth century, to exterminate the Waldenses of Piedmont, and appropriate to themselves all their property. The Christians of Val Louise, in Dauphiny, were actually exterminated, burned alive, and suffocated in the caves in which they had sought refuge. Four hundred infants were found dead in their mothers' arms, and 3,000 perished in the struggle.

Lorente calculates, from official reports, that in the forty years prior to the Reformation, the Inquisition alone burned 13,000 persons and condemned 169,000. The latter half of the fifteenth century was a time of Satan's raging against the saints. But in spite of racks and prisons and sword and flame, the voices of the witnesses of Jesus were still raised in behalf of the truth, and against the power and pretensions of antichrist.

At last, however, as the fifteenth century drew to a close, the furious crusade seemed about to accomplish its object. The beast had all but conquered and killed the witnesses, according to the prediction. The strong figure employed of the witnesses lying dead for three and a half days, means, of course, that their testimony was silenced. They no longer prophesied; they were silent, helpless, extinct for a brief period. They were worn out. The wild beast from the abyss had prevailed against them. For the moment the struggle was over.

The fulfillment of this part of the vision was at the opening of the sixteenth century, just before the Reformation movement commenced. Hear Mosheim's description of the crisis. "As the sixteenth century opened, no danger seemed to threaten the Roman pontiffs. The agitations excited in former centuries by the Waldenses, Albigenses, Beghards, and others, and afterwards by the Bohemians, had been suppressed and extinguished by counsel and by the sword. The surviving remnant of Waldenses hardly lived, pent up in the narrow limits of Piedmontese valleys, and those of the Bohemians, through their weakness and ignorance, could attempt nothing, and thus were an object of contempt rather than fear." Milner, the Church historian, says that at this date, though the name of Christ was professed everywhere in Europe, nothing existed that could properly be called evangelical. All the confessors of Christ, "worn out by a long series of contentions, were reduced to silence." "Everything was quiet," says another writer; "every heretic exterminated." This was not, of course, literally true. The Lord knoweth them that are His, and had even in that darkest hour of the night that precedes the dawn, His own who served Him secretly. But so far as collective testimony before Europe was concerned, the witnesses were dead! Their enemies gloried in the fact. The Lateran Council congratulated itself that Christendom was no longer afflicted by heresies, and, as one of its orators said, addressing Leo X, "Jam nemo reclamat, nullus obsistit." "There is an end of resistance to the Papal rule, and religious opposers exist no more." And again, "The whole body of Christendom is now seen to be subjected to its head, i.e. to thee." Leo commanded a great jubilation, and granted a plenary indulgence in honor of the event. Dean Waddington, describing the close of this council, says: "The pillars of Rome's strength were visible and palpable, and she surveyed them with exultation from her golden palaces." "The assembled prelates separated with complacency and confidence, and with mutual congratulations on the peace, unity, and purity of the apostolic Church." "The power of Rome was de facto paramount in the Church." So Neander says: "The edifice of an unlimited Papal monarchy had at that time come victoriously out of all the preceding flights, and established itself on a firm basis. In the last Lateran Council at Rome, the principle of an unlimited Papal power was established, in opposition to the principle of general councils, and the Waldenses and Hussites had no more any importance to fight against the Papacy." So another writer 7 says: "At the commencement of the sixteenth century Europe reposed in the deep sleep of spiritual death. There was none that moved the wing, or opened the mouth, or peeped."

The witnesses were dead! Never before, and certainly never since, was Rome able to congratulate herself that heresy was extinguished and heretics exterminated from the face of Christendom. It is a fine, striking hieroglyph of the crisis that the prophecy presents. There stands the fierce wild beast monster from the abyss! He has prevailed against his defenseless human victims. The struggle has been long and hard; it has made him all the more savage and impatient: but it is over at last! His jowls still drop with gore, his eyes are red with blood as he stands glaring with his fierce eyes on the pale, cold, silent corpses of Christ's two witnesses, so long empowered from above to resist and defy all his might.

As John watched the sad scene, did there not recur to his mind scenes in the amphitheaters of pagan Rome, scenes such as Dore has imagined and painted for us, scenes with which the exile of Patmos was all too familiar? The arena strewn in the pale moonlight with the cold, stiff corpses of the faithful witnesses of Christ; and the victorious wild beast, glutted and sufficed with their flesh and blood, standing guard over the remains! That was the symbol. The reality was ù wimessing Churches silenced by long and bloody persecution. The time ù A.D. 1514, the close of the last Lateran Council, which proclaimed to the world in a formal, official manner the fact that all opposition to Rome had ceased.

Now note the sequel: In 1517 the Reformation began ù the movement which, like a snowball growing ever greater as it rolls along, has in the year 1887 one hundred and tiny millions of adherents, all professing the faith of Christ in opposition to the apostasy of Rome! Witnessing Churches ù Protestant Churches sprang up everywhere, and have been multiplying ever since.

What shall we say? Is not this a resurrection of the witnesses? Rome had crushed them, had she? So she thought! But she knew better before fifty years had rolled by! She knew better when Germany threw off her yoke, and England withdrew from her communion, and Holland resisted her legions, and the trumpet of Protestant defiance deafened her ears, and the earthquake of Reformation revolution shook her throne, and when the outburst of heavenly light so illumined the minds of men that they laughed at her once dreaded excommunications, sat unmoved under the thunders of her interdicts, and boldly tearing the mask of mother Church from her face, exposed her as the mother of harlots and abominations of the earth!

They were dead, were they, the witnesses of Christ? They had no longer any voice to testify, any courage to struggle, any fortitude to resist? So Rome fancied ù till the spirit of life from God entered into them, and they rose up a mighty host to proclaim the glad tidings through Europe, to do and dare and die in their myriads, denouncing Rome's "doctrines of devils," with such boldness and power as to arrest the attention of the world, and to produce a revolution of unexampled greatness in Christendom. Rome reeled on its seven hills as if shaken by an earthquake, and a "tenth part" of the Babylonian "city" fell.

England, one of the ten kingdoms into which the western Roman empire had been divided, fell away ù separated from Latin Christendom. Thousands perished in the terrible struggle which ensued in many lands, and Rome was worsted in her warfare. The rise of Protestantism was, as the very name attests, the resurrection of the witnesses; the Reformers themselves recognized it as such, and their enemies also. Pope Adrian, Leo's successor, wrote in a brief to the Diet of Nuremberg, "The heretics Huss and Jerome seem now to be alive again in the person of Luther."

The Reformation of the sixteenth century commenced in the year 1517. The translation and publication of the Word of God, the definition of Protestant doctrine, and the founding of Protestant Churches occupied the next half-century, while the liberation of Protestant States from Papal dominion was not completed till the century which followed. During much of this period the "war" of the "wild beast" against the "witnesses" continued, and with it the sufferings, "sackcloth" testimony, and slaughter of the latter.

The birth of Protestant Churches and nations in the first half of the sixteenth century did not however, as we know, mark the close of Rome's bitter and bloodthirsty opposition to the truth. The Papal war against the witnesses continued to rage all through that century and all through the next with undiminished hatred and cruelty. But there was one great difference. In pre-Reformation times the beast had the best of it; he "prevailed against" the saints; he wore them out, and was at last so far victorious that for a few brief years he completely silenced all corporate testimony to the truth. But after the marvelous resurrection of the witnesses, after the uprising of powerful Protestant communities, duly organized on a permanent basis and backed up by civil power, the Papacy was never again able to silence the witnessing Churches as a whole, never again able to prevail against them simultaneously in all quarters. Her victims had been transformed into her powerful enemies; and while Rome prevailed against the reformers in some lands, they prevailed against her in others. Henceforth Roman Christendom was divided into two camps; and, as of old, the house of Saul grew weaker and weaker, and the house of David stronger and stronger, so there was a gradual loss of power on the part of the Papacy and the Papal nations; and as time passed on, a gradual growth in political influence, material prosperity, intellectual enlightenment, and social condition, on the part of Protestant nations. But at first the struggle was a sore one. Just as Pharaoh pursued the people after he had been compelled reluctantly to let them go, and pursued them to the annihilation of his own power, so Rome pursued the young Protestant Churches of Europe to her own undoing in the end. She stirred up opposition and international conflicts, instigated blood massacres and cruel exiles and banishments, and plunged the reformed communities into a sea of sorrow and trouble: witness the terrible massacre of St. Bartholomew with its 60,000 victims in France, the Marian persecutions in England, the cruel slaughter in six brief years of 18,000 Protestants in the Netherlands, the desolating Thirty Years' War in central Europe, and the revocation of the Edict of Nantes, which in 1685 exiled 400,000 Huguenots from France and caused the death of nearly as many more. This may be regarded as the last great act of the Papal war against the witnesses. Protestantism had to pass through a long drawn out agony before Rome recognized, not its right to exist, for she still denies that, but its existence and growth as a fact against which it was useless to fight.

It was not till the close of the seventeenth century, not until the glorious Revolution which placed William of Orange on the throne of England in 1689, that Protestantism was firmly established in England. This event took place about three and a half years after the revocation of the Edict of Nantes. Papal supremacy had been abrogated in England in 1534, but in the reign of Mary and again under the Popish Stuarts its very existence was imperiled afresh. The Peace of Ryswick, at the close of 1697, first completely established the civil and religious liberty of Protestants.

All this proves that while the first stage of the resurrection of the "witnesses" took place at the commencement of the Reformation movement of the sixteenth century, their exaltation to political power and supremacy, the establishment of Protestantism, occupied a much longer interval. Like all other similar great movements, the Reformation, starting from an epoch, extended over an era. Space forbids the exposition of the chronology of this most remarkable period, including its relation to the 1,260 years of prophecy. Suffice it to say, that the interval from A.D. 1534, the date of the abrogation of Papal supremacy in England, and the publication of Luther's Bible in Germany, to A.D. 1697-8, the date of the complete establishment of Protestantism at the Peace of Ryswick, is separated by exactly 1,260 lunar years from A.D. 312-476, or the period which extended from the fall of paganism at the conversion of Constantine to the fall of the western Roman empire.

I have not attempted, nor could I in the compass of this lecture attempt, to expound fully the wonderful Reformation vision of the book of Revelation. I have only glanced at its leading features. There is in it very much more of the deepest interest which I dare not touch at this time because it would take me too far. But have I not said enough to convince you that the great and blessed revival of true doctrine and of spiritual life which took place between three and four centuries ago, and which we call the Reformation, was both foreshadowed in Jewish history and foretold in Christian prophecy, and that in connection with each of these wonderful predictions the seal of God's approval is conspicuously set on the movement? What is the vision of Revelation 10? One of a divine interference, giving back to the Church the Bible and the preaching of the gospel, and formally separating between apostate Christendom and the true Church. What is the retrospective narrative told by the angel? It is the story of witnessing Churches, sustained for long centuries amid sorrow and poverty and shame, destroyed at last as corporate bodies by the ferocious attacks of the Roman beast, resuscitated however after a very brief interval, and exalted to political power in spite of all enemies. Such is the prediction; such have been the facts. How came that strange prediction to be incorporated 1,800 years ago with these sacred writings? Realize, if you can, the stupendous marvel of the fact that it is here in this book, and that myriads of men of all nations were for ages engaged, all unconsciously to themselves, in fulfilling it. Realize, if you can, the sublime tenderness and sacred sympathizing approval with which the Savior uttered those simple words, "My two witnesses." Yes, Lord, they were Thy witnesses, those poor, persecuted Lollards and Huguenots, those martyred Waldenses and Paulicians! Thy witnesses, Thou blessed Sufferer, who didst Thyself resist unto blood, striving against sin!

They were witnesses to Thy grace, to Thy glory, to Thine all-sufficient atonement, to Thine only high priesthood and sole mediatorship; and for this they suffered, for this they died! They suffered with Thee; they shall reign with Thee, according to Thine own word, "Where I am, there shall also My servant be." "My two witnesses"! Ah, Lord, how Thou didst love Thy faithful martyrs! How Thou dost hate the cruel and evil system which for ages made bitter war upon them, and would fain do so still! In persecuting them did it not persecute Thee? Oh, how often didst Thou ask of pope and prelate, as of Saul of Tarsus in earlier days, Why persecutest thou Me?" As we think of these things, must we not share the feelings of the psalmist, and say, "Do not I hate them, O Lord, that hate Thee? Am I not grieved with them that rise up against Thee?" Far, far be it from us to sympathize with the persecutors and lightly esteem the true witnesses, as is the fashion with too many in our days! Let us rather maintain against the great enemy of the gospel the same testimony they held fast amid his fiercest onslaughts, and thus share with them the honor of being numbered by Christ among His faithful witnesses.

## Notes

1. *"A New System of the Apocalypse," p. 214.*
2. *Haggai 2:4-9.*
3. *Malachi 3:1.*
4. *D'Aubigne "History of the Reformation, " vol. 1, p. 163.*
5. *D'Aubigne "History of the Reformation, " vol. 2 p. 129.*
6. *Reference not available.*
7. *Cunninghame.*

# Concluding Remarks on the Practical Bearing of the Subject

We trust that the lectures to which you have listened have produced in your minds the profound conviction that the existence and character of Romanism ù the entire history of the Papacy was foretold in the Bible long ages before that evil power arose in the earth. If so, the conviction will bear fruit, for knowledge influences conduct. Several practical results of an important nature should follow, otherwise we should not have cared to expound to you, this great subject. And first, let your knowledge of this truth confirm and deepen your confidence in the divine inspiration of Scripture. None but God can thus foresee and foretell the events of a long series of unborn ages. In these symbolic prophecies the history of twelve or thirteen centuries is written in advance. Compare them with anything else in the entire circle of literature, and you will realize that they stand apart as a thing unique, like a living man in a gallery of statues.

The miracle of the existence of these prophecies in the book, and of their fulfillment in the facts of history, is so great that few minds can grasp it. That not only twelve or thirteen, but twenty-five centuries of history should have fallen out exactly as it was foretold in the days of Daniel they would, is a marvel that nothing but the Incarnation itself can exceed. It is a stupendous miracle in the world of mind, that world which rises high above the world of matter. It evinces more markedly the finger of God than any mere physical sign, however great, could do. It appeals to the intelligence of the human mind; it challenges the recognition not of the senses, but of the conscience. It sets a seal of supernatural wisdom on the entire Bible. None but God could have delineated beforehand the Papal power. Its very unnaturalness forbids the possibility of its being the fruit of human imagination. That a power claiming to act for God, to be "as God," and enthroned in the temple of God or of the Christian Church, should yet be His most determined enemy, the opposer of His truth, the destroyer of His saints, the great agent of Satan in the earth; that it should, by fraud and corruption and false pretenses, rule the world for ages from the very same seven-hilled central city whence it had already been ruled for other ages by military force; and that Roman rule should, in its Christian stage, shed more saintly blood than in its pagan stage ù all this could never have been anticipated by man, but only foretold by God. It is a demonstration which candor cannot resist of the divine inspiration of this holy book.

Is not this a practical result? Let criticism carp as it may, it cannot blind our eyes to this gigantic fact, that twenty-five centuries of history have, in their leading outline, exactly corresponded with Bible predictions. We are bound to conclude that the page that bears the prophecy was written by a divinely guided pen. The tremendous importance of this conclusion I need not indicate. I solemnly charge you to reverence this book. It will judge you in the last day. Heaven and earth may pass away, but not a jot or tittle of the word of God shall ever fail. Trust its promises! They are as true as its predictions. Tremble before its warnings and its threats! They will as assuredly be fulfilled as its prophecies have been. Study its sacred pages, never think you know it all; it is as fathomless in its wisdom as is the mind from which it emanates. I have been studying it for more than thirty years, and I am convinced that it has oceans of truth which I have not yet explored. How few really study it? and yet it has riches of wisdom which exceed those of all the libraries on earth. And remember that as certainly as it unveiled beforehand the past history of the Church in the world, so surely does it unveil and illuminate her critical present and her glorious future. The guide book that has proved true thus far may be trusted till we reach the goal.

Secondly, there are personal, social, and civil duties as regards Romanism and the Reformation arising from the truth we have learned which are of primary importance, and which I must indicate and urge on you before I close.

What is the present position of Romanism in the world? and what the condition of the Reformed Churches? You must be able to answer these questions before you can clearly see your own practical duties in relation to this subject.

As to Romanism, I have shown you that its present stage is that of decay, and swiftly approaching destruction. Its rise took place one thousand three hundred years ago; it reached the height of its dominion five hundred years ago; it received its first fatal blow in the Reformation over three hundred years ago, its second in the French Revolution at the end of the last century, and a third in the unification of Italy and the liberation of Rome itself from Papal rule in 1870. The final blow is yet to fall, at the fast approaching advent of Christ, as described at the end of the nineteenth chapter of Revelation.

To enable you to realize the extent and steady increase of this consumption and decay of Romanism, I will mention a few facts and give you a few figures.

**1.** Just before the Reformation Rome boasted that heresy was extinct in Christendom. Not a Protestant existed; she had slain the witnesses of Jesus. Now the number of Protestants is variously estimated at from one hundred and thirty-six to one hundred and fifty millions of mankind. In the national convention of Protestants held last year in Glasgow, the last figure was given as the correct one. Including the Greek, Coptic, and Armenian Churches, there are two hundred and fifty millions of professing Christians opposed to Rome, and only one hundred and eighty millions subject to her. She has therefore no claim whatever to supremacy or universality, but is in a minority, as compared with other Christians.

**2.** Romanists have, during the present century, increased sixty millions, owing to the natural growth of population. At the end of the last century they numbered one hundred and twenty millions; now they are one hundred and eighty millions. But Protestants have in the same period grown from forty millions to one hundred and fifty millions. In other words, Romanists have increased fifty percent, and Protestants two hundred and seventy-five percent. Going on at the same ratio, Protestants will, by the end of this century, equal or exceed Romanists in the world. Had they increased at the same rate, the Papacy would now have had four hundred and fifty millions of adherents, instead of only one hundred and eighty millions. It is a decadent cause throughout the world. Among the English-speaking populations the proportions are still more remarkable, and when it is remembered that this section of mankind includes the most enterprising, prosperous, and powerful nations of the earth, the facts are most suggestive. Out of the hundred millions who speak English, only one-seventh are Romanists, including all the Catholics in Ireland and America, in Africa and our colonies. Everywhere among the intelligent, educated English-speaking races Romanism is an effete religion, and its votaries are being absorbed by the purer and more vigorous faith. In America it declined twenty per cent in the ten years between 1863 and 1873. In Montreal alone there are five congregations of ex-Romanists. Even in Ireland Romanism is decreasing and Protestants are increasing; that is, the disproportion between the two grows less each decade.

As regards the United Kingdom, the facts are most remarkable and cheering. At the beginning of this century the Romanists numbered one-third of the population. Now they are only one-seventh. The proportion of Romanists has decreased from one-third to one-seventh, and that of Protestants has increased from two-thirds to six-sevenths. In other words, whereas in 1801 every third man was a Papist; now only every seventh man is such. The population has in this interval increased from sixteen to thirty-five millions. Protestantism has trebled its numbers, and now reaches over thirty millions, while Romanism remains stationary at about five millions. Had it thriven like Protestantism it would have had fifteen millions.

Now these statistics tell their own tale. As surely as Romanism rose in the sixth century and culminated in the thirteenth, so surely is it decaying and falling in the nineteenth. Not only has it lost all temporal sovereignty and all direct political power, but it has ceased to hold its own in the world, and especially in the foremost nations of it, even as regards its adherents. It is consuming and wasting, diminishing while others are increasing, and losing even the semblance of a right to the proudly arrogated title of catholic.

But this is only one aspect of the subject. There is another, and a very important one. Romanism is, and has been all through this century, and especially during the last fifty years...

# MAKING A DESPERATE EFFORT TO SECURE A RENEWED ASCENDANCY IN OUR OWN EMPIRE, AND ESPECIALLY IN ENGLAND.

It has enormously increased its working staff and its working centers. During the last quarter of a century, that is from 1850 to 1885, its priests in Great Britain have increased by 1,641, its churches, chapels, and stations by 866, its monasteries and convents by 558, and its colleges by 20. This immense and rapid growth is not owing to any proportionate increase of adherents, though it is of course designed to secure such an increase. But it indicates "the determination of the Papacy to try issues on the grandest scale with Protestantism in its stronghold." We have to face a deliberate and desperate effort on the part of this wealthy, highly organized, and centralized system, to weaken and, if possible, subjugate the champion of Protestantism in the earth. The present perplexities of England are the result.

Whether we believe it or not, we are again in the old battle, which we thought had been won at the Reformation and at our Revolution. It is the struggle for power between the priests of Rome and the people of England. The one, a party small in number, but organized, united, and unwearied. The people, the majority, but divided, distracted, and deceived.

The Church of Rome has never concealed her claim. Her chief, Dr. Manning, has repeatedly asserted it. She is to lay down the laws which we are to obey. Our Government is to receive and enforce them. Her success now in Ireland is only a step in her imperial progress. She will never rest till she has gained her ends, till our throne has ceased to be Protestant, and our Parliament is subservient to her will. Nor is her scheme unreasonable, though, as yet, incomplete. She has gained a section of the Anglican clergy, who adopt her principles, use her worship, and teach her dogmas. She returns a considerable section of the members of the House of Commons, who think, speak, and vote as she desires. She uses this section to bring pressure to bear on Government and parties. To the Liberals she speaks the language of Liberalism; to the voluntaries she is a voluntary. A large body of the English dissenters, and two-thirds of the Free Church of Scotland, have fallen into her trap, and are now her tools. In Parliament she is strong. She moves members through their constituen-cies. She fills some of the public offices with her creatures.

She assails all by importunity, flattery, or threats. She has gained a premier, who is possibly her disciple certainly her accomplice; through him she commands a cabinet. She works incessantly through the press. No publication is too small for her hand, none too strong for her agency. She is served by a host of devoted troops, who work with all their soul for her, under all sorts of names, in all places and disguises; reporters, writers for the press, literary and scientific men, ministers of State, preachers in the pulpits of the Church and of dissent, masters of schools, inspectors and examiners. She enters families by governesses, tutors, nurses, and domestics. She has secured a large section of our upper classes, and every day she gains more. She draws them by shows, by music, by taste, by frivolity and reflection, by dissipation and remorse. She works on the hearts of women by their fancies, their love of pleasure, and their fear of pain. She makes the wealth of men her exchequer, and the influence of the rich becomes hers. From the marquis down to the carpenter, she considers none below her notice or too strong for her power.

Against this disciplined and able confederacy, you the English people ù have to stand. And for such a fight you are ill prepared. Your impulse is right, your disposition is good; but impulse and feeling are insufficient against unscrupulous and unwearied conspirators. You are divided by parties, distracted by business, weakened by indifference. Yet the issue is great. It is, whether we are to keep the rights and liberties which our forefathers gained? Your freedom stands on your faith; and if your faith fails, your freedom will fail. That is the lesson of your own history; for all that we ever won of liberty was had through the strength of Protestant convictions. I ask you to weigh the issue. It is no light matter. It is your life. Don't despise or underrate your adversary, but don't flinch or quail before him. Rome has in her service the highest intellect and the most untiring zeal. She is served with the talents of the ablest and the passions of the keenest. She uses the vices of men as well as their virtues; and she has no restraints. She adapts herself to all forms of government and all states of society. She plies every class with arguments suited to its habits, and she can prevail as well with the accomplished and jaded man of fashion as with the illiterate peasant. The history, which I now put before you, tells you what strides she has made in England in the last forty years. It is for you to decide whether she will go on till she has mastered you, or whether you will re-assert your power and compel her to obey your laws. That is the real question. I have given you the facts; draw your own conclusions, and act like thoughtful men." 1

We urge you carefully to study the pamphlet to which these words form the preface. It is a catalogue of facts, and they prove that all our Protestant privileges are in peril, and that it behooves us to be on our guard. Rome makes no secret of her object; it is to reunite England to Latin Christendom by reestablishing the Papal supremacy here. "If England is ever to be reunited to Christendom," says Cardinal Manning, "it is by submission to the living authority of the vicar of Jesus Christ. The first step of its return must be by obedience to his voice, as rebellion against his authority was the first step of its departure." 2 He proceeds to show that religious toleration is a complete delusion, that the true Church can tolerate nothing but absolute and unconditional submission. "Neither true peace nor true charity recognize tolerance; the Church has a right to require every one to accept her doctrine"; that "the duty of the civil power is to enforce the laws of the Church, restrain evil doers, and punish heresy." "It is astonishing," he writes, "how small is the space rightfully left to the exclusive domination of the civil power..Even in passing laws, Parliament must defer to the Church. The State may enact a law, but it must see that it in no way contravenes the higher laws of the Church." 3

Dr. Manning plainly asserts that Rome has entered on a struggle between the supremacy of the pope and that of the Crown, that it is a struggle for life and death, and that it embraces the whole question of the Reformation in these countries. As Colquhoun remarks, "It is the old battle fought under the Plantagenets, whether the law of England is to be sovereign and supreme, or whether we are to have a confederacy of Roman priests, aided by treacherous English priests, braving English law, defying the British Parliament, and trampling on the sovereign's crown."

One of the avowed objects of the "Catholic Defense Society" is the removal from our statute book of the coronation oath and the Act of Settlement, which limit the possession of the crown of England to Protestants. Cardinal Manning considers that Rome has the full right to depose a Protestant sovereign.

The election of a prince in a Christian community cannot be put in the category of a purely civil act. If therefore an heretical prince is elected, or succeeds to the throne, the Church has a right to say, "I annul the election, or I forbid the succession." Or again, if a king of a Christian nation falls into heresy, he commits an offense against God,...and against his people..Therefore it is in the power of the Church, by virtue of the supreme authority with which she is vested by Christ over all Christian men, to depose such a prince, in punishment of his spiritual crime, and to preserve his subjects from the danger of being led by his precept and example into heresy or spiritual rebellion. 4

There is no mistaking this doctrine. Leo XIII has a perfect right to depose Queen Victoria; nay, more, it would be a bounden duty for him so to do, if he had the power. He has not, and he is never likely to have that power; but meantime we have foolishly given him the power to cause serious political trouble in her realm, and he is availing himself to the full of the opportunity.

This is, be it observed, no antiquated claim quoted from mediaeval times; it is published in England in this nineteenth century by one who is styled the Cardinal Archbishop of Westminster. And it is no mere theory, no mere fancy sketch; it is a working drawing, as architects would say, a practical scheme which Rome is steadily endeavoring to carry out.

The chances of his ever bringing England back under his sway are very remote; but if "home rule" could be obtained for Ireland, it becomes atonce a Papal kingdom and a perpetual menace to England. This therefore is an object to be attained by any and every means. The chief result of home rule is to be the extirpation of Protestantism in Ireland. "The woes of Ireland are due to one single cause ù the existence of Protestantism in Ireland. The remedy can only be found in the removal of that which causes the evil..Would that every Protestant meeting-house were swept from the land! Then would Ireland recover herself and outrages be unknown." 5

That this attempt would be made is not to be questioned. Cardinal Manning insists that it is a sin, and even an "insanity," to hold that men have an inalienable right to liberty of conscience and of worship, or to deny that Rome has the right to repress by force all religious observance save her own, or to teach that Protestants in a Catholic country should be allowed the exercise of their religion. "Catholicism," says a Romish magazine, "is the most intolerant of creeds; it is intolerance itself, because it is truth itself. The impiety of religious liberty is only equaled by its absurdity."

Conceive what home rule in Ireland would be in the light of these statements!

A most important point to be borne in mind in the consideration of this question is, that Romanism is not a religion merely, but a political system. We are of course bound to allow the Roman Catholics the liberty of conscience which we claim for ourselves; but we are not bound by any law, human or divine, to allow them the right of conspiring for the overthrow of our liberties, Government, and empire. Adam Smith well says: "The constitution of the Church of Rome may be considered the most formidable combination that was ever formed against the authority, and security of civil government, as well as against the liberty, reason, and happiness of mankind." 6

Peace and prosperity are impossible under Papal and priestly rule, as all history attests. "The Papacy," says Prince Bismarck, "has ever been a political power which, with the greatest audacity and with the most momentous consequences, has interfered in the affairs of this world." The question before our country now is, whether we are willing to make a further and most decisive advance on the road in which we have already traveled too far, and to grant to an alien and antagonistic political power a most real practical supremacy over five millions of the queen's subjects in Ireland, including a million of loyal Protestants in that land.

I cannot close these lectures without urging you to study the subject more thoroughly, and to get well grounded in your Protestant principles. A dangerous laxity on doctrinal matters marks the present day.

Multitudes hardly know what they believe, or why they believe what they do. In Reformation days people knew the ground on which they had become Protestants; but we have been so long sheltered behind the bulwarks erected by our fathers, that we have forgotten that we may have to defend our own civil and religious liberties, and neglected to furnish ourselves with arms for the conflict. It does not do however to be unprepared and defenseless in these perilous times. Let me urge you to read up carefully the history of the Reformation and something of the Romish controversy. Read up also the history of your country in the days of the Stuarts, when a dark conspiracy existed to enthrall England once more, and to force our free Protestant land back under the terrible tyranny of

Rome. A similar conspiracy exists again now. Call at John Kensit's, 18 Paternoster Row, and purchase some of his cheap and popular Protestant pamphlets. They will open your eyes as to this great subject. Get some armor, and gird it on, for believe me, you will have to do battle for the liberties that have made England what she is this day. Ignorance is weakness; knowledge is power. When you know with some degree of fullness and accuracy what it is to be a Protestant, how you will prize the privilege of bearing the name, and resolve that none shall rob you of it!

Above all, ground yourselves firmly in a comprehension of the three Bible foreviews of Romanism to which I have directed your attention, for the sword of the Spirit is the Word of God.

Lastly, I would urge you to avoid all tampering with the bastard Romanism which is called RITUALISM, or High Churchism, and which abounds, alas! all over England. It is simply Romanism slightly diluted, Popery disguised with a thin veil. Wherever you have a "priest" instead of a preacher, an "altar" instead of a communion table, wax candles instead of the sunshine of divine truth, ceremonial instead of sound doctrine, sacraments instead of saving grace, intoned liturgies instead of spiritual worship, gorgeous vestments instead of gospel truth, tradition and "the Church" instead of "as it is written," and crossings instead of Christ ù there you have Romanism, no matter what it may be called. Beware of it, however attractive the architecture and the incense, the music and the solemn ceremonial. Think of the apostles and their upper chamber; remember that Judaism gave us "a shadow of good things to come," not a model to be imitated, and that all this outward show is not worship "in spirit and in truth," such as God our Father seeks from His people now. The Apostle Paul styles this sort of thing a return to "the weak and beggarly elements," to bondage, and says of those who in his day had been beguiled by ceremonies, "I am afraid of you," etc. Let not these things beguile you from the simplicity in Christ. What! will you play with a poisonous snake because it has a gaily speckled back? Keep clear of all danger to your eternal interests. The pitfalls of Popery are concealed by fair flowers, but they will none the less be your ruin if you fall into them. The Bible brands it as antichristianity, and traces its origin to Satan. I warn you to stand aloof from the whole thing if you would not be involved in its solemn judgments.

Remember that there is only "one Mediator between God and man"; that there is but "one sacrifice for sins," offered "once" for all and "for ever." Through the "one Mediator," by the "one sacrifice," "draw nigh to God, and He will draw nigh to you." You need no mediator between yourself and Christ. The priest is a false intruder there. Jesus calls you to come to Himself. He is both human and divine. He is bone of your bone, and flesh of your flesh, yet without sin. God is in Him. He is one with us and one with God. Suffer nothing to come between your soul and Him. Suffer no saint, no angel, no virgin, no priest, to come between you and

Jesus Christ. Go to Him for the pardon of all your sins. Make to Him your confessions. He can absolve you, and will, yea, does, if you truly believe in Him. Priestly absolution is a lie. It is a blasphemous pretense. The sentence, "I absolve thee," whether from the mouth of Romish priest or Protestant minister, is profane. Be not deluded by it. Your fellow sinner cannot absolve you from the sins you have committed against God. Turn from these idols and vanities. Jesus is all you need. His blood is sufficient to atone, and cleanses those who simply trust in Him 'from all sin." "Search the Scriptures," they testify of Him. Come to Him that you may have life. His heart is touched with the feeling of our infirmities; none can sympathize as He can; none can help as He. To you, to each one, He says, "Him that cometh unto ME I will in no wise cast out." "Heaven and earth shall pass away, but MY WORDS shall not pass away."

"Lord, to whom shall we go? THOU hast the words of eternal life." Thou alone art ALL we need, for Thou alone art "ALL IN ALL."

## Notes

1. *J. C. Colquhoun: "Progress of the Church of Rome towards Ascendancy in England traced through the Parliamentary History of Forty Years." London: Macintosh, 24, Paternoster Row, E.C.*
2. *"Essays on Religion," p. 19.*
3. *Ibid., p. 458.*
4. *Ibid., pp. 458,459.*
5. *"Catholic Progress."*
6. *"Wealth of Nations," p. 237.*

Printed in Great Britain
by Amazon

48975772R00097